Jane Austen: *Northanger Abbey/Persuasion*

ENIT KARAFILI STEINER

Consultant Editor: NICHOLAS TREDELL

© Enit Karafili Steiner 2016

All rights reserved. No reproduction, copy or transmission of this publication may be made without written permission.

No portion of this publication may be reproduced, copied or transmitted save with written permission or in accordance with the provisions of the Copyright, Designs and Patents Act 1988, or under the terms of any licence permitting limited copying issued by the Copyright Licensing Agency, Saffron House, 6–10 Kirby Street, London EC1N 8TS.

Any person who does any unauthorized act in relation to this publication may be liable to criminal prosecution and civil claims for damages.

The author has asserted her right to be identified as the author of this work in accordance with the Copyright, Designs and Patents Act 1988.

First published 2016 by
PALGRAVE

Palgrave in the UK is an imprint of Macmillan Publishers Limited, registered in England, company number 785998, of 4 Crinan Street, London, N1 9XW.

Palgrave Macmillan in the US is a division of St Martin's Press LLC, 175 Fifth Avenue, New York, NY 10010.

Palgrave is a global imprint of the above companies and is represented throughout the world.

Palgrave® and Macmillan® are registered trademarks in the United States, the United Kingdom, Europe and other countries.

ISBN 978–1–137–43217–9 hardback
ISBN 978–1–137–43216–2 paperback

This book is printed on paper suitable for recycling and made from fully managed and sustained forest sources. Logging, pulping and manufacturing processes are expected to conform to the environmental regulations of the country of origin.

A catalogue record for this book is available from the British Library.

A catalog record for this book is available from the Library of Congress.

Printed in China

READERS' GUIDES TO ESSENTIAL CRITICISM SERIES

CONSULTANT EDITOR: NICOLAS TREDELL

Published

Thomas P. Adler	Tennessee Williams: *A Streetcar Named Desire/Cat on a Hot Tin Roof*
Pascale Aebischer	Jacobean Drama
Lucie Armitt	George Eliot: *Adam Bede/The Mill on the Floss/Middlemarch*
Simon Avery	Thomas Hardy: *The Mayor of Casterbridge/Jude the Obscure*
Paul Baines	Daniel Defoe: *Robinson Crusoe/Moll Flanders*
Brian Baker	Science Fiction
Annika Bautz	Jane Austen: *Sense and Sensibility/Pride and Prejudice/Emma*
Matthew Beedham	The Novels of Kazuo Ishiguro
Richard Beynon	D. H. Lawrence: *The Rainbow/Women in Love*
Peter Boxall	Samuel Beckett: *Waiting for Godot/Endgame*
Claire Brennan	The Poetry of Sylvia Plath
Susan Bruce	Shakespeare: *King Lear*
Sandie Byrne	Jane Austen: *Mansfield Park*
Sandie Byrne	The Poetry of Ted Hughes
Alison Chapman	Elizabeth Gaskell: *Mary Barton/North and South*
Peter Childs	The Fiction of Ian McEwan
Christine Clegg	Vladimir Nabokov: *Lolita*
John Coyle	James Joyce: *Ulysses/A Portrait of the Artist as a Young Man*
Martin Coyle	Shakespeare: *Richard II*
Sarah Davison	Modernist Literatures
Sarah Dewar-Watson	Tragedy
Justin D. Edwards	Postcolonial Literature
Michael Faherty	The Poetry of W. B. Yeats
Sarah Gamble	The Fiction of Angela Carter
Jodi-Anne George	*Beowulf*
Jodi-Anne George	Chaucer: The General Prologue to *The Canterbury Tales*
Jane Goldman	Virginia Woolf: *To the Lighthouse/The Waves*
Huw Griffiths	Shakespeare: *Hamlet*
Vanessa Guignery	The Fiction of Julian Barnes
Louisa Hadley	The Fiction of A. S. Byatt
Sarah Haggarty and Jon Mee	William Blake: *Songs of Innocence and Experience*
Geoffrey Harvey	Thomas Hardy: *Tess of the d'Urbervilles*
Paul Hendon	The Poetry of W. H. Auden
Terry Hodgson	The Plays of Tom Stoppard for Stage, Radio, TV and Film
William Hughes	Bram Stoker: *Dracula*
Stuart Hutchinson	Mark Twain: *Tom Sawyer/Huckleberry Finn*
Stuart Hutchinson	Edith Wharton: *The House of Mirth/The Custom of the Country*
Betty Jay	E. M. Forster: *A Passage to India*
Aaron Kelly	Twentieth-Century Irish Literature
Elmer Kennedy-Andrews	Nathaniel Hawthorne: *The Scarlet Letter*
Elmer Kennedy-Andrews	The Poetry of Seamus Heaney
Daniel Lea	George Orwell: *Animal Farm/Nineteen Eighty-Four*
Rachel Lister	Alice Walker: *The Color Purple*
Sara Lodge	Charlotte Brontë: *Jane Eyre*
Philippa Lyon	Twentieth-Century War Poetry
Merja Makinen	The Novels of Jeanette Winterson
Stephen Marino	Arthur Miller: *Death of a Salesman/The Crucible*
Matt McGuire	Contemporary Scottish Literature
Timothy Milnes	Wordsworth: *The Prelude*

Jago Morrison	The Fiction of Chinua Achebe
Merritt Moseley	The Fiction of Pat Barker
Carl Plasa	Toni Morrison: *Beloved*
Carl Plasa	Jean Rhys: *Wide Sargasso Sea*
Nicholas Potter	Shakespeare: *Antony and Cleopatra*
Nicholas Potter	Shakespeare: *Othello*
Nicholas Potter	Shakespeare's Late Plays: *Pericles/Cymbeline/The Winter's Tale/The Tempest*
Steven Price	The Plays, Screenplays and Films of David Mamet
Berthold Schoene-Harwood	Mary Shelley: *Frankenstein*
Nicholas Seager	The Rise of the Novel
Nick Selby	T. S. Eliot: *The Waste Land*
Nick Selby	Herman Melville: *Moby Dick*
Nick Selby	The Poetry of Walt Whitman
David Smale	Salman Rushdie: *Midnight's Children/The Satanic Verses*
Enit Karafili Steiner	Jane Austen: *Northanger Abbey/Persuasion*
Patsy Stoneman	Emily Brontë: *Wuthering Heights*
Susie Thomas	Hanif Kureishi
Nicolas Tredell	Joseph Conrad: *Heart of Darkness*
Nicolas Tredell	Charles Dickens: *Great Expectations*
Nicolas Tredell	William Faulkner: *The Sound and the Fury/As I Lay Dying*
Nicolas Tredell	F. Scott Fitzgerald: *The Great Gatsby*
Nicolas Tredell	Shakespeare: *A Midsummer Night's Dream*
Nicolas Tredell	Shakespeare: *Macbeth*
Nicolas Tredell	Shakespeare: The Tragedies
Nicolas Tredell	The Fiction of Martin Amis
David Wheatley	Contemporary British Poetry
Martin Willis	Literature and Science
Matthew Woodcock	Shakespeare: *Henry V*
Gillian Woods	Shakespeare: *Romeo and Juliet*
Angela Wright	Gothic Fiction
Michael H. Whitworth	Virginia Woolf: *Mrs Dalloway*

Forthcoming

Pat Pinsent	Children's Literature
Britta Martens	The Poetry of Robert Browning
Nick Bentley	Contemporary British Fiction
Keith Hughes	African-American Literature

From the same author

Editor. *Called to Civil Existence: Mary Wollstonecraft's A Vindication of the Rights of Woman*. New York and Amsterdam: Rodopi, 2014.

Editor. *The History of Lady Julia Mandeville,* by Frances Brooke. London: Routledge, 2013.

Author. *Jane Austen's Civilized Women: Morality, Gender and the Civilizing Process*. London: Routledge, 2012.

**Readers' Guides to Essential Criticism
Series Standing Order ISBN 978-1-4039-0108-8**
(outside North America only)

You can receive future titles in this series as they are published by placing a standing order. Please contact your bookseller or, in the case of difficulty, write to us at the address below with your name and address, the title of the series and the ISBN quoted above.

Customer Services Department, Macmillan Distribution Ltd, Houndmills, Basingstoke, Hampshire, RG21 6XS, UK

CONTENTS

INTRODUCTION 1

Provides a brief overview of Austen's literary biography and outlines the goals and structure of this guide.

CHAPTER ONE 7
From Pen to Print

Highlights key aspects of the writing and publication of *Northanger Abbey* and *Persuasion* in relation to the genre of the novel. Ponders Jane Austen's 'Advertisement to Northanger Abbey' and Henry Austen's 'Biographical Notice' that revealed Austen's identity as the author of the six novels.

CHAPTER TWO 18
Contemporary Reception, 1818–1840s

Considers the immediate reactions to *Northanger Abbey* and *Persuasion* up to mid-century pronouncements about the novels' mimetic and imaginative elements. Discusses in detail R. Whately's long review that likened Austen's skill of characterization to Shakespeare's and commended her Aristotelian balance between action and character. Includes commentaries by W. Wordsworth, S. T. Coleridge, C. Lamb, R. Southey and C. Brontë.

CHAPTER THREE 29
Victorian Readers, 1850s–1900s

Engages with Austen's rise to prominence in the second half of the nineteenth century. Some critics speak of the novels' selective realism, concealed art and the possibility that Austen's wit may harbour 'feminine' cynicism. Others regret her narrow and ahistorical art. Includes criticism by G. Lewes, J. Kavanagh, M. Oliphant, M. A. Ward, W. B. Clymer, R. Simpson, W. F. Pollock and H. James.

CHAPTER FOUR 47

The 'Cult of Jane' and the Rise of the Novel, 1900s–1950s

Explores Austen's booming popularity, delineating the shift from gentle Jane to subversive Austen. Critics debate *Northanger Abbey*'s Gothic parody and drama and *Persuasion*'s irony, conflicting ideologies and the movement from character to personality. Austen emerges as the first modern novelist. Includes criticism by R. W. Chapman, D. W. Harding, R. Farrer, V. Woolf, E. Bowen, M. Lascelles, M. Mudrick, N. Frye, A. Wright, J. Mathison, L. Trilling, I. Watt and R. S. Crane.

CHAPTER FIVE 67

The Text, the Unconscious and Commodity, 1950s–1990s

Discusses interpretations based on critical approaches such as formalist, deconstructionist, psychoanalytic and Marxist. Narrative strategies, genre criticism and the realities of capital are some of the chapter's key points. Includes criticism by J. Duffy, A. W. Litz, C. A. Weissman, N. Page, L. Brown, J. Phelan, T. G. Wallace, P. Morrison, A. Sokolsky, F. Restuccia, J. Vernon and J. Thompson.

CHAPTER SIX 87

Political and Historical Austen, 1950s–1990s

Presents interpretations that question the image of an ahistorical Austen and examine class and gender relations in the light of contemporary discourses. Links these interpretations to the rise of feminist criticism. Includes criticism by A. Duckworth, M. Butler, R. Kiely, M. Poovey, R. Hopkins, M. Kirkham, C. Siskin, C. L. Johnson, A. Walzer, J. Wiltshire, M. Jencic, D. Looser, D. Hoeveler, M. Loveridge, R. Sales, M. Waldron and P. Knox-Shaw.

CHAPTER SEVEN 107

New Millennium, New Directions

Explores the ongoing interest in questions of gender, aesthetics and history in the twenty-first century. Organizes the critical debates under the following headings: masculinity, history, revisions and narration, the gothic and professional sublime and romanticism reconsidered. Includes criticism by M. Kramp, C. Miller, J. Harris, A. K. Mellor, J. Heydt-Stevenson, J. Barchas, P. Gay, C. Tuite, C. Franklin, A. Frey, K. Kickel, W. Deresiewicz, D. Lynch, E. K. Steiner and M. Sodeman.

CHAPTER EIGHT 130

From Words to Image and Sound

Discusses some of the most influential filmic adaptations of *Northanger Abbey* and *Persuasion* and the mixed responses they have elicited. Addresses the question of fidelity pertaining to the transfer of content from one medium to another, and the intertextual relationship between the adaptations. Includes criticism by K. Sutherland, R. Sales, S. Parrill, D. Looser, A. Collins, T. G. Wallace, S. Cardwell, J. Shears, R. Dickson, C. M. Dole and J. Wiltshire.

CONCLUSION 143

Provides an overview of the most significant shifts in the interpretations of *Northanger Abbey* and *Persuasion*. Discusses areas of future research.

NOTES 151
BIBLIOGRAPHY 168
INDEX 178

INTRODUCTION

In a letter to her sister in 1809, Jane Austen complained of a lack of inspiration, writing: 'I am looking about for a sentiment, an illustration, a metaphor in every corner of the room. Could my Ideas flow as fast as the *rain* in the Storecloset [sic], it would be charming.'[1] This confessed dearth of ideas by a novelist of Austen's stature offers solace to any writer familiar with the ebbs and flows of creativity. However, it is hardly descriptive of Austen's career and even less so of the last decade of her life, in which she published the six novels that would make her one of the world's most enduring and beloved novelists: *Sense and Sensibility* (1811), *Pride and Prejudice* (1813), *Mansfield Park* (1814), *Emma* (1815), *Northanger Abbey* (1818) and *Persuasion* (1818). Three of these novels grew from earlier drafts, while the other three were entirely fresh material. Austen saw the first four through the press but did not live to welcome the publication of *Northanger Abbey* and *Persuasion*, which, although different in gestation, shared the fate of a posthumous publication. As in the case of *Sense and Sensibility* and *Pride and Prejudice*, a long hiatus separated the drafting and publishing of *Northanger Abbey*, whereas *Persuasion* was completed within a year (August 1815–August 1816).[2]

The present guide explores the critical history of *Northanger Abbey* and *Persuasion* from their publication in 1818 to the first decade of the twenty-first century. It delineates the diachronic evolution of the criticism of these novels in the context of key moments of literary and social theory, highlighting the themes and concerns that have prompted continuous interpretations throughout the years. The last chapter provides an overview of influential filmic adaptations of the texts and the critical responses elicited by them. In view of the posthumous joint publication of *Northanger Abbey* and *Persuasion*, the rationale for a guide that combines these novels is, thus, far from random or dictated by marketing goals. In fact, the guide approximates what was cast together from the start.

Chapter 1 explores the production of *Northanger Abbey* and *Persuasion*, providing a contextualization of Austen's writing and revisions of the novels as well as the circumstances of their joint posthumous publication in a four-volume set. It also selects and elaborates on certain diehard ideas from Henry Austen's 'Biographical Notice' that prefaced the four volumes. In his 'Notice', Henry Austen introduced the novels as the last works of his sister Jane, whose name had never before appeared in any of her previous works.

1

Henry Austen's introduction shaped the immediate responses of Austen's contemporaries as reflected primarily in the reviews and private letters discussed in Chapter 2. Some readers considered the novels to be worthy successors of the early ones, while others were disappointed with Austen's final works. One reviewer, for example, appreciated *Northanger Abbey*'s comical tone and sound morality but could not recommend *Persuasion*'s critique of parental interference. Another, Archbishop Whately, wrote a long review which deserves particular attention for its critical assessment of Austen as an author and of her last two novels next to works by other English novelists from Defoe to Edgeworth. Moreover, Whately initiated a critical tradition that compares Austen to Shakespeare for treating the characters of fools as discerningly as the characters of sense, and for admirably conveying every character's individuality. Austen is also commended for being among the few writers who achieve an Aristotelian balance between natural incidents and unforeseen *dénouements*.

Chapter 3 considers the reputation of Austen's work and interpretations of *Northanger Abbey* and *Persuasion* in the Victorian period. Most Victorian responses, although not proper pieces of criticism on each individual novel, raise topics and lines of thought that are pursued in the twentieth century. In their letters and reviews, Victorian readers discuss Austen's novels as a clear product of the early nineteenth century: *Northanger Abbey* as a specimen of Anne Radcliffe's romances and *Persuasion* as a domestic sentimental novel. Advocates of the works praise Austen's faithful character descriptions, witty perceptiveness and concise language, while detractors begrudge the limitations of a woman novelist who, although exquisitely capable in the narrow sphere of domestic comedy, cannot aspire to the ranks of what Mathew Arnold distinguished as great art. Thus, in the nineteenth century two coexisting and enduring lines of criticism emerge: one that applauds Austen's realism and economy of style and the other that attributes her realism to a deplorable lack of imagination. The most efficient defence comes from critics who recognize Austen's aesthetic acumen in her ability to select and condense meaningful details from amidst the innumerable particulars of everyday life. Between these two positions, there are readers for whom the novels' defining feature is the ironical distance, which in itself is an expression of the author's scepticism if not cynicism. After her nephew's publication of *A Memoir of Jane Austen* (1870), in particular the second edition in 1871, which contained an incomplete transcript of the first ending of *Persuasion* as well as other pieces from her juvenilia manuscripts, the individual novels are spoken of in evolutionary terms: many argue that *Persuasion*, despite its affiliation to earlier novels, achieves unequalled excellence. The chapter elaborates on pronouncements by critics such as G. H. Lewes, Charlotte Brontë, Julia

Kavanagh, Mary Augusta Ward, Margaret Oliphant, Richard Simpson, Leslie Stephen and Henry James.

Chapter 4 looks at the reception of Austen and her work in the first half of the twentieth century. From the publication of Austen-Leigh's *Memoir*, followed by that of Austen's private letters, the public appreciation of the novels has continually been conflated with the life of the author. Paradoxically, the popularity reflected in the swelling numbers of Austen's admirers, or self-christened Janeites, springs from the readers' very personal experience of the novels and their author. Around this time, to know the novels means to know the author, both of which function as markers of exclusive taste. A trend of commercialization is also on the rise, often provoking valuable critical insights and a pressure to read the novels through an academic lens. Apart from several serious pieces of criticism that keep faith with Janeite devotion, while chipping away at the image of a mild and unconscious artist, this period sees the first scholarly edition of Austen's novels, and the first of any British novel. Now, interpretations of the novels, which at times had been regarded as exhausted by previous criticism, are open to new possibilities: The narrator is often viewed as a moralist and subtle humourist in the footsteps of worthy eighteenth-century predecessors. *Northanger Abbey* comes to be seen as a fiction of social critique and an original reweaving of Gothic material, rather than an inferior youthful production, while *Persuasion* is praised for inaugurating a great novelty with its heroine who unites quiet action with intensified tenderness (a Victorian view that persists throughout the twentieth century). D.W. Harding's 'Regulated Hatred', which draws largely on *Northanger Abbey*, although by far not the first piece to comment on Austen's pitiless wit, delivers a severe blow to the cult of 'gentle Jane' with its psychoanalytically inspired misanthropic Austen. *Persuasion*, on the other hand, awakens interest for its highly finished characterization. If the most sanguine commentaries of the nineteenth century celebrate Austen's affinity with Shakespeare, those of the first half of the twentieth century place her among the giants of European literature next to Flaubert and Balzac. For F. R. Leavis, Austen is the first modern novelist, without whom there could have been no George Eliot, Henry James or Joseph Conrad, whereas for Ian Watt, the British novel comes of age under her pen.

The second part of the twentieth century experiences a veritable boom of critical engagement due not least to the prominence of literary theory in the humanities. As a result, *Northanger Abbey* and *Persuasion* benefit from historical and theoretical interpretations belonging to two main trends: one that focuses on the structure, language and the fabric of the texts, and the other that untangles the novels' complicity with contemporary cultural and historical processes. Chapters 5 and 6 discuss approaches that respectively illustrate these trends. Chapter 5 looks at readings influenced by theoretical perspectives such as psychoanalysis, structuralism, deconstruction and Marxism, whereby the latter serves as a bridge to theories that foreground historicization – the feminist and New Historicist interpretations proposed in Chapter 6.

After the literary prominence to which early-twentieth-century critics like Chapman, Leavis and Watt had elevated Austen, sustained historicization seemed a necessary step. Accordingly, the novels are investigated within a framework that attempts to reconstruct the history of the novel genre. Such studies contribute to an enlarged sense of Austen's artistry as being embedded in and moulded by the literature of the eighteenth century, a recognition that further debilitates the myth of the 'unconscious genius'. In its early stages, this historical perspective aligns Austen with Augustan common sense and satire. Accordingly, *Northanger Abbey* reads as a parody of the excesses of the Gothic fiction that inundated Austen's contemporary print culture. Other critics, however, claim that the novel's Gothic burlesque validates the very aesthetics that it seems to undermine. Hence, the moral of the novel is at stake and this moral could throw light upon and be best established by Austen's politics. The ultimate question then is: Do her novels stand for 'whatever is, is right' or rather welcome energies that seek to remake society?[3] Alistair Duckworth and Marilyn Butler argue for an aesthetically and morally conservative Austen. However, they have difficulty squaring Anne Elliot's subjectivity and the abandonment of the estate with the conservative paradigm. Claudia Johnson's book-length study of each of the six novels, in contrast, rebukes a conservative reading of *Northanger Abbey*. For Johnson, Austen's parody hints at politically sensitive material that is meant to emancipate readers like Catherine, as well as educate those who, like Henry Tilney, do not contribute any substantial truth to the Gothic.

Furthermore, the question of Austen's literary indebtedness and political allegiances requires an examination of the novels' status within Romantic aesthetics and politics: How Romantic in themes and treatment is her work? Anne K. Mellor proposes Austen's novels as compelling representations of cross-currents of feminine Romanticism, whereby feminine and masculine are not grounded in the writer's or characters' sexuality (for Mellor, the poetry of John Keats evinces traits of feminine Romanticism). Other critics explain the irony and parody in *Northanger Abbey* with Austen's Romantic sensibility. *Persuasion*'s lyricism, on the other hand, evokes aesthetics redolent of Romantic poets, in particular Byron's poetry. In addition, key Romantic themes, such as subjectivity and its relationship to one's environment, generate important psychoanalytic readings as well as an increasing feminist scholarship for which the agency of a Catherine Morland or an Anne Elliot becomes synonymous with Austen's progressive or conservative orientation.

The first decade of the twenty-first century sees unwavering interest in the broader context that informed Austen's writing and her reception. Kathryn Sutherland's *Austen's Textual Lives: From Aeschylus to Bollywood* (2005) asks for a critical assessment of the work of previous centuries in the making of the Austen encountered in academia and popular culture. Therefore, Chapter 7 explores the pervading sense in Austen criticism that the novels and their criticism absorbed the spirit of their time in its variety of low- and high-culture sensibilities, philosophical and political events, and print market ideologies. Particular emphasis is laid on political events, social phenomena, names and places mentioned in *Northanger Abbey* and *Persuasion*. Janine Barchas's *Matters of Fact in Jane Austen* (2012) is the most recent representative study of this trend. The context of the Napoleonic Wars, during which *Northanger Abbey* was revised and *Persuasion* written, gains importance, with criticism zooming in on the historical climate and the novels' attitudes towards history. The culmination of a contextual approach reaches its climax with Jocelyn Harris's *A Revolution Almost beyond Expression: Jane Austen's Persuasion* (2007). Harris, following Sutherland's call for meticulous attention to textual elements, starting from punctuation and word choice, tackles the revised chapters of *Persuasion*. From a quarter less interested in book history, the novel's formal qualities, for some an aspect overshadowed by the influence of New Historicism, receive new attention in D. A. Miller's *Jane Austen: The Secret of Style* (2003), where Miller identifies an ahistorical and impersonal narratorial voice as the hallmark of Austen's style. Only two years later, Jill Heydt-Stevenson's study of the language and vocabulary of the novels depicts a narrator in touch with the bawdy idiom of her time. Other studies contribute to uncovering the novels' engagement with Romantic aestheticism as well as Enlightenment ideas of the self, education, nature and gender.

Ongoing engagement with the novels' appeal and legacy prompts Claudia Johnson's *Jane Austen's Cults and Cultures* (2012), another study that further illuminates the reception histories of *Northanger Abbey* and *Persuasion*. Johnson picks up on Sutherland's conclusion, which argues that the first scholarly edition of Austen's novels in 1923 by Chapman, with its 'faux Regency' typeface, projects nostalgia for a bygone world.[4] Johnson adds that even his contextualizations end up skewing the historical cues, for example, when he devotes a very long note to the location of the Little Dragoons where Frederick Tilney (a minor character) serves, but treats with silence the London riots mentioned by Eleanor, which, as later critics have argued, are no fictional embellishment. On the contrary, they refer to real violent and popular dissent in reaction to food scarcity and political instability.[5]

The eighth and last chapter of the guide traces the afterlives of *Northanger Abbey* and *Persuasion* on screen. It provides readers with an overview of each adaptation before introducing them to the critical responses they have elicited. Questions of textual fidelity, historical contextualization, casting and music have been at the centre of the debates. Critics have addressed the inevitable difficulties that directors face, as they seek to preserve the key tenets of the novels: for instance, the literary seedbed of *Northanger Abbey* with its direct references to Ann Radcliffe's fiction and the atmosphere of the Napoleonic Wars or the Romantic aestheticism that pervades *Persuasion*. Some directorial decisions are regarded as poor compensations for the limitations of a modern audience for whom things must be made explicit that Austen's readership would have known implicitly. For example, the rendering of the abbey in 1987, on screen an ominous medieval castle, is criticized for trading Catherine's growing apprehension of a household led by a despotic General Tilney for an externally Gothicized emphasis on the sinister aura of the abbey. Casting, too, remains a bone of contention. Critics disagree about the suitability of Sally Hawkins in the role of Anne Elliot in the 2007 version of *Persuasion*. Not all of them think her jittery performance superior to that of Amanda Root in the 1997 adaptation.[6] Others insist that the 1997 adaptation deserves praise for its sense of realism and rejection of nostalgia.

To date, Palgrave's *Readers' Guides to Essential Criticism* provides two volumes that explore and review the critical history of four of Jane Austen's novels: the first volume, edited by Sandie Byrne in 2004, focuses on *Mansfield Park*, and the second, written by Annika Bautz in 2010, on *Sense and Sensibility, Pride and Prejudice* and *Emma*. The present guide on *Northanger Abbey* and *Persuasion* completes the circle that surveys the critical history of all six of Austen's completed novels.

CHAPTER ONE

From Pen to Print

Five months before *Northanger Abbey* and *Persuasion* saw the light of print, Jane Austen passed away. She had prepared both novels for publication, but first physical weakness and then terminal illness prevented her from approaching potential publishers. Her brother Henry and her sister Cassandra, confidante and heiress to Austen's literary property, undertook to publish them. They approached John Murray, publisher of *Emma* and of the second edition of *Mansfield Park*. Murray duly accepted their proposal, announcing the publication of the new novels on 20 December 1817 (1818 on the title page).[1] Thus, had Austen been alive, on the day of her 42nd birthday on 16 December 1817, she could have boasted herself the author of six published novels.

Northanger Abbey and *Persuasion* came out as a four-volume set, each novel taking up two volumes. The title page read: 'NORTHANGER ABBEY: | AND PERSUASION. | BY THE AUTHOR OF 'PRIDE AND PREJUDICE', | 'MANSFIELD PARK', & c. | WITH A BIOGRAPHICAL NOTICE OF THE AUTHOR. | IN FOUR VOLUMES. | VOL. I. | LONDON: | JOHN MURRAY, ALBEMARLE-STREET. 1818'.

Two things distinguished this set from Austen's earlier publications. First, although the title page, like those of her other novels, did not feature her name, it promised to reveal it in a biographical notice. This was written by her brother, probably with Cassandra's help, and acknowledged Austen as the author of the six novels published until then anonymously. Second, the edition featured an unprecedented prefatory remark made by the author herself. In 'Advertisement, by the Authoress, to Northanger Abbey', Austen, explaining that the novel dates back to 1803, entreats readers to allow for the lapse of years that have rendered the novel's 'manners' and 'opinions' obsolete.[2] No such remark accompanied *Persuasion*. The reason for this different treatment lay in their composition history.

Writing *Northanger Abbey* and *Persuasion*

Jane Austen considered herself a writer long before seeing any of her works in print. So did her family, who read, circulated and frequently commented on her manuscripts. She wrote with a clear audience in mind, which from the beginning prefigured the intimate family and social circles at the centre of her novels.[3] Of her writing habits, we know that she had no room of her own but a desk in the family sitting room. There, she composed letters and most of her novels, about which, however, only her closest relations knew. She herself described her writing in rather modest terms as 'the little bit (two Inches wide) of Ivory on which I work with so fine a Brush, as produces little effect after much labour?'[4] However, readers familiar with Austen's irony cannot miss the defence of her own creative process contained in this metaphor. After all, she is said to have laid claim to originality by saying: 'I am much too proud of my own gentlemen ever to admit that they are merely Mr A. or Major C.'[5]

Pride was mixed with a critical attitude towards her creations. Contrary to the myth of Austen's instinctive and effortless style that lingers in some criticism, her writing involved corrections, unfinished bits, dead ends and a great deal of revising. Indeed, some of her most beloved novels owe their present form to Austen's revisiting them. Both *Northanger Abbey* and *Persuasion*, although to different extents, rely on this critical practice.

Northanger Abbey belongs to the first years of Austen's career. Prior to this novel, she had as a teenager composed three manuscript volumes now referred to as juvenilia. Unlike Fanny Burney who destroyed the musings of her youth, Austen provided a fair copy of the three volumes in 1793. In those early years, she also drafted *Sense and Sensibility* and *Pride and Prejudice*, and a few years later, between 1798 and 1799, she worked on a piece titled 'Susan', the first manuscript of *Northanger Abbey*. This important piece of information comes from Cassandra, who, shortly after Austen's death, drew up a list of the genesis and development of her sister's novels. In the case of *Northanger Abbey*, mentioned last in her list, she writes: 'North-hanger Abbey [sic] was written about the years 98 & 99.'[6]

Austen's 'Advertisement, by the Authoress, to *Northanger Abbey*' explains the composition of the novel in the following manner:

■ This little work was finished in the year 1803, and intended for immediate publication. It was disposed of to a bookseller, it was even advertised, and why the business proceeded no farther, the author has never been able to learn. That any bookseller should think it worth while to purchase what he did not think it worth while to publish seems extraordinary. But with this, neither the author nor the public have any other concern than as some observation is necessary upon those parts of the work which thirteen years have made comparatively obsolete. The public are entreated to bear in mind that thirteen years have passed since it was finished, many more since it was begun, and that during that period, places, manners, books, and opinions have undergone considerable changes. (*NA* 13) □

The novel was started while Austen was still living in her birth home Steventon and 'was finished and intended for publication' by the time she and her family had moved to Bath, the city where most of the plot of *Northanger Abbey* unfolds. Upon family advice and with the help of Henry's connections, she offered the manuscript, still titled 'Susan', to Benjamin Crosby & Co., who paid ten pounds, advertised it as *Susan; a Novel, in 2 vols.* in the list of 'New and Useful Books' in *Flowers of Literature for 1801 & 1802* (1803) but never published it. He never gave a reason for withholding from print a work for which he had already paid, hence Austen's surprise at this 'extraordinary' business decision.

Six years later, in April 1809, conceivably exasperated by Crosby's unaccountable behaviour, Austen wrote him a letter under the pseudonym Mrs. Ashton Dennis, in which she reminded him of their agreement, adding that, if Crosby's firm did not intend to publish the novel, she would approach another publisher. Crosby wrote back that he would relinquish his rights on the manuscript only upon receiving the ten pounds the firm had paid six years ago. As far as we know, Austen did not pay anything or make further attempts at publication while the manuscript remained with Crosby for another seven years. In 1816, after refunding the ten pounds and thus securing the copyright of 'Susan', she returned to the manuscript, changed the title and the name of the heroine to 'Catherine' and wrote the advertisement quoted above. In a letter to one of her nieces, four months before her untimely death, she wrote: 'Miss Catherine is put upon Shelve [sic] for the present, and I do not know that she will ever come out.'[7] The experience with Crosby had clearly disheartened her and most of her hopes in this letter look forward to the publication of a new novel, *Persuasion*.

Unlike *Northanger Abbey*, the composition history of *Persuasion* is straightforward. According to Cassandra's chronology, it was started on 8 August 1815 and finished on 6 August 1816, its completion thus coinciding roughly with the last touches put on 'Catherine' (later *Northanger Abbey*). The starting of *Persuasion* also coincides with the first signs of Austen's illness and many critics have attributed the novel's melancholy mood to the author's failing health. However, perhaps the most striking fact is that she could complete *Persuasion* within a year in spite of such unfavourable circumstances.

The only slight complication in the composition of the novel regards its concluding chapters. Austen began drafting chapter 10 of the second volume on 8 July 1816 and added the words 'Finis. July 16. 1816' at the end of an intended Chapter 11. This was followed by a paragraph and 'Finis. July 18, 1816'. However, finding the ending unsatisfactory, she produced another version, in which the early Chapter 10 is transformed into the present Chapters 10 and 11 and the early Chapter 11 into Chapter 12.[8] In March 1817, in the same letter where she wrote about putting 'Miss Catherine' on the shelf, she also announced the existence of a new creation: 'I have something ready for Publication, which may perhaps appear about a twelvemonth hence.'[9] It was 'something' that she feared might not be to everybody's liking, although one 'may *perhaps* like the Heroine, as she is almost too good for me'.[10] Moreover, it was something with the provisional title 'The Elliots', which under Cassandra and Henry Austen's collaboration with John Murray became *Persuasion*.

One Edition and Two Novels

John Murray, who counted Byron and Sir Walter Scott among his authors, readily accepted the manuscripts for Austen's final works. The novels appeared on 20 December 1817 (although, as noted above, the official date on the title page read 1818) in a four-volume set. They were advertised in *The Courier* on 17 December 1817 and in *The Morning Chronicle* on 19 December 1817. Initially, 1,750 copies were printed, of which 1,409 sold rapidly and 283 sold later at cut price. These were quite high numbers, considering that the first edition of a novel amounted to an average of 500 to 750 copies.[11] Austen would have made £518.6.5 from the sales, which was more than the £221 she had made from her last novel *Emma*.[12] The last 283 copies moved in 1820 and there was no second edition until May 1833.

The Courier advertised *Northanger Abbey* as a 'Romance' and *Persuasion* as a 'Novel'. These different appellations for two works that in modern perception belong to the same genre have to do with the development and the status of the novel in the long eighteenth century, the period spanning the Glorious Revolution of 1688 and the Reform Act of 1832. During the eighteenth century, the terms 'romance' and 'novel' had not yet solidified, although there were attempts to draw a line between the two or to show an evolutionary connection. Already in 1691, William Congreve associated 'romance' with a love tale that involved improbable incidents, 'lofty Language, miraculous Contingencies and Impossible Performances that elevate the Reader into a giddy Delight which leaves him flat upon the Ground whenever he gives of'.[13] In contrast, novels 'are of a more familiar nature; Come near us, and represent to us Intrigues in practice'.[14] One comprehends how vexed the relationship between novel and romance is when considering that, in Richardson's novels, one of the most serious charges against the heroine is the indulgence of romance reading, an escapist and frivolous activity, clearly very different from the experience of *Pamela*, *Clarissa* and *Sir Charles Grandison* that Richardson was proposing to his own readers.

Later in the century, this distinction was confirmed by Clara Reeve in *The Progress of Romance* (1785), where she sharply distinguished romance as 'an heroic fable, which treats of fabulous persons and things' and novel as 'a picture of real life and manners, and of the times in which it is written'.[15] For Reeve, romance lay at the novel's origins or, in her words, 'the Novel has sprung out of [romance's] ruins'.[16] Reeve was not alone in explaining the popularity of the novel at this time as a continuation of the aesthetic pleasure introduced by romance. One reviewer writes in 1796:

> ■ To the old romance, which exhibited exalted personages, and displayed their sentiments in improbable or impossible situations, has succeeded the more reasonable, modern novel; which delineates characters drawn from actual observation, and, when ably executed, presents an accurate and captivating view of real life.[17] □

Northanger Abbey does not fit squarely with the understanding of romance as a fantastic fable of the past, nor do its characters resemble 'exalted personages'. However, one of the novel's most contested concerns revolves around the question of probability: could General Tilney have murdered his wife? The investigation driven by this question as well as explicit references to Ann Radcliffe's plots align *Northanger Abbey* with the Gothic tales that crowded the circulating libraries. These were full of sensational incidents, formulaic plots and language reminiscent of the early romance that Congreve and Reeve describe. Perhaps, the title chosen by Cassandra and Henry suggested a stronger affiliation than Austen had intended.

Ironically, *Northanger Abbey*, the only work in which Jane Austen mounts the following defence of the novel as a genre, was not advertised as one:

> ■ Yes, novels; – for I will not adopt that ungenerous and impolitic custom so common with novel-writers, of degrading by their contemptuous censure the very performances, to the number of which they are themselves adding – joining with their greatest enemies in bestowing the harshest epithets on such works, and scarcely ever permitting them to be read by their own heroine, who, if she accidentally take up a novel, is sure to turn over its insipid pages with disgust. Alas! if the heroine of one novel be not patronized by the heroine of another, from whom can she expect protection and regard? I cannot approve of it. Let us leave it to the Reviewers to abuse

such effusions of fancy at their leisure, and over every new novel to talk in threadbare strains of the trash with which the press now groans. Let us not desert one another; we are an injured body. Although our productions have afforded more extensive and unaffected pleasure than those of any other literary corporation in the world, no species of composition has been so much decried. From pride, ignorance, or fashion, our foes are almost as many as our readers. (*NA* 36) □

The reasons for Austen's discontent with the depreciation of the novel and its enthusiasts have to do with the print culture and reading practices of her time.

The Novels and Their Time

Austen lived and wrote in a period in which book production and reading exploded to an unprecedented extent: book trading became a lucrative activity for hundreds of entrepreneurs who ran bookshops, printing shops and circulating libraries to which readers subscribed for an affordable fee. Increasingly, this flourishing trade offered the possibility for writers to live by the pen and free themselves from the ties of patronage. Indeed, the last three decades of the eighteenth century saw a four-fold increase in publication, while readership numbers grew rapidly as books were sold in smaller formats at lower prices and distribution networks became more efficient.[18]

The increase was dramatic, especially in the numbers of novels (alternately titled 'history', 'tale' or 'romance'): in 1775, Austen's birth year, thirty-one new novels were published; by 1818, *Northanger Abbey* and *Persuasion* were two among sixty-one new publications.

The status of the novel was also hotly discussed in the periodicals of the day. Austen's observation that novels had almost as many readers as foes is probably not far from the truth. The reviewers were merciless: 'reviewing a novel became something of a sport, critics often seemed to compete for the most insulting or sarcastic dismissal'.[19] Not surprisingly, three quarters of all novels published between 1770 and 1820 were anonymous. Often, additions such as 'By a Lady' (Austen adopted this appellation on the title page of *Sense and Sensibility*) would reveal the gender of the author, if such a commodified tag could be trusted.

The effects of the novel on the reader were deemed to range from dangerous to harmless and the novels themselves from corrupting to useless. One of the most influential writers of the eighteenth century, Samuel Johnson, thought that the 'works of fiction' avidly read by the readers of his time derived their charm from exhibitions of 'life in its true state' rather than remote sentiments, habits and actions. However, this element of authenticity, depending on the author's moral tendency, harboured potential to improve or to harm.[20] Johnson's assessment of the genre's power to excite emulation illuminates the closing sentences of *Northanger Abbey*, where the narrator leaves it to the reader to decide whether the story tends 'to recommend parental tyranny, or reward filial disobedience' (*NA* 235). Johnson's cautious stance recognizes both the nature of the interest that the new genre had for readers and how it could shape individuals and social morals.

His observation certainly did more justice to the novel than comments that belittled its impact. Another critic's exclamation offers a glimpse into the kind of scathing criticism that novelists, in Austen's words, 'the injured body', encountered: 'Will the labour of reviewing novels be never again compensated by a little rational entertainment?' laments a reviewer in 1791.[21] Criticism was even more severe towards prose works that drew on the taste for mysteries, superstitions, persecutions, ruins and remote places which, since Horace Walpole's *The Castle of Otranto* (1764), had come to be labelled as Gothic.[22] Such productions provoked accusations, similar to those brought against the old romances, of improbable plots and shocking accidents. However, Walpole turned the tables on the proponents of realist novels by claiming that this kind of literature had traded the elevations of imagination for the flatness of ordinary life: 'the great resources of fancy have been damned up, by a strict adherence to common life'.[23] Against this aesthetic backdrop, *Northanger Abbey* with its bipartite structure bridges depictions of real-life Bath and social activities with the Gothic themes of crime and persecution that haunt Catherine Morland during her stay at the Abbey.

Of all the novels published from 1788 to 1807, 30 per cent belonged to the Gothic genre. Around the time that Austen drafted *Northanger Abbey*, Gothic fiction had 38 per cent of the market share in novel production.[24] But by 1820, that is, only two years after the publication of *Northanger Abbey*, Gothic tales took less than 10 per cent of market share. Hence, Austen's assessment that her novel could be out of step with readers' taste was justified.

Persuasion, in contrast, resonated more closely with contemporary aesthetic taste and national concerns. The interweaving of the eight-year-long romance between Anne Elliot and Captain Wentworth with the latter's naval career offered a canvas on which the novel could suggestively sketch events around the Napoleonic Wars. In *Persuasion*, Austen contemplates retrospectively this time of national anxiety and sacrifice. The novel was begun in a time of peace, after Napoleon Bonaparte's escape from Elba and his ultimate defeat at Waterloo in June 1815. Twenty-two years of war with France had come to an end, bringing relief but also the necessity to ponder the losses and a future without war. It is important to keep in mind that the time of composition does not coincide with the novel's narration time. *Persuasion*'s story starts to unfold in the summer of 1814, while Admiral Croft and his wife are coming back from sea to rent Kellynch Hall, because 'peace is turning [...] Navy officers ashore' (*P* 10). Here, peace refers to the allies' victory over Napoleon and his exile to Elba in April 1814. Three months later, in June 1814, the Treaty of Paris marked the end of war, before it was sparked again by the return of Napoleon in March 1815. By Michaelmas, 29 September 1814, Sir Walter hands over his estate to the Crofts, and in October, Captain Wentworth, while visiting his sister's new dwelling, enters Anne's life. A month later there is the excursion to Lyme, in which Louisa's injury awakens Wentworth to the consequences of his flirtations. Mary's letter on 1 February 1815 informs Anne (and the reader) about Louisa's engagement with Captain Benwick, an event that fuels the hope of reconciliation in Anne and Wentworth. Only a few weeks separate Anne's receipt of this letter from the revealing moment at the White Hart, so that *Persuasion* ends just before the news of Napoleon's escape reaches British shores. Thus, there is a conscious choice on Austen's part to situate the rekindling of romance between her protagonists in the temporary peace of 1814. We will see in the following chapters how this decision has inflected interpretations of the novel's cautiously happy ending.

The Portrait of an Author

The four-volume set of *Northanger Abbey* and *Persuasion* came along with a first glimpse into Jane Austen's life and character in the 'Biographical Notice' written by her brother Henry. It must have been of significant attraction to readers who knew the earlier novels but lacked any insights into the author's life. For almost half a century, Henry Austen's remained the only public biographical pronouncement until the appearance of the first biography, *A Memoir of Jane Austen*, by Jane's nephew James Edward Austen-Leigh in 1870. In her lifetime, Austen had recoiled from publicly assuming authorship. The writer of the note hopes that not mere curiosity but a more profound appreciation lies behind the readers' interest in the deceased author. Indeed, the note, although much shorter than the biography of 1870, strongly shapes the Victorian perception of Austen and her works.

After a succinct synopsis that traces the novelist's passage from Steventon, her birthplace, to Bath, Chawton and Winchester, the place of her untimely death, the note attempts to bring Austen's character alive. The image that emerges is one of poised goodness and instinctive genius. Both pictures will in later criticism become synecdoches for her art. We are told that Austen, 'quiet, yet graceful' in her deportment, was capable of producing lines 'replete with fancy and vigour' until the very last days of her life, when she, too weak to use a pen, wrote with a pencil (*P* 4, 5). Words like 'quiet' and 'tranquil' alternate with 'communicative' and 'playful' (*P* 5, 7). Henry Austen seems to anticipate the charges of idealism called forth by such a perfectly balanced portrait, when writing:

> ■ If there be an opinion current in the world, that perfect placidity of temper is not reconcileable to the most lively imagination, and the keenest relish for wit, such an opinion will be rejected for ever by those who have had the happiness of knowing the authoress of the following works. (*P* 5) □

While it is impossible to draw a line between reality and idealization, Henry's descriptions are illuminated by some of Austen's own creations. The possibility of the symbiosis of a serene disposition with a lively imagination replicates Anne Elliot's dismissal of the 'too-common idea of spirit and gentleness being incompatible with each other' (*P* 139).

There are two other striking resemblances between the Jane of the 'Biographical Notice' and the characters of her novels. First, when relating the last days of his sister's life in Winchester, where she was under constant medical care, Henry writes:

> ■ She supported, during two months, all the varying pain, irksomeness, and tedium attendant on decaying nature, with more than resignation, with a truly elastic cheerfulness. (*P* 4) □

Anne Wentworth detects and admires a similar attitude in Mrs. Smith: 'here was that elasticity of mind, that disposition to be comforted, that power of turning readily from evil to good' (*P* 125). Second, with a generosity that 'sought, in the faults of others, something to excuse, to forgive or forget' and 'where extenuation was impossible [...] had a sure refuge in silence', Henry's Austen starts to resemble Jane Bennett in *Pride and Prejudice*, who in all judgements 'make[s] allowance enough for difference of situation and temper' (*P* 5).[25] On the other hand, while 'the frailties, foibles, and follies of others' do not escape her inquisitive intelligence, Henry assures the reader that 'even on their vices did she never trust to comment with unkindness' (*P* 5). However, Austen's letters, incomplete as the versions that have reached us are (Cassandra Austen selected the letters, cutting out many passages), show that their writer was equally capable of candour, kindness and acerbic irony, a quality that Henry Austen attributes to his sister's partaking 'in all the best gifts of the comic muse' (*P* 6). In the next centuries, Austen's irony, the thrust and implications of her comic gift become contested ground.

The letters also shed a different light on Austen's perception of her own work as a novelist, an aspect upon which the 'Biographical Notice' dwells with considerable emphasis, maintaining that she became an author entirely from taste and inclination, without entertaining any professional aspirations whatsoever:

> ■ Neither the hope of fame nor profit mixed with her early motives. [...] It was with extreme difficulty that her friends, whose partiality she suspected whilst she honoured their judgment, could prevail on her to publish her first work. (P 5–6) □

It may be true that Austen's early writing experiments as a teenager were not driven by thoughts of posterity or recognition that went beyond the family circle. Indeed, she preferred to publish anonymously and Henry's boasting in fashionable circles that the writer of *Pride and Prejudice* was his sister did not lead to a wide public outing. In Henry's account, Austen was shy of fame and famous people, a claim that he supports further in the expanded 'Biographical Notice' that prefaces the novels of the 1833 edition.

Most of Austen's biographers have accepted Henry's reticent Austen who put up with her brother's indiscretion about the authorship of her novel but remained unmoved in her reclusive ways. Recently, Claudia Johnson has offered a more nuanced interpretation, questioning the motive behind Austen's avoidance of notoriety and wondering whether it was a matter of character or of social circumstances. As Johnson argues, the letters evince Austen's pleasure at her growing reputation as a writer in literary circles:

> ■ Whether Austen's uneasiness with notoriety was genuinely her own, or whether it was to one degree or another foisted on her by her family, Jane Austen – as distinct from 'Jane Austen' – surely did not dwell among untrodden ways.[26] □

As for concerns of profit, Austen's letters abound in both hopeful and dispirited comments about the publication terms and sales of her novels. Upon the publication of *Sense and Sensibility*, for instance, she had savoured the joy of financial reward: 'I have now therefore written myself into £250. – which only makes me long for more.'[27] She was no stranger to the rules of the print market, knew the habits of her readership and followed the careers of fellow writers who also represented competition in economic terms. Her most famous comment in this regard was spurred by Walter Scott's publication of *Waverley* (1814), his first novel:

> ■ Walter Scott has no business to write novels, especially good ones. – It is not fair. – He has Fame and Profit enough as a Poet, and should not be

taking the bread out of other people's mouths. – I do not like him, & do not mean to like Waverley if I can help it – but fear I must.²⁸ ☐

Indeed, in comparison to Scott or female writers like Maria Edgeworth or Fanny Burney, Austen's profit was moderate. While Edgeworth, the leading female novelist of the day, amassed £11,062.8.10 from the sales of her novels and Burney £4,280, Austen received only £668 during her life, a sum that would have yielded a yearly income of £90.²⁹

The writer of the 'Biographical Notice' hopes that the posterity of a work of art need not rely on sale numbers. His reasons for such expectations lie with the works themselves and the exceptional skills of the artist that created them. In Austen's case, the instinctual delineation of the characters 'from nature [...] but never from individuals' is the jewel in the crown of a novelist who pursued perfection even in her private correspondence or daily notes: 'Every thing came finished from her pen' (*P* 7). This assessment reiterates Walter Scott's praise of the truthful depiction of manners and perfectly rounded characters in his review of *Emma*. It was an 'intuitive and almost unlimited' skill, Henry Austen writes (*P* 7). We encounter here the seeds for two lines of criticism: the first embraces, often quite uncritically, the view of Austen as the bright and intuitive rather than conscious genius, and the second, convinced by the highly finished characters, claims that under her pen domestic comedy reached perfection. In the next chapter, we will look at the influence the 'Biographical Notice' had on the immediate reception of the novels. Several reviewers accepted Henry's version of Austen as an intuitive perfectionist, but they also saw in it an opportunity to address the mimetic quality, called by Henry drawing from nature, in terms of the novels' scope, technique and morality.

CHAPTER TWO

Contemporary Reception, 1818–1840s

In the first year of their publication, *Northanger Abbey* and *Persuasion* were reviewed in *The British Critic*, *Blackwood's Edinburgh Magazine* and *The Gentleman's Magazine*. The last of these dwelled principally on Henry Austen's biographical note, but the first two offered discussions of Austen's style within the larger context of prose fiction, with frequent references to the vexed novel–romance relationship and the moral value of these literary forms. The most sustained analysis was Archbishop Richard Whately's lengthy article that appeared in *The Quarterly Review* three years later. Austen's passing prompted all reviewers to retrospectively assess her artistic contribution with the result that less attention was paid to the novels. Whately's analysis of *Persuasion*, which he preferred to *Northanger Abbey*, was an exception; it would be the second half of the nineteenth century before comparable assessments of the novels would be made.

Mimesis

During Austen's lifetime, unease about the novel as a genre was coupled with the unprecedented ascendancy of women writers. As the reviewer of Mary Wollstonecraft's *A Vindication of the Rights of Woman* in 1792 declared, 'Women we have often eagerly placed near the throne of literature: if they seize it, forgetful of our fondness, we can hurl them from it.'[1] While the majority of novel readers and writers were women, reviewers of the novels were mostly male and felt at times threatened by their counterparts' increasing numbers. However, constrained to cater for the novelistic taste of their readership, reviewers devoted attention to novels of their choice, often with the disclaimer that their 'fair' readers expected it of them.

The British Critic, the first to take notice of *Northanger Abbey* and *Persuasion*, explains with some reluctance that in order to preserve the wide-ranging spectrum of the journal, one or two superior novels have been chosen to be presented to the public.[2] The reviewer acknowledges that works like *Northanger Abbey* and *Persuasion* are worth this effort and that they demonstrate that good novels are 'perhaps, among the most fascinating productions of modern literature'.[3] The reviewer singles out the speech of the *dramatis personae* as Austen's main artistic skill. Rather than being described through the narrator's 'definitions', her characters reveal themselves to the reader through their own words and thoughts.[4] Not only does this technique distinguish one character from another, so that each acquires a unique personality on the page, but these self-representations have real-life resonances: 'we instantly recognize among some of our acquaintance, the sort of person she intends to signify, as accurately as if we had heard their voices'.[5] Later analysis of Austen's style will attribute the immediacy of characterization to her mastery of dialogue and the free indirect discourse that zooms into the characters' perceptions of people and situations.

The British Critic reviewer links this technique to the author's 'talent for observation' and her ability to translate the observed into written words, an ability that is likened to a painter's. Her compositions bear an 'exact and striking resemblance' to the realities they portray and it is from the 'perfect truth' of such imitation that readers derive pleasure, similar to that experienced by viewers of a painting that captures a minute similitude of a real-life object. In order to keep up this illusion of reality and to stay within the bounds of people who 'meet together every night, in every respectable house in London', the narrator must avoid exaggerations (like those of the romance), 'vivid and poetical sort of descriptions' and violent and improbable turns of plot.[6] The reviewer admits that there is a deplorable loss of imagination in this restrained choice of subject and style. However, it is a lack at the service of mimetic pleasure and rootedness in a typically English cultural environment.

Two months later, *The Edinburgh Magazine* elaborated these two points in a more concise review. This reviewer also concedes that Austen may have confined herself to 'a narrow walk' of ordinary people of no 'vehement passions', but within these boundaries she evinces a 'seemingly exhaustless invention'.[7] He explains the perception of Austen's subject matter as being limited and temperate in socio-literary terms: the wars with France and the prevailing taste for strong sensations have produced a readership that can be satisfied only with the 'highest seasoned food'. Her novels represent almost an anomaly in a time where 'real life Napoleons' hold public attention in suspense and works capitalizing on extraordinary, even 'fantastic characters', 'wild and monstrous' plots and 'national peculiarities' such as Scottish and Irish dialects (Maria

Edgeworth and Sir Walter Scott are mentioned), and exotic interests (as in Byron's *Corsair*) have inured the reader to the enjoyment of domestic fiction, which the reviewer calls 'familiar cabinet pictures'.[8] Against this literary backdrop, Austen's novels seem to operate without the 'slightest strain of imagination'.[9] Interestingly, her absence of imagination does not stand in contradiction to her almost 'exhaustless invention', suggesting that, although the novels' narrow scope necessitates reduced imagination, creativity within this scope raises them above common observations. These are observations of manners to be found in any town or village in England, the reviewer insists, but they are clothed in liveliness, humour and pathos. It is possibly herein that Austen's exquisite invention lies: she succeeds in raising interest in the familiar. Because her works accomplish this feat, they simultaneously evoke a paradoxical sense of affinity and uniqueness:

> ■ The singular merit of her writings is, that we could conceive [...] any one of her fictions to be realized in any town or village in England, [...] that we think we are reading the history of people whom we have seen thousands of times, and that with all that perfect commonness, both of incident and character, perhaps not one of her characters is to be found in any other book, portrayed at least in so lively and interesting a manner.[10] □

The reviewer draws two concluding remarks from this recognition: first, because the novels' attraction resides in style, the stories themselves are subordinated to artistic invention (*The British Critic*, too, considered the novels to have 'little narrative').[11] Second, due to their foundation in English domesticity and their exceptional prose, Austen's works will be rediscovered and read by later generations together with those of Henry Fielding and Samuel Richardson. The reviewer prophesies that when this happens, 'we have no hesitation in saying, that the delightful writer [...] will be one of the most popular of English novelists'.[12] Clearly, Austen's posterity is viewed in the tradition of the greatest writers of the eighteenth-century domestic novel, an affiliation that will be further elaborated by Ian Watt in his seminal *The Rise of the Novel* (1957), as discussed in Chapter 4.

The Question of Morality

Despite its praise of the genre as 'perhaps, among the most fascinating productions of modern literature', *The British Critic* expresses doubts about the novel's improving impact on the readers.[13] *Persuasion* does not escape these doubts and it is possible that they provoke the reviewer's preference for *Northanger Abbey*. In a matter of a few lines, *Persuasion* is found to be deficient in its morality: while it bears the same artistic signature and merits as the earlier novel:

> ■ we certainly should not number its moral, which seems to be, that young people should always marry according to their own inclinations and upon their own judgment; for that in consequence of listening to grave counsel, they defer their marriage, till they have wherewith to live upon, they will be laying the foundation for years of misery, such as only the heroes and heroines can reasonably hope even to see the end of.[14] □

Surprisingly, the morals of *Northanger Abbey* are not called into question, although the issues of morality and filial obedience force themselves on the reader's attention in the closing sentence, where a defiant narrator leaves 'it to be settled by whomsoever it may concern, whether the tendency of this work be altogether to recommend parental tyranny, or reward filial disobedience' (*NA* 235). The reviewer of *The Gentleman's Magazine*, too, dispensing with detailed commentaries, prefers *Northanger Abbey* to *Persuasion* for its plot and 'moral tendency'.[15] Among these early reviews, only *The Edinburgh Magazine* distinguishes between the novels in terms of mood rather than morality: *Northanger Abbey* is said to partake of a 'lively' style, while *Persuasion* is more 'pathetic'.[16] For this reviewer, there is no doubt that Austen remains faithful to the Christian sentiments that permeate her other novels, even though such sentiments are not openly displayed.

In his article in *The Quarterly Review* (1821), Richard Whately, archbishop of Dublin and writer, explains that the novels' morality complements their entertainment value. Since Sir Philip Sidney, the chief goal of good literature had been to instruct and delight, that is, to offer moral insights to readers by keeping them genuinely interested in the work itself. Whately argues that not only did Austen understand the potential of the novel to balance the aims of instruction and entertainment, but she excelled in their mutual amplifications according to the logic that aesthetic pleasure heightens the reader's willingness to adopt moral lessons. There are two important ideas in Whately's analysis: the first involves the status and value of the novel as a genre, and the second, Austen's superiority as a novelist.

Whately defends the genre of the novel in terms of its instructive power: the new 'prose-fiction', as he calls it, is an effective vehicle of moral improvement. So much so that it has superseded explicit and 'formal' tracts or essays concerned with moral issues. The essays contained in *The Spectator* and *The Rambler*, for instance, fall into the category of such formal productions, in which morality is expressed through generalized precepts. In contrast, the novel chooses the language of the particular; it conveys similar ideas by the examples illustrated 'in the course of conversations suggested by the circumstances of the speakers, and perfectly in character'.[17] Whately reminds the readers that, if they allow that biography is the most instructive reading (a common opinion at the time), then they must concede comparable worth to the novel, which is 'a kind of fictitious biography'.[18]

Austen excels in this field because she lets the events and characters of these fictitious biographies illuminate morality without being obtrusively didactic. Unlike Maria Edgeworth, who thought of the moral first and then of circumstances and characters to illustrate it, Austen did not treat her tales as accessories or subordinates to premeditated instruction. Indeed, her novels inculcate virtue most effectively due to the fact that morality always springs from the actions of individuals. As Whately puts it, 'If instruction do not join as a volunteer, she will do no service.'[19] He seems to have more confidence than other critics in the reader's ability to discern good from bad examples and abstains from any cautionary remarks about the necessity of making moral lessons unequivocal.

Whately's assessment of the novel is among the most positive we encounter in the long eighteenth century. It also echoes Austen's defence of novel readers in *Northanger Abbey*, who, under the pressure of public disdain towards the novel, must feign interest in *The Spectator*'s improbable plots, 'unnatural characters' and outdated 'topics of conversation' (*NA* 37). Hence, both Austen and Whately attribute to the genre modern appeal and sensibility. Confident of this appeal, Whately states in the opening lines of his review that the times are past in which the study of the novel was preceded by the critic's apology or condescension.

When it comes to any specific morality, the reviewers are quite vague (with the exception of *The British Critic*'s displeasure at *Persuasion*'s support of filial independence). However, their comments on Austen's taste, 'fine sense' and 'delicate humour' link instructive power to the observation of human weaknesses and strengths.[20] In particular, she appears as a psychological portraitist attracted to depictions of human folly and affectation. Nonetheless, this predilection for the ridiculous is not interpreted as a sign of misanthropy. On the contrary, while it leads readers to critical assessments of each character, it does not induce a profound questioning of sociability. Her humour is not 'satire' and her comedies are 'innocent amusement',[21] as *The British Critic* explains:

> ■ [T]he follies which she holds up to us, are, for the most part, mere follies, or else natural imperfections; and she treats them, as such, with good-humoured pleasantry; mimicking them so exactly, that we always laugh at the ridiculous truth of the imitation, but without ever being incited

to indulge in feelings, that might tend to render us ill-natured, and intolerant in society.²² ☐

The novels therefore steer clear of morbid social critique by reflecting some of the reader's own 'absurdities [...] back upon one's conscience'. Through this inclusionary technique, readers recognize their own flaws in fiction and are compelled to submit to self-interrogation, which in return serves to reintegrate them, in an improved state, into the social order. In light of this, we can perhaps understand why another critic enthuses over Austen's 'most charitable view of human nature'.²³ More importantly, the novels' sociable morality complements the reviewer's experience of the author as a 'most fascinating companion' and 'one whom we had long known and loved'.²⁴ Such personal attachment that conflates author and text peaks in the attitudes of Janeite readers at the end of the nineteenth century (see Chapter 4).

Plot, Character and Shakespeare

Whately's review represents the first elaborate discussion of *Northanger Abbey* and *Persuasion*. Although primarily interested in the question of morality, Whately makes an interesting connection between the instructive authority and the larger narrative frame of the novel as prose fiction. For him, the more a work of fiction aligns itself with the rules of probability and naturalness, the greater its moral impact on its readers. He derives the definitions of probability and naturalness from the categories of plot and character. Earlier reviewers had found little to say about Austen's plots, maintaining that the stories' few variations and overturns were in themselves not worthy of special attention. However, the combination with the characters rendered them beautiful and simple at the same time. The issue of probability had already been discussed in connection to the extravagances of the romance genre that Austen's novels wisely avoided. However, there was an exception to this practice. According to *The British Critic*, *Northanger Abbey* introduces improbable incidents and characters. In particular, General Tilney is considered to be a fanciful creation removed from the novelist's 'usual taste and judgement'.²⁵ Before the publication of this review in March 1818, Maria Edgeworth, in her private correspondence, expressed similar reservations:

■ The behaviour of the General in *Northanger Abbey*, packing off the young lady without a servant or the common civilities which any bear of a man, not to say a gentleman, would have shown, is quite outrageously out of drawing and out of nature.²⁶ ☐

But what does drawing out of or according to nature imply? For this, we have to turn to Whately's distinction between probability and naturalness.

Whately argues that incidents are improbable when the chances are against them. Many eighteenth-century tropes fall under this category: when in the moment of their direst need the protagonists meet exactly the person who can release them from it; or when an unexpected piece of news, communicated at the right moment, leads to the resolution that characters and readers have been hoping for (this would suggest *deus ex machina*, that is contrived, *dénouements*; Austen's teenage work abounds in such lucky contrivances). The naturalness of event and character resides in the very logic that holds them together. When the people described act contrary to their assigned dispositions they become unnatural. For instance, a young and retired heroine, surrounded by 'narrow-minded and illiterate' adults, who displays the knowledge only experience and learning can afford is unnatural. Hence, naturalness has to do with 'consistency of character', while probability refers to likely occurrences. However, Whately acknowledges that improbable circumstances or unnatural characters can be encountered in real life itself, which explains the existence of such expressions as 'lucky or unlucky accident' or 'inexplicable or unaccountable' behaviour.[27]

The natural and probable do not necessarily coexist in fiction. They do not, for example, in Henry Fielding's novels, in which 'a perfect consistency of character' is preserved in the course of 'extraordinary adventures'.[28] For this reason, Fielding's *Tom Jones* is improbable but nonetheless natural. In view of these categories, Austen's novels are 'nearly faultless': they display a balance of unity of action and consistency of character in which neither of the two is subordinated to the other. It is, Whately writes, as if Austen had applied Aristotle's precepts *à la lettre*.

When attempting to clothe in words the novel's extraordinary aesthetic qualities, Whately relies on Shakespeare. He is the writer who, in Aristotle's spirit, did not impose his voice on his characters but allowed them to speak according to their nature, thus creating a truly dramatic universe. Austen achieves a similar effect through the conversations that fill her novels. Like Shakespeare, her observational and representational skills are not limited to witty and wise characters. Her fools (or weaker characters) reveal themselves with equal verisimilitude. The objection that her fools are tiresome, because they remind one too much of folly in real life, meets with Whately's downright dismissal: he argues that, while there is no point in quarrelling about differences of taste, readers who complain of Austen's tediousness must find the *Merry Wives of Windsor* and *Twelfth Night* tiresome. This comparison to Shakespeare saves Austen from another charge of tediousness: the detailed description of character. Whately argues that if one decided to strip from

Shakespeare's plays everything that has no intrinsic value or independent merit, one would rob the plays of half of their charms. Without the minute details, spectators and readers would hardly be so enthralled by the characters.

Of all characters, Austen's women are the best-realized. In this, she has no precedent. Unlike other women novelists, who are found deficient in rendering their heroines' interiority, Austen does not shy away from depicting 'naked a female mind'.[29] Her heroines are 'anxious to attract the attention of agreeable men, as much taken with a striking manner, or a handsome face, as unequally gifted with constancy and firmness' and as influenced by fashion or circumstances as men.[30] Thus, psychological complexity rather than moral perfection elevates them above the average novelistic heroine.

The Novels

The reviewers have less to say about *Northanger Abbey* and *Persuasion*. The novels are quite rapidly evaluated according to notions of morality and mimesis of character and plot. While *The British Critic* repudiates *Persuasion* for its doubtful moral lesson and declares *Northanger Abbey* to be 'one of the very best of Miss Austen's productions' that repays 'the time and trouble of perusing it', *The Edinburgh Magazine* finds equal merit in them: *Northanger Abbey* is 'more lively' and *Persuasion* 'more pathetic'.[31] It is noteworthy that these reviewers, despite Austen's fears, do not regard *Northanger Abbey*'s Gothic theme and style as outdated. Whately reverses the preference of *The British Critic*, finding only a few words of praise for *Northanger Abbey* before proceeding with a thoughtful assessment of *Persuasion*.

Northanger Abbey, he writes, is a worthy representative of the Gothic genre, although, due to its lack of plot and moral sophistication, it holds an inferior position among Austen's novels. However, Whately admits that he cannot resist including a comment on Austen's humorous treatment of John Thorpe's refusal to drive his sister 'because she has such thick ankles' and his 'horse that cannot go less than 10 miles an hour' or his 'sober consumption of five pints of port a day'.[32] Whately identifies John Thorpe as a representative of a category of its own – the character of the hard-drinking, 'Bang-up Oxonian' – while Isabella Thorpe embodies the category of husband-hunting middle-class woman.[33] With tangible relish for Austen's double-edged prose, Whately draws on John Morland's words to sum up the narrator's (and reader's) condemnation of Isabella: 'I can never expect to know such another woman' (*NA* 149).[34]

Persuasion earns a more detailed analysis from Whately. It is a work of mature age, he argues, and it does not disappoint in showing the novelist at the height of her powers: it is second to none of her earlier productions, 'if not superior to all'.[35] Like in all of Austen's novels, readers find in it humorous entertainment, although to a lesser degree. Indeed, many silly or conceited characters are described with the 'minute fidelity to nature' of Hogarth's prints, a technique which ensures both entertainment and social critique (note that the novel is linked to the satirist tradition of the eighteenth century, contradicting *The British Critic*, who argues that Austen 'never dips her pen in satire').[36] Despite its humorous delineations, Whately describes *Persuasion*'s chief interest as being 'tender' and 'elevated', thus vaguely echoing the reviewer of *The Edinburgh Magazine*, who emphasizes the novel's pathos. Whately points out the isolation of Anne Elliot in the midst of her unworthy family, claiming that in Austen's universe the solitude of her heroines epitomizes the human condition: Anne is 'the only one possessed of good sense, (a quality which Miss Austin is as sparing of in her novels, as we fear her great Mistress, Nature, has been in real life)'.[37] As the events are related from the perspective of the extraordinary, but lonely, Anne Elliot, the novel's pathos outweighs the humoristic vein.

In Whately's vocabulary, the 'infinite spirit and detail' of Anne's perspective endows *Persuasion*'s prose and story with elegance:

■ First, dread of the meeting, – then, as that is removed by custom, renewed regret for the happiness she has thrown away, and the constantly recurring contrast, though known only to herself, between the distance of their intercourse and her involuntary sympathy with all his feelings, and instant comprehension of all his thoughts, of the meaning of every glance of his eye, and curl of his lip, and intonation of his voice. In him her mild good sense and elegance gradually re-awake long-forgotten attachment.[38] □

In addition, elegance (as in its Latin origins 'select with care') also applies to *Persuasion*'s morality. According to Whately, in her previous novels, Austen promotes prudence instead of romantic enthusiasm. In her last novel, however, there is doubt whether Anne Elliot would have better followed her inclinations or listened to Lady Russell's cautious advice. Far from being frustrated by the novel's uncertain morality, Whately celebrates it as 'the proper medium', which compels the reader to test the bounds of prudence and love.[39] Whately's personal endorsement goes to love, which is recognized as a powerful stimulus to moral improvement. Anne embodies a Christian kind of love, a passion that overcomes self-centredness and self-admiration, by imaginatively drawing the self towards the other's wants and inclinations. In 1823, possibly influenced by Whately's rhetoric, *The Retrospective Review* writes of an 'angelic' Anne 'to whom all instinctively turned for counsel, sympathy and consolation'.[40]

Apart from these critical pronouncements, *Northanger Abbey* and *Persuasion* received little attention. The reasons for this neglect may rest with the contemporary *Zeitgeist* – the spirit of the age – and the developing taste for novels that delved into the period's social ailments, such as poverty, homelessness and legal injustice. Austen's novels, in contrast, were seen as antiquated comedies of manners. Even those who admired her humour, for example, Mary Shelley, whose *Frankenstein* shared the same year of publication with *Northanger Abbey* and *Persuasion*, found her philosophical views less developed.[41] The Shakespearean actor William Macready described *Northanger Abbey* as 'heavy' and putting 'too long a strain of irony on one topic',[42] while Henry Crabb Robinson's disappointment was such as to reduce his estimation of Jane Austen, for he thought of the novels as being 'little more than galleries of disagreeables' and their protagonists 'scarcely out of the class of insignificants'.[43] Brian Southam, who offered the first sustained critical analysis of Austen's manuscripts in 1964, rightly concludes that Austen's contemporary readers seem not ready to follow the challenge of 'her disconcerting account of the ways and values of their society'.[44] They shrunk back from the implications of her satire and appeased their discomfort by speaking, at best, of her 'nicely-regulated vein of humour'.[45]

1830s–1840s

The most significant event in the following decade was the appearance of the six novels in the *Standard Novels* series published by Richard Bentley in 1833. From 1818 to 1833, there had been no new editions and it is to be presumed that the novels had fallen into obscurity. Bentley's series, however, placed Austen among novelists like Horace Walpole, Elizabeth Inchbald, William Godwin, William Beckford, Madame de Staël, Catherine Gore, Mary Shelley and Edward Dulwer-Lytton. Cassandra Austen sold the copyright to Bentley, who reprinted them at six shillings a volume (until then, the novels had been marketed at 15s, 18s and 21s). He also accompanied them with illustrations that reflected a Victorian taste of fashion, dissociating them from the Regency period in which they originated. Although it took about four years for the copies of this edition to sell, the fact that there was a second one in 1837 is proof of a revived interest. However, considering that for almost twenty years the novels were not reprinted, popular attention seems to have been short-lived.

It is a recurring conviction in the reviews of the first half of the nineteenth century that Austen had not achieved the popularity she deserved. Readers had been deceived by the 'unpromising materials' of her novels (that is, scenes of common life among the middling ranks) and had failed to appreciate the superb artistry with which those materials had been handled. Her greatest achievement resided in the very concealment of the art that made the characters the readers' intimates and their conversations anything but 'bookish'.[46]

Among Austen's Romantic contemporaries, Robert Southey, Poet Laureate from 1813 to 1843, praised the novels unequivocally as having 'passages of finer feelings than any others of this age'. Coleridge, according to his daughter Sara, shared Southey's high opinion, whereas Wordsworth conceded that, albeit admirable copies of life, they lacked 'the pervading light of imagination'.[47] This lack, already identified by the very first reviewers of *Northanger Abbey* and *Persuasion*, continued to be advanced even by Austen enthusiasts. George Henry Lewes, a literary critic, journalist, philosopher and admirer of Austen, seems to have written to Charlotte Brontë that Austen did not have a poet's 'eloquence' or 'sentiment' and 'none of the ravishing enthusiasm of poetry'. Nonetheless, in the same letter, he exhorts Brontë to 'learn to acknowledge her as one of the greatest artists, of the greatest painters of human character'.[48] He calls Austen 'the prose Shakespeare'.[49] However, Brontë did not submit to this 'strange lecture': 'Can there be a great artist without poetry?' she asks. Her answer is distinct: Austen may be 'sensible' and 'real', but without poetry and sentiment, 'she cannot be great'.[50] The intellectual conversation between George Henry Lewes and Charlotte Brontë has come to represent the culmination of the Romantic case against Austen, which conceives of the novels as faithful representations of surfaces, rather than profound probes into the psyche in its oscillations between self-command and overwhelming passions.

The second half of the nineteenth century, however, sees an increasing appreciation of the novels and a refinement of Lewes's commentaries on Austen's unpoetic but perfectly dramatic art. In continuation of these discussions, Chapter 3 presents interpretations that argue for Austen's technique of selective realism that creates a purportedly smooth surface beneath which the careful reader senses the stirrings of a cynic mind. Of all her novels, *Northanger Abbey* emerges as the clearest expression of this tension between surface and depth, parody and drama, laughter and critique.

CHAPTER THREE

Victorian Readers, 1850s–1900s

The second half of the nineteenth century saw the publication of the first biography of Jane Austen, *A Memoir of Jane Austen* (1870) by her nephew James Edward Austen-Leigh, alongside new editions of the novels in 1857, 1870 and 1897. Despite renewed interest in Austen's work and life, there is little critical engagement with *Northanger Abbey* and *Persuasion*, whereas *Pride and Prejudice*, *Emma* and *Mansfield Park* seem to be favourites with readers for whom Austen is uncontestably one of the greatest novelists. On the other hand, there is more sustained analysis of key features of her art.

In particular, critics discuss with increased discernment the nature and implications of the novels' realism. One of the most interesting developments of this period's criticism is the connection established between the novels' commitment to realism and Austen's self-restraint. More often than not, the latter equates with the repression of those imaginative impulses that threaten the novels' perfect mimetic illusion. Although this connection is not utterly new, some Victorian critics recognize in it the actual proof of Austen's irony and even cynicism, implying that wit and humour not only depend upon the absence of sentimentality but also betray the narrator's distanced coldness. Hence, we encounter here the first intimations that Austen's novels may not be as benign and harmless as thought earlier in the century. In order to trace this development, the present chapter begins with commentaries pertaining to Austen's novelistic art (these outnumber discussions of any particular novel), before turning to the criticism of *Northanger Abbey* and *Persuasion*.

Selective Realism

George Lewes, journalist and critic, and Richard Simpson, Shakespearean scholar, offer two of the longest and most influential articles of the period. Lewes's piece, written in 1859, is partly motivated by what he considers to be Austen's paradoxical afterlife, noticing that few beyond literary circles know Austen as an author, despite her novels being widely read and enjoyed.[1] In a similar vein, in 1870, Simpson ponders her peculiar status, writing that she is great in the history of literature but insignificant in the history of men of letters.[2] Lewes believes that the future will rectify the asymmetry between the reputation of the novels and that of their author, since Austen's 'indestructible excellence' transcends literary fashions and ages.[3] He classifies her representations of character among those of the most illustrious dramatists, never mind that her subjects are not grand and her 'dramas of homely common quality'.[4] The sensation-seeking mass of readers misses the double life of her prose hidden beneath the unrippled surface of ordinary pictures. For Lewes, this double life, the very secret of Austen's simple tales, hinges on the narrator's knowledge of human character and 'how it is acted upon by education and circumstance'.[5] Simpson, too, insists that verisimilitude should not be confounded with mere imitation and that critical judgement lies at the core of Austen's artistic faculty. In this, he declares, she is truly Shakespearean.[6]

Lewes acknowledges that previous critics, Scott being the most renowned of them, had praised Austen's description of everyday life. However, he also laments that the general tenor of such praise leaves this innovative mimetic excellence undefined. Indeed, the word 'description' is misleading, he cautions. It is rather in the art of 'dramatic presentation' that the novel's strength and uniqueness reside. Austen refrains from telling us her characters' feelings and instead creates the circumstances and conversations through which the characters reveal themselves. Her power is 'dramatic ventriloquism' and, in this, she is the least intruding narrator of all.[7] Not even descriptions of physical appearance interfere with the idea we create of each character by simply eavesdropping on their words and thoughts. Like the dramatist, who does not rely on descriptions, knowing that the characters will be embodied in flesh and blood on stage, Austen trusts that her characters will take shape in the reader's mind through their own personality. However, because so much construction of character depends on subjective perception and must happen without narratorial guidance, certain relations between mental and physical organization are bound to be missed by the reader. (Lewes's ingenious remark hints at the novels' open-endedness and their appeal for very diverse readerships.) To illustrate Austen's originality, Lewes draws a comparison to two giants of European realism, Balzac and Dickens: both, he claims, would have not been content without making the reader see their characters, while Austen wants to make us know them.[8] Knowing also dissociates Austen's characters from Charlotte Brontë's: Jane Eyre and Rochester, for example, are 'vigorous sketches, but the reader observes them from the *outside*, he does not penetrate their souls, he does not know them'.[9]

Comparisons to other novelists proved enlightening. The question was, if Austen dealt with pictures of the household, a common practice in eighteenth- and nineteenth-century fiction, what set her realism apart? In her 1862 article, Julia Kavanagh, novelist and biographer, located this difference in the experience of femininity. She argued that the writings of women display at least one of three qualities: delicacy, tenderness and sympathy. Austen's novels thrive on delicacy, whereas, for instance, Aphra Behn's *Oroonoko* thrives on sympathy. Delicacy enables Austen to paint rather than analyse life. Moreover, it renders her prose deceptively realistic, because it represents life tamed, levelled and subdued in unnatural stillness. Life never runs as smoothly as in her novels, Kavanagh concludes.[10]

In 1870, Margaret Oliphant, an influential critic and novelist, furthered the conversation around the novels' realism, by insisting on their author's experience as a member of a certain class. William F. Pollock had earlier observed that the social range of Austen's characters did not exceed that of a baronet and rarely moved below the professional and commercial ranks.[11] Oliphant does not argue for a ladylike Austen, although she writes of the 'genteel way' in which her characters endure only a few hardships. She anchors Austen's observant style in the reality of the landed gentry. Thus, if her characters seem to lead quite unruffled lives, it is because Austen chooses to restrict her craft to the social sphere she knows most intimately.[12]

We see here a new development: next to the Victorian social novel and its ambition for a panoramic view of social stratification, Austen's fiction seems limited and even self-indulgent. Although Oliphant goes on to praise Austen's remorseless truthfulness within her own class, Victorian readers only occasionally conceive of the novels as the domestic *tableaux* representative of the English household that they were thought to be upon publication. Indeed, as literature of a bygone England which, as one critic puts it, 'we can scarcely believe was England only half-a-century ago', they ooze antiquated charm.[13] The few deeper concerns that surface in the novels are dealt with so 'lightly and gently' that they could arise only from the workings of a placid and content mind.[14] In Leslie Stephen's estimation, Austen's 'delightful world of well-warmed country-houses' ignores the daily struggles of ninety-nine per cent of the population.[15] Against this backdrop, Simpson writes that:

■ [i]ndeed there is nothing in her novels to prove that she had any conception of society itself but only of the coterie of three or four families mixing together, with differences of intellect, wealth, or character, but without any grave social inequities. Of organized society she manifests no idea. She had no interest for the great political and social problems which were being debated with so much blood in her day. The social combinations which taxed the calculating powers of Adam Smith or Jeremy Bentham were above her powers.[16] □

This view will be intensely contested by late-twentieth-century scholars. However, Simpson's assertion that Austen's apolitical art 'could rise to contemplate the soul as a family, but not as a republic' is a persisting charge.[17]

Even Austen's most enthusiastic admirers admit that such a narrow social field affects not only the novels' mimetic scope but also the richness of intellectual ideas and the readers' responses to them. For example, George Pellew, writer of the first dissertation on Austen's *oeuvre* in 1883, attributes to George Eliot the ability to provoke higher thoughts and deeper sympathy in readers, because she belongs to that genus of writers who 'represent in typical characters the aspirations and intellectual life of a whole generation'.[18] In contrast, far from arousing emotional identification by capturing the *Zeitgeist*, Austen capitalizes on the 'real though unexciting pleasure' derived from enduring observations of human nature. Consequently, her realism, unlike Eliot's, evinces universal rather than historical or political acumen.[19] Only in light of these considerations does Pellew admit that Eliot is a great author in a sense in which Austen is not and did not aspire to be.

For less congenial critics, Austen's mimesis is merely parochial 'maiden lady realism' removed from philosophic or universal realism.[20] Her gender sets the parameters of her 'provincial' fiction: she observes from a woman's point of view what no man would notice, invests herself more deeply and with better results in her female characters and does not venture into the unknown region of male sociability which explains the absence of only-men scenes.[21] The novels themselves are the 'lightest bubbles on the great stream of existence' brightened by Austen's 'genius'. In particular, the courtship plot that rewards a young lady with a profitable match motivates such views. Not simply did Austen write about her class, but also about the typical concern of a spinster of her class: marriage.[22] Thus, not surprisingly, as one critic puts it in 1889, Austen's readers form quite a controversial community: they 'either award them [the novels] unbounded praise or find them insufferably dull'.[23]

Concealed Perfection of Artifice

Comments on Austen's 'dramatic ventriloquism', feminine delicacy, 'genteel' handling of social evils and flawed characters prompt critics to carefully examine the novels' narrative technique. For example, if (according to Lewes) the narrator's goal is to make the reader know the recesses of the characters' psyche, which stylistic elements enable this internal (rather than external) assessment of character? Which artistic devices produce certain effects?

As we have seen in the previous chapter, critics speak of Austen's style as a wondrous veil that beautifies her rather simple stories, and of portraits of a perfect finish that disguises the very efforts at the heart of the creative process. One critic puts it in the following terms:

> ■ Her style is very rich, and not only rich with the palpable meaning which in each individual sentence she has to express, but rich also in those swift, indescribable associations which well chosen words recall, allusions to past reading, the reflected sparkle of past thinking, the fragrance of past feeling.[24] □

Two key features seem to shape her prose: exactness of expression and multifarious lexical possibilities. Not only is every sentence well-gauged for its context, but also the words evoke a series of associations in the reader, thus generating a variety of meanings. Expressions such as 'sparkle of past thinking' and 'fragrance of past feeling' testify to the difficulty critics encounter when attempting to pin down the particularities of Austen's style. Not surprisingly, Pollock writes of the concealment of the 'machinery of representation' and of characters that never leave the narrative frame in spite of this frame's invisibility; whereas another critic maintains that the elusiveness of such 'art-concealing art' accounts for the novels' modernity.[25]

Pollock, however, is among the first to raise the veil of invisibility and offer more precise analysis. For him, dramatic power depends on the characters being recognizable in their individuality, which demands that the minutest markings of character be at the service of individual personality. Pollock insists that in Austen's hands this recognizability does not produce stereotypes. On the contrary, as no worn-out words or catchphrases are deployed to reveal the characters, the reader can never predict what a person will say or do. However, their words and actions, although unexpected, lead the reader deeper into the truth of their individuality. Simpson, too, hints at this selective method in a rather elliptic remark: 'She is so true because she is consciously exceeding the truth.'[26] Read next to Pollock's observation on the characters' language and its simultaneous recognizability and unpredictability, Simpson's remark suggests that the novels present distilled truthfulness.

Along similar lines, Mary Augusta Ward, a novelist, essayist and niece of Matthew Arnold, writes of Austen's mastery of condensation, which Ward deems the most defining quality of her art. Ward explains that in works of literature condensation requires discrimination, that is, the capacity to choose, from a myriad of parts that create what we call daily life, only those details that when put together will fit into one whole universe. She likens the work of the discerning novelist to that of the clear-sighted gardener who skilfully prunes the tree in view of its potential. In literature, Ward writes:

> ■ [i]t implies the determination to avoid everything cheap and easy – cheapness in sentiment, in description, in caricature. In matters of mere language it means the perpetual effort to be content with one word rather than two, the perpetual impulse to clip and prune rather than expand and lengthen.[27] □

Only the superior artist knows what to prune and what to infuse with imagination.

Ward's analysis picks up on the economy of style that Lewes equates with the highest achievement of art ('the *truest* representation, effected by the *least expenditure* of means').[28] However, she not only describes it with unprecedented clarity but also provides explicit illustrations from the novels. She singles out, for example, Anne Elliot's silent rapture upon detecting Captain Wentworth's jealousy of Mr. Elliot, which, for Ward, demonstrates brilliantly Austen's infusion of details of sober truth with poetry. Here we enter into Anne's thoughts enhanced by the narrator's intervention:

> ■ Their union, she [Anne] believed, could not divide her more from other men than their final separation. Prettier musings of high-wrought love and eternal constancy could never have passed along the streets of Bath than Anne was sporting with from Camden Place to Westgate Buildings. It was almost enough to spread purification and perfume all the way. (P 155) □

This passage stands as a specimen of the style that makes the novels the classics that they are: 'terse' but 'suggestive', poetical but free from 'vulgarity' and 'commonplace'.[29] Thus, Ward and Lewes are the first to classify Austen's novels as fictions of selection. Ward advises those who prefer expansion – or in Henry James's words 'saturation' – to seek it elsewhere. Equally important is the connection that Ward makes between concentration and Austen's 'temper of self-restraint'.[30] Narrative control through the condensation of wisely selected details, be they thoughts, conversations or emotional responses, testifies to the author's ethos of self-discipline.

For others, concentration and selection imply conscious exclusion, which, in Austen's case, produces the sifting away of all 'that takes real wear and tear of spirit'.[31] Richard H. Hutton likens this technique to a 'fine feminine sieve' that amuses the readers without taxing their attention with conflicted realities. In a witty and gendered hypothesis, Hutton conjectures that if Tennyson's Lady of Shalott had seen Austen's pictures on her mirror, she would have been 'satisfied without plunging into the stream of life'.

Restraint and Irony

Conflations of Austen's psychological make-up and the tenor of her work occur frequently after the biographical insights reached the public through the pronouncements of her family members. Henry Austen's comments on his sister's uneventful life and mild disposition reveal, for some critics, the reason behind the novels' tranquil scenes. Neither the author nor her creations step out of 'the humdrum of easy-going respectable life' and, under such untroubled circumstances, Austen cannot but 'be calm and neat in arranging every thread of the narrative she has to weave', in choosing the right words and evoking the right images.[32] Selection and condensation appear as much the novels' recipe as Austen's own living experience.[33] In Anne Thackeray's words, Austen's 'machinery is simple' but she operates it 'with unerring precision'.[34] No wonder that her fiction is not a world of exalted heroism or extraordinary passions.

Even critics who grant her tenderness of heart hasten to add that this does not imply sentiment. Her imagination is 'sustained', 'cool' and 'comfortable' and her pathos at best touching.[35] She governs her craft with characteristic patience, 'perfectly calm, perfectly self-conscious'.[36] Poise defines her imagination, her treatment of human joy and sorrow and, most importantly, as Simpson argues, her wit.

Next to the 'art-concealing art', the nature and implications of Austen's wit are the most discussed stylistic features. But what type of humour is hers? Does she belong to the ironist school of Cervantes or Swift? According to Simpson, she does not, because her humour, unlike Cervantes's or Swift's, does not adhere to an implicit but understood 'common measure'.[37] Perhaps it is Austen's control over imagination, which keeps her from running away with her humour, that does not compare well to Cervantes's and Swift's extravagances and accounts for Simpson's simplification of these writers' ironic intricacies. However, by pointing out the lack of a common ground against which the reader can test Austen's irony, Simpson anticipates the notion of unstable irony, in which no secure standpoints are shared by reader and narrator. This lack impacts the morality of the stories and discloses Austen's view of 'virtues, not as fixed quantities, or as definable qualities, but as continual struggles and conquests and progressive states of mind'.[38] Simpson therefore more readily aligns Austen with Thackeray and Charles Lamb, who couple their wit with critical judgement and have an eye for the humorous in ordinary life, even though none of them has Austen's mastery over imagination. Indeed, because she is first and foremost a critic rather than a poet, imagination never outstrips judgement in her novels.[39]

Such emphasis on controlled and restrained imagination expands and gives an analytical body to more subjective evaluations of irony. It underlies perceptions of her irony as 'gentle' but 'cold'.[40] Indeed, as one critic puts it, the narratives' subtle satirical strokes can succeed only if unclouded by colourful emotionality.[41] Therefore, her humour tends to tickle rather than provoke loud laughter.[42] However, some critics are less willing to explain restraint by Austen's good sense or artistic decorum. For Oliphant, gentle irony fails to do justice to the narrator's 'fine stinging yet soft-voiced contempt'.[43] Austen stands by as a half-smiling onlooker who occasionally sympathizes with sufferers, but the 'gentle disdain of the possibility that meanness and folly and stupidity could ever really wound any rational creature' prevents her (and her readers) from feeling truly sorry. While still drawing on words like 'gentle' and 'soft', Oliphant introduces the jarring eventuality that, notwithstanding its mild tone, the attitude feeds on derision and cynicism. Most interestingly, Oliphant defines this stance of the cynical, restrained onlooker as 'essentially feminine':

■ The position of mind is essentially feminine, and one which may be readily identified in the personal knowledge of most people. It is the natural result of constant, though probably quite unconscious, observation in which a young woman, with no active pursuit to occupy her, spends, without knowing it, so much of her time and youth. [...] A certain soft despair of any human creature ever doing good to another – of any influence overcoming those habits and moods and peculiarities of mind which the observer sees to be more obstinate than life itself – a sense that nothing is to be done but to look on, to say perhaps now and then a softening word, to make the best of it practically and theoretically, to smile and hold up one's hands and wonder why human creatures should be such fools, – such are the foundations upon which the feminine cynicism which we attribute to Miss Austen is built.[44] □

Oliphant returns with emphasis to the feminine character of Austen's cynicism, leaving the reader wondering how it contrasts with masculine cynicism. Although her gendered differentiation is hard to grasp without its masculine counterpart, it seems that this feminine cynical state of mind stems from a social position that restricts gentry women to the activity of observation and acceptance of things as they are. From this position, Austen, 'softly feminine and polite, and so remorselessly true', delineates with tolerance and controlled contempt ('not absolute', Oliphant insists) the absurdities of a humankind that she holds in low regard.[45]

Alice Meynell reiterates this view, writing in 1894, that Austen watches her characters like the characters watch one another, with intense curiosity but little tenderness. In the absence of sympathy, such close observation attests to the narrator's 'exceeding cynicism'.[46] George Saintsbury, a staunch admirer of Austen's and self-declared Austenite, takes issue with the charge of cynicism. He attempts to redefine this 'misused' word by reminding the reader that its conflation with gentle and oblique satire obfuscates its original association with 'rough and snarling invective'. Austen may be called a cynic only in this misunderstood sense of the word; she is as much a cynic as anyone who is not a fool and refuses 'to live in a fool's paradise'.[47] Clearly, Saintsbury tones down the distrustful aloofness that Oliphant and Meynell reckon to be characteristic of Austen's attitude.

It is noteworthy that Oliphant's distinction of the cynical feminine perspective contrasts with other critics' emphasis on her unfemininity, in particular Lewes, who praised her as having 'nothing of the doctrinaire [...] not a trace of a woman's mission'.[48] Lewes's Austen seems to be more innocent and much under the influence of Henry's biographical notice. Oliphant, on the other hand, insists that disbelief, rather than hope, and amused resignation, rather than missionary zeal of improvement, underlie Austen's apparent tolerance. Austen has judgement, but she is neither her characters' judge nor censor. The faculty to see and delineate states of minds and motivations detached from an accepted standard of right or wrong constitutes her feminine humour.

We encounter here, in slightly different terms, the lack of a stable moral ground noted by Simpson. Like Oliphant, he perceives Austen as an author distanced from her creations, who sat 'apart on her rocky tower, and watched the poor souls struggling in the waves beneath' with 'amused and ironical complacency'.[49] Nonetheless, for Simpson, Austen is a kind albeit complex humourist, because her novels do not collapse the characters and the narrator's consciousness. On the contrary, while speaking words of faith through her characters, she knows how to convey her own sense of scepticism.[50]

Besides similar comments on emotional coldness, feminine cynicism and scepticism, there are critics who dismiss Austen's ironic complexity and view her humour as excessively mild and without 'a single flash of biting satire'.[51] More often than not, these are also the very critics who lament the narrow, class-biased and glossed reality of her novels. However, when undertaken, explorations of humour and style shed new light on Austen's abilities as a novelist, who, far from merely observing and painting the surfaces of life, is driven by an unsettling spirit of inquiry.

Northanger Abbey

After the publication of Austen-Leigh's *Memoir*, a chronological relation between Austen's early writings and *Northanger Abbey* emerges. Austen-Leigh had revealed that his aunt started writing in her teens, and Simpson in his long review of *Memoir* indicates that her first completed novel, *Northanger Abbey*, grew out of these teenage writings, to which it owes its parodic vein. Austen, like Shakespeare, sharpened her artistic vision by observing and setting up an ironical distance between herself and her contemporaries, the traces of which can be found in the burlesque tone of *Northanger Abbey*. The term 'parody', however, needs careful qualification because

> ■ her parodies were designed not so much to flout at the style as at the unnaturalness, unreality, and fictitious morality, of the romances she imitated. She began by being an ironical critic; she manifested her judgment of them not by direct censure, but by the indirect method of imitating and exaggerating the faults of the models, thus clearing the fountain by first stirring up the mud. This critical spirit lies at the foundation of her artistic faculty.[52] □

According to Simpson, this is a three-pronged faculty that imitates, enquires and mocks simultaneously. For this reason, her parody is quite complex and new: it penetrates the styles and ideas of predecessors and contemporaries, absorbing selectively what it deems true to nature and laughing at their aberrations. *Northanger Abbey* deploys parody to confront readers with 'the unreality of the notions of life which might be picked out of Mrs. Radcliffe's novels'.[53] A more nuanced review interprets Austen's choice of a realistic foundation for her novels as an act of emancipation from the excesses of, and prejudices against, novels. However, her emancipation is devoid of any sign of contempt for her rivals or desire to eclipse them. On the contrary, as some passages in *Northanger Abbey* demonstrate, she acknowledges the value of the genre and contributes to its renewal without denigrating its past.[54]

Kavanagh participates in this discussion, suggesting that the critical distance between *Northanger Abbey* and its Gothic contemporaries materializes in the narrator's refusal to exaggerate and her reluctance to inspire high-wrought ideals. Catherine Morland is the very embodiment of this attitude. Referring to the description of Catherine's childhood and puberty in the first chapter of the novel as that of an unconventional and unheroic protagonist, Kavanagh writes that Austen introduces her first heroine by negatives and recommends her through cold laughter. Yet, to dismiss Catherine would mean to misinterpret Austen's mockery, because, although inexperienced and at times laughable, Catherine embodies the pleasant and innocent counterpart to Isabella Thorpe, who is Austen's main target:

> ■ The selfish enthusiasm, the foolish ardour, of this girl were fit food for satire – for such satire especially as Miss Austen loved; for to deceit, assumption, and mere simple silliness she was inexorable.[55] □

In addition, Kavanagh makes two important points: first, Isabella is instrumental to Catherine's infatuation with the plots and props of Ann Radcliffe's Gothic romances, and second, the narrator discloses Isabella's hollowness through conversation. For example, Isabella's puzzling connection between Miss Andrew's expertise regarding every Radcliffe novel and her netting of the 'sweetest cloak you can conceive' is downright absurd and proof of Austen's triumph over her character's folly (NA 25). Similarly, in conversations redolent of, if not superior to, Oliver Goldsmith's irony, obnoxious John Thorpe betrays himself with the simple-minded question he puts to nearly every character that comes his way: 'Does he want a horse?' (NA 54).[56] Kavanagh illustrates with these examples what Agnes Repplier aptly observes some thirty years later, namely, that the reader is not warned in advance of Isabella's or John Thorpe's absurdities: 'they stand convicted on their own evidence'.[57]

Generally, the critics agree that Austen's first novel fails to rise to the artistic heights that she proved capable of achieving. Some argue that, despite excellent character-drawing such as the Thorpes (who do not let the main characters monopolize the reader's attention), the story lacks finish. In particular, the relationship between Catherine and Henry Tilney is sketchy, largely due to the insufficient charisma of the latter, who although 'a perfect gentleman' of 'some quiet humour' is 'rather a stick'.[58] And in spite of the interest one takes in Catherine's development from romantic playfulness to love, the final outcome shows an amateur artist who, wary of intricate breadth and variety, tries her hand at a manageable subject. Nonetheless, Catherine deserves praise for her 'artless beauty' and Austen for creating an impulsive and plain heroine before Jane Eyre.[59] In 1894, Saintsbury summarized *Northanger Abbey*'s debated status as follows:

> ■ To some the delightful freshness and humour of *Northanger Abbey*, its completeness, finish and *entrain*, obscure the undoubted critical fact that its scale is small and its scheme after all, that of burlesque parody, a kind in which the first rank is reached with difficulty.[60] □

More importantly, critics recognize the unmistakable seal of Austen's style in the similarities that *Northanger Abbey* bears to her other writings. In 1885, Ward saw the most direct parallels between Austen's private letters (published by Lord Brabourne) and Catherine's good humour, frankness and spontaneity, claiming that *Northanger Abbey* and the letters partake of the same bright and youthful energy.[61] Simpson, on the other hand, contributed to the division of the six published novels into early and mature works, with *Northanger Abbey*, *Sense and Sensibility* and *Pride and Prejudice* belonging to the first group. All three novels draw on what Simpson calls a 'polemical bias' with roots in literary tradition. If *Pride and Prejudice* revolved around the long-standing stereotype of love at first sight, and *Sense and Sensibility* tested the sentimental education derived from poetry against the hard facts of life, *Northanger Abbey* pushed to 'the verge of caricature' the unrealistic expectations raised by Gothic romances.[62] The treatment of secondary characters, such as Isabella and John Thorpe, draws *Northanger Abbey* closer to the early novels, for example, characters like John Dashwood and his wife in *Sense and Sensibility*. The Thorpes's and the Dashwoods' greatest deficiency lies not in intellect but in moral understanding, although only the mature novels establish a correlation between wickedness and a deficient moral sense.[63]

Persuasion

Following Simpson's distinction between early and mature novels, one would expect critics to place *Persuasion* at the pinnacle of Austen's artistic development. This, however, is not always the case: *Persuasion* has the strange fate of being viewed as both the weakest and the most accomplished of the six published novels. Lewes, who predicted Austen's much deserved and long-awaited recognition, found little to say in praise of *Persuasion*:

> ■ Even *Persuasion*, which we cannot help regarding as the weakest, contains exquisite touches, and some characters no one else could have surpassed.[64] □

Lewes's disclaimer and vague recommendation of some of the characters is further developed by other critics. Pollock, sparingly though not as reticently as Lewes, writes that *Persuasion* has entered collective memory for containing Anne Elliot, 'the most perfect in character and disposition of all Miss Austen's women', and for having renewed the fame of such places as Lyme Regis and the Cobb through Louisa Musgrove's accident.[65] (Pollock's observation is confirmed in a private letter by Henry James, where he mentions a friend who, inspired by the novel, visited the Cobb and, after finding it as beautiful as described in the novel, decided to reside there.)[66] Hutton, too, while comparing Anne with Elizabeth Bennet, the most beloved of Austen's heroines, prefers the former. Anne may not possess Elizabeth's 'bright and mischievous playfulness', but she is a character of a more refined grace, strongly reminiscent of the author described in Austen-Leigh's *Memoir*.[67]

The character of Anne Elliott occupies the centre of most discussions of *Persuasion*. Some see her as a novelty in Austen's fiction and others as a revisited embodiment of her earlier heroines. American literary journalist W. B. Clymer argues that Anne represents several new combinations: her 'womanly sensibility' – recognisable in her patience, submissiveness and tenderness, but compatible with sound reason – is tried in a completely new situation.[68] We have to go to other critics to unpack the claim of novelty. Kavanagh's reading illuminates particularly well the gender aspect of Clymer's analysis. For Kavanagh, this last novel deepens the fear and suffering of unrequited love that Austen approached in *Sense and Sensibility* and *Mansfield Park*. *Persuasion* explores this theme more powerfully, because Anne's unfeeling family, the advice of her best friend, her own loss of youthful bloom and the flirtations of younger rivals put her in a more desolate position than other protagonists. Indeed, Kavanagh attributes unmatched originality and enduring literary influence to Anne's portrayal:

■ Here we see the first genuine picture of that silent torture of an unloved woman, condemned to suffer thus because she is a woman and must not speak, and which, many years later, was wakened into such passionate eloquence by the author of *Jane Eyre*. □

Austen, thus, heralds a feminist tradition of fiction dealing with the unspeakable agony of female desire. (Anne Thackeray may be influenced by this review when writing in 1871 that Anne is so womanly that it is impossible not to feel affection for her.[69]) Kavanagh argues that *Persuasion*'s tone may be more restrained, its expressiveness less subdued, but its suffering is not less keen and painful than its successor's – a tone, moreover, well-sustained throughout the narrative and not neutralized by the happy end. For Kavanagh, 'the shadow of disappointment, secret grief, and ill-repressed jealousy' cast over Anne Elliot never dissipates.[70] Kavanagh's analysis of *Persuasion* remains memorable for linking Austen's restraint not with modesty, delicacy or distaste for emotionality (Kavanagh herself laments Austen's coldness in other novels), but with gender constraints on female erotic desire. In addition, she also establishes continuities between Jane Austen and Charlotte Brontë in areas in which others had seen only differences.

Simpson enriches this interpretation of Anne Elliot by affiliating her to *Sense and Sensibility*'s Elinor Dashwood as a character of 'sense'. Judging from the pervasive emotional if not mournful drift of the story, Anne Elliot revisits and recants the ideas advanced by Elinor. For Simpson, Austen's creation of Anne Elliot sets right the belief that she had meant to divorce reason and sentiment, 'intellect and passion', in her early work. This intention motivates the choice of a story in which love and esteem coexist and fuel a mutually constant attachment. Simpson reads the revisionist trajectory from Elinor to Anne Elliot as typical of Austen's career. Her growth as a novelist consists in the covering of the same ground, while 'trying other ways to produce the same effect, and attempting the same ends by means less artificial, and of more innate origin'.[71] Similarly, Anne Thackeray understands Anne Elliot to be a mature, chastened and cultivated embodiment of the early 'bright-eyed heroine'.[72] Clymer, too, praises *Persuasion*'s pathos, especially poignant in the penultimate chapter of the novel, which equals in excellence Thackeray's chapters about Waterloo in *Vanity Fair* (1847). The superiority of this finale places Austen on a level with Percy Bysshe Shelley: towards the end of their careers, his *oeuvre* grew better and her scope wider.[73]

Persuasion revisits not only Austen's earlier novels, but also the works of other writers. For example, Simpson suggests that Anne be read as a translation of Shakespeare's Viola in *Twelfth Night* into the nineteenth century:

■ Like Viola, she never tells her love, or rather never talks of it after its extinguishing, but sits like patience on a monument smiling at grief; the green and yellow melancholy feeds on her, and wastes her beauty. Like Viola, too, she meekly ministers to the woman who is unknowingly her rival.[74] □

Such alignment with Viola underlines both Anne's agency and meekness, a combination upon which the novel itself and future critics dwell with insistence. Simpson also highlights more text-related similarities which prompt him to conjecture that Austen must have read *Twelfth Night* during the composition of *Persuasion*'s last chapters. Anne's eulogy of female constancy during her dialogue with Captain Harville in the penultimate chapter, for example, parallels the exchange between Duke Orsino and Viola:

■ ORSINO
    There is no woman's sides
    Can bide the beating of so strong a passion
    As love doth give my heart. No woman's heart
    So big, to hold so much. They lack retention. □

To which Viola responds:

- We men may say more, swear more, but indeed
  Our shows are more than will, for still we prove
  Much in our vows, but little in our love.[75] ☐

Viola's valorization of women's love as less showy and more profoundly felt resonates with Anne's insistence on women's lasting attachments: it is 'loving longest, when existence or when hope is gone' that she claims for her own sex (P 189). It is what Simpson calls the exquisitely beautiful 'song of the dying swan', in which Austen proves herself capable of unsuspected poetical tenderness.[76] However, Clymer deems the comparison to Viola to be more fanciful than justified, since Viola's language and expression of love bears emotional notes that one could hardly imagine being uttered by Anne. Nonetheless, he admits that Sir Walter Elliot, 'consequential, pompous and vain, is a not altogether unworthy descendant of Malvolio'.[77]

Henry James seems to be an exception to the opinion that *Persuasion* treated emotionality differently. Without much elaboration, James mentions Anne and Emma in the same breath as two characters who convey impressions as intense as the female protagonists of George Sand or Balzac, albeit less outward and explicit.[78] Ward adds that precisely the lack of outward 'raptures' and 'despairs', as well as the controlled poetic vein coupled with vivid imagination, makes Austen's style 'a typical English embodiment of the drier and more bracing elements' of French literature.[79]

Although there is general consensus that the appearance of Anne Elliot at the end of Austen's career compensates for the unsentimental vein of her other novels, this is not unanimously regarded as a marker of excellence. On the contrary, Austen's attempt to abandon the self-assigned boundaries of detached wit and to move into the sphere of 'romance and sentiment' may have harmed the general interest of the story.[80] As one critic writes in 1866, despite the heightened emotional appeal of Anne Elliot's and Wentworth's romance, *Persuasion* does not surpass *Mansfield Park* or *Pride and Prejudice* in plot structure and organization of characters. In *Persuasion*, the characters are rather separate studies and not well-connected in groups. In their separateness, they lack wit and finish.[81]

Such an interpretation is countered by Kavanagh's observation about the secondary characters, who (like those of *Northanger Abbey*) betray their folly, moral weaknesses and assumptions through their speech. Austen rarely describes them, but she wittily puts in their mouths revealing words. Sir Walter Elliot stands as a case in point:

■ Sir Walter Elliot is handsome; we are merely told so, but we never forget it, for he does not. [...] And his worship of personal appearance is perfectly unaffected and sincere. Sir Walter Elliot's good looks have acted on him internally; his own daughter Anne rises in his opinion as her complexion grows clearer.[82] □

In a similar vein, Saintsbury singles out Mrs. Musgrove's regrets over her dead son as a typical stroke of Austen's satire, which stems from 'an epicurean delight in dissecting [...] her fools and mean persons'.[83] It is a civil, restrained but also 'ruthless delight in roasting and cutting up a fool' that she learned from Addison's *Spectator* (mentioned in her diatribe in *Northanger Abbey*). According to Oliphant, Austen's wit in *Persuasion* is not only undeniable, but also even out of bounds and responsible for making every secondary character a foolish foil to the superior protagonist lovers, a strategy that Oliphant holds for 'an old imperfection'.[84]

Simpson, on the other hand, finds *Persuasion*'s wit more refined and its main characters exceptionally well-sustained throughout the narrative. Sir Walter Elliot serves as an example of the progress of wit: he is the last and most superior of Austen's fools. A comparison to *Pride and Prejudice*'s Mr. Collins illuminates the narrator's perfected knowledge of character. According to Simpson, Mr. Collins's fixed ideas govern his talk more than his life, and, in this sense, Austen's ridicule remains external. In contrast, Sir Walter's main preoccupations, namely his rank and good looks, rule his lifestyle and relationships. With Sir Walter's portrayal, Austen has fully understood the Aristotelian maxim that 'all things, even stones, fishes, and fools, pursue their proper end'.[85] In him, internal motivations match external behaviour and the degree of absurdity corresponds to that of naturalness. As for the main characters, Simpson argues that *Persuasion*'s protagonist couple is the first in which no internal inconsistencies can be found. While in other novels (he mentions *Pride and Prejudice* and *Emma*), the characters' shortcomings are out of step with their general nature, Anne and Wentworth's failures are integral to the ideas they represent: she embodies strength of mind throughout the narrative, her initial weakness notwithstanding, and Wentworth remains worthy of her love in spite of his anger-motivated flirtations.[86]

In terms of style, *Persuasion* remains faithful to the recipe of concentration and restrained authorial intervention. Clymer argues that these two elements interweave most effectively in the scene of Louisa Musgrove's accident, which is so bare of description that it calls for the readers' own mental stage directions. The passage to which Clymer refers is quoted here:

■ He advised her against it, thought the jar too great; but no, he reasoned and talked in vain, she smiled and said, 'I am determined I will': he put out his hands; she was too precipitate by half a second, she fell on the pavement on the Lower Cobb, and was taken up lifeless! There was no wound, no blood, no visible bruise; but her eyes were closed, she breathed not, her face was like death. The horror of the moment to all who stood around!

Captain Wentworth, who had caught her up, knelt with her in his arms, looking on her with a face as pallid as her own, in an agony of silence. 'She is dead! she is dead!' screamed Mary, catching hold of her husband, and contributing with his own horror to make him immoveable; and in another moment, Henrietta, sinking under the conviction, lost her senses too, and would have fallen on the steps, but for Captain Benwick and Anne, who caught and supported her between them.

'Is there no one to help me?' were the first words which burst from Captain Wentworth, in a tone of despair, and as if all his own strength were gone.

'Go to him, go to him,' cried Anne, 'for heaven's sake go to him. I can support her myself. Leave me, and go to him. Rub her hands, rub her temples; here are salts; take them, take them.' (P 91–2) □

Clymer notes that most information can be derived from the words of the characters and very little from the omniscient narrator. The inattentive reader may find the scene tame, but careful perusal manifests its rapidity and exactness of character representation and situation chiefly through dialogue. In comparison to other authors who often rely on dialogue (e.g. Anthony Trollope), Austen resists supplementing her characters' conversations with her own comments. Her dialogues are as concise as they are revealing.[87] Clymer explains that, for this reason, her characters are never overcome by an obtrusive narrator or the novel's general subject matter. This is to say that, due to the narrator's ability to restrain her interventions and conceal her presence, the reader does not experience the characters as puppets.[88]

In conclusion, the second half of the nineteenth century reads *Northanger Abbey* and *Persuasion* as the two ends of Austen's artistic spectrum, with the first being indebted to her juvenile writings and the latter as a final revisiting of earlier themes. Repeatedly, critics attempt to qualify the nature of the novels' realism, maintaining that the difficulty of this task arises from the narrator's unique ability to create deceptively simple realities and to keep her intrusions into the narrative to a fruitful minimum. *Northanger Abbey* explores the relationship between fiction and reality, purging the heroine's Gothic exaggerations, albeit not at the expense of the heroine or the genre itself. *Persuasion* exhibits more willingness to delve into the realities of human, in particular, female suffering, a novelty that prompts critics to argue for the expansion of Austen's scope in her last novel. Female representations not only engross

Austen's attention, but also remain the primary focus of criticism: Catherine's artlessness and Anne's sensible tenderness overshadow the presence of Henry Tilney or Captain Wentworth. More often than not, irony emerges as the thread running through *Northanger Abbey* and *Persuasion*. In both, Austen's irony is internal, that is, embedded in characterization and dependent on the narrator's restrained interventions. Generally, the characters lay bare their follies or moral weakness through their own words. For this detachment, Austen's humour verges on cynicism and her poise on emotional coldness. To a certain degree, *Persuasion* seems to escape this charge, since several critics project onto Anne Elliot the dignified equanimity of the author herself. This assumption contributes to the rise of the subculture of Janeites, Austen's devotees who take a keen and enthusiastic interest in anything pertaining to her life and social world. The birth and impact of this cult is discussed in the following chapter.

CHAPTER FOUR

The 'Cult of Jane' and the Rise of the Novel, 1900s–1950s

In 1905, Henry James writes that the public recognition that Jane Austen's well-wishers had fervently awaited and predicted had arrived with the inevitability and force of a high tide. However, James, although himself an admirer, fears the tide has risen above the mark of Austen's artistic merit, blown beyond the critic's objective judgement by the commercial wind of strategic bookselling, the 'publishers, editors, illustrators, producers of the pleasant twaddle of magazines' who promote their '"dear", our dear, everybody's dear Jane so infinitely to their material purpose'.[1] What had happened in the last years of the nineteenth century to explain Austen's becoming a household name and an incomparable favourite with whom the reader was on a first-person basis?

Devotees and Austenphobes

Let us first address the novels' presence in the print market that James holds responsible for Austen's booming popularity. After Austen-Leigh's *Memoir* and Lord Brabourne's edition of Austen's *Letters* (1884), two other family members cater to the public taste for biography: first, James Austen Leigh's son William and grandson Richard Austen-Leigh compose the lengthy *Jane Austen, Her Life and Letters: A Family Record* (1913); then, seven years later, Mary Augusta Austen-Leigh's *Personal Aspects of Jane Austen* expanded the focus of earlier biographies, by elaborating on Austen's connections to social communities and events beyond the parochial sphere that commentators had presumed since Henry Austen's biographical notice. Interest in Austen culminated in Elizabeth Jenkins's *Jane Austen: A Biography* (1938), the first literary Austen biography. In the meantime, there had continuously been new editions of the novels: the cheap Routledge editions in 1883, the six-penny series in 1886, the deluxe *Steventon Edition of Jane Austen's Works* (1882), Macmillan's effusively illustrated issues in 1890 and Reginald Brimley Johnson's ten-volume set for Dent in 1892, reprinted five times within five years. Not surprisingly, the number of Austen's readers grew along with the public appreciation of her as one of the greatest British novelists.

However, as James's vexed comment shows there was something odd about this kind of literary enthusiasm. In Austen's case, it related to the commodification not only of her work, but also of her person, which was reflected in the ways readers thought and felt about her as an author. As early as 1818, one reviewer laments that Austen's untimely death had robbed the reading community of a 'most fascinating companion [...] whom we had long known and loved'.[2] Hence, biographies and personal accounts kindled what had been a lingering flame from the immediate reception of the novels, an intimacy that is best captured by one of the ablest Victorian commentators, George Saintsbury, writer of *A History of Nineteenth-Century Literature* (1896) and of the preface to the illustrated edition of *Pride and Prejudice* in 1894, where he proudly declares himself a member of 'the sect – fairly large and yet unusually choice of Austenians or Janeites'.[3] The latter term has entered the idiom of Austen scholarship, acquiring features that distinguish it from the appreciation and literary investment of, say, Shakespeareans, Miltonians, Johnsonians or Dickensians. It is a term that reduces the distance between reader, author and novels, alluding to a more personal and affectionate bond between them, an attitude espoused by academics and amateurs alike. For example, A. C. Bradley, professor of English and Shakespearean scholar, introduces himself at a lecture on Austen given at Cambridge in 1911 as one of the 'faithful' who enjoy conversing and comparing notes about their idol.[4]

Shared reverence creates ties among many of Austen's readers, as Rudyard Kipling's humorous and now famous short story 'The Janeites' (1924) shows. Kipling's piece revolves around the shell-shocked Humberstall, who while a soldier during World War I is introduced into a secret society of Austen readers with a password inspired by *Northanger Abbey*: 'Tilniz an'trap-doors'. In the trenches, the solidarity of this '[h]appy little Group' seems to be the most reliable support system.[5] Curiously, after the war, the novels were recommended as restorative reading therapy, in which veterans could find relief from their devastating past and regain a foothold in real life through the tranquillizing portraits of untroubled country-life.[6]

In the beginning, Janeites were predominantly male readers, the most influential among them publishers, professors and literary critics who inaugurated enduring lines of criticism. Within this group, R. W. Chapman deserves particular mention for producing the first scholarly edition of Austen's novels (and the first of any British novel) in 1923.

Austen's admirers enthused over Chapman's pioneering work, while her detractors met with sneering incredulity the fact that a scholarly practice until then reserved for exceptional poets and dramatists had been applied to a novelist, in particular, to Jane Austen, whose artistic achievement had been inflated by undiscerning 'votaries', as H. W. Garrod put it in his talk held at the Royal Society in London in 1815.[7] Garrod, who openly disliked and saw no value in Austen, and James, who regarded her as one of the greatest writers, shared the irritation at what Claudia L. Johnson outlines as one of the defining features of Janeism:

■ a self-consciously idolatrous enthusiasm for 'Jane' Austen and every primary, secondary, tertiary (and so forth) detail relative to her.[8] □

However, Garrod also rails against the academics who had elevated Austen to the literary Olympus (Chapman's edition being the last act in this process of intellectual deification). He calls them down for speaking of her as 'divine' and imposing censorship, as if criticizing Austen was 'as bad as speaking against the Prayer Book'.[9]

As is often the case, disagreement proved fruitful: the confrontation between admirers and detractors stirred readers to plumb the novels' depths. Garrod's depreciation of Austen as an ahistorical, apolitical, intolerably sensible, asexual, husband-hunting 'slip of a girl', who was interested in feminine trivialities and was insensitive to natural beauties, furnished her supporters with material upon which to build their defence. Yet there was one charge which Janeites conceived of as a downright affront to their beloved Jane and that was the charge of cynicism. With ostensible zest, Garrod poked fun at Janeites' most dear claim, namely, that although a humourist, Austen indulged in no bitterness or harsh satire. Garrod explodes this myth in his reading of *Northanger Abbey*, demonstrating the lamentable range of Austen's characters and the undertone of her attitude:

■ In *Northanger Abbey* a heroine who is a romantic little fool marries a high-brow cynic – for no better reason than that she *is* a little fool and he a cynic.[10] □

He claims that this novel, like the letters, evinces 'a malicious acuteness of vision'. As for *Persuasion*'s Anne, she merely points up to a promised land of 'milk and water'.[11]

It is a charge that Chapman (and others) cannot let rest. The very absence of the expected 'honey' in *Persuasion*'s promised land provokes Chapman's diatribe against Garrod's generalizations: How can a man of Garrod's perception ignore the artistic growth from the 'simplicities of *Sense and Sensibility*' to the 'twilight tints of *Persuasion*'? What is watered down in a novel whose White Hart scene Chapman reads for the twentieth time 'with a beating heart, as though it were still possible that true love might be frustrated'? And in the language of a faithful Janeite, he confesses that Catherine Morland, Garrod's 'romantic little fool', was his early love. Without disguising his affiliation, Chapman adds that he assumes the role of the spokesperson for 'all of us – all lovers of Jane Austen', whom Garrod dubs 'votaries'. In their names, he denounces Garrod's greatest injustice: 'He has accused Jane Austen of cynicism', and by doing so, he has made 'odious' the author who has been loved like few other authors for delighting her readers with creatures 'of flesh and blood' such as Anne Elliot.[12]

The exchange between Garrod and Chapman manifests the hardening of critical lines that coincided with (and resulted from) Austen's institutionalization in the academy and her increasing notoriety in popular culture. Garrod's comments on Austen's malicious tendency, amplifying earlier observations on her contempt, cynicism and coldness, countered the vision of Jane the gentle humourist that Janeites cherished. Admittedly, subjective dislike and negligent analysis weakened Garrod's argument. However, the field of Austen studies was to change radically when similar claims were put forward by those who enjoyed and valued the novels as keenly as the Janeites – albeit for different reasons.

From 'Gentle Jane' to Subversive Austen

Generally, the readers of the early twentieth century perceive Austen's wit as gentle mockery, going as far as conceding that 'she laughed, mocked at things very gently and decorously, but she still mocked'.[13] Some mitigate the thrust of her humour by arguing for the intuitive rather than intentional wit of 'dear Jane', who unconsciously but lucidly depicted the more privileged middle-class English through the genre of the comedy of manners.[14] When endorsing earlier commentators' claims of cynicism, some hurry to specify her affinity with the greatest eighteenth-century novelists (such as Fielding and Smollet), adding that, unlike theirs, her cynicism springs from a humanist disposition, 'an infinite fund of tenderness', as one critic puts it.[15] Eventually, opinions like Oliphant's and Meynell's on controlled contempt and biting cynicism, or Kavanagh's on emotional coldness (see Chapter 3), receive their due weight in a line of criticism initiated by D. W. Harding's essay 'Regulated Hatred: An Aspect of the Work of Jane Austen' (1940).

Here, Harding speculates that the hype about Austen, bolstered by the multitude of readers and critics who recommend her novels as favourable and soothing depictions of civil society, has shut the door on many who may happen to be her best readers.[16] Harding belonged to those deterred by the prevailing opinion of a gentle and tame Jane – until he read her and found to his great surprise that she had been misread all along. From his own reading experience, Harding learns that Austen calls for meticulous care because 'her books are, as she meant them to be, read and enjoyed precisely by the sort of people whom she disliked'.[17] Perhaps unwittingly, he allows, Austen constructed her prose in ways that make the misreading the least laborious of all readings.

With admirable attention to the text, Harding (a student of English at Cambridge before choosing a career as a psychologist) sheds light on the slovenly reading skills responsible to a great extent for the myth of gentle Jane. He writes:

■ Fragments of the truth have been incorporated in it but they are fitted into a pattern whose total effect is false.[18] □

He then turns to a passage in *Northanger Abbey* to demonstrate the necessity of thorough reading techniques and the misleading effect of selective ones. In his chosen passage, Henry Tilney, confronted with Catherine's allegations against his father, appeals to her sense of probability:

■ Does our education prepare us for such atrocities? Do our laws connive at them? Could they be perpetrated without being known, in a country like this, where social and literary intercourse is on such a footing, where every man is surrounded by a neighbourhood of voluntary spies, and where roads and newspapers lay everything open? (*NA* 145) □

The clause 'every man is surrounded by a neighbourhood of spies' reveals for Harding everything that most readers overlook: namely, that such a sentence does not sit well with a generous character like Henry Tilney or with his arguments about the transparent laws and civilized culture of the age. So Harding asks: why slip such a paranoid view of pervasive surveillance into Henry's grave lecture? Spoken by Henry and bracketed by his eulogies, the acerbic comment is likely to go unnoticed and leave the reader unperturbed. Austen then has it both ways: she manages to sneak in the comment but avoids open confrontation and 'exaggerated bitterness', by cushioning it with acceptable material (the idea of Austen not being openly polemical is already hinted at by nineteenth-century reviewers – see Chapter 3).

Harding deepens this view in his analysis of *Persuasion*. Here, two attitudes, satire towards the character and satire towards the public (easily missed by the reader), coalesce and provide a more sophisticated picture than in *Northanger Abbey*. In the first chapter of the novel, the exposition of Elizabeth Elliot's failed courtship with Mr. Elliot starts as satire towards Elizabeth, upon whose calculations and pride the reader is supposed to frown:

> ■ There was not a baronet from A to Z whom her feelings could have so willingly acknowledged as an equal. Yet so miserably had he conducted himself, that though she was at this present time (the summer of 1814) wearing black ribbons for his wife, she could not admit him to be worth thinking of again. The disgrace of his first marriage might, perhaps, as there was no reason to suppose it perpetuated by offspring, have been got over, had he not done worse. □

However, here, according to Harding, the satire changes direction and targets the readers who have been lulled by their own superiority over the character:

> ■ but he had, as by the accustomary intervention of kind friends they had been informed, spoken most disrespectfully of them all [...]. (*P* 13)[19] □

Harding concludes that Austen, shrewd observer that she was, had understood that mockery would be acceptable as long as it was perceived to provide good laughter without being disruptive. Caricature (a definition also used by critics to describe Isabella, John Thorpe and Sir Walter Elliot among other characters) was Austen's preferred device because no clear line separates caricature from serious portraiture. Between these two, Harding locates the 'eruption of fear and hatred' which revolts Austen's admirers, because, to use Chapman's own words, it makes the beloved novelist 'odious'.[20]

Harding shows that simmering and subversive animosity accounts for the omnipresence of the Cinderella trope, which Austen modifies into the pattern of the admirable heroine raised by unworthy parents. In *Northanger Abbey*, the isolation of the heroine/princess from other characters accentuates her superior moral judgement and justifies the final reward of marriage to a worthy hero/prince. In *Persuasion*, the Cinderella theme foregrounds Anne's need for affection through the mother's death and the presence of the human godmother Lady Russell. Much of the novel's tension stems from Anne's irresolution towards Lady Russell:

> ■ It is in *Persuasion* that Jane Austen fingers what is probably the tenderest spot for those who identify themselves with Cinderella: she brings the idealised mother back to life and admits that she is no nearer to perfection than the mothers of acute and sensitive children really are.[21] □

Harding ends his analysis by insisting that he offers his interpretations to those readers who seek neither escape nor relief in the novels, but 'a formidable ally' against all things that Austen found hateful.[22]

Hence, by 1940, not only new motivations for turning to Austen emerge, but also a new practice of reading her works. Against A. C. Bradley's well-meant but belittling remark that the novels generated enjoyment and conversation, the stakes of Austen criticism are raised to commitment to scrupulous argumentation and critical controversy.

Form and Social Critique

Before the controversy sharpened between Janeites, whom Harding reckoned simple-minded readers, and the iconoclasts of Harding's ilk (in Chapman's words) who sought discontent and subversion where there was none, Austen criticism, under New Critical and Formalist influences, was already marked by an increased emphasis on the novels' textual aspects, although none of these analyses ventured to read them as much against the grain as Harding.[23]

Due to its affiliation to the Gothic, *Northanger Abbey* was particularly apt to draw this kind of attention. As early as 1901, John Louis Haney revealed that the titles of the Gothic novels discussed by Catherine and Isabella, far from being Austen's mock inventions, appeared between 1793 and 1798.[24] Further developed by Michael Sadleir in 1927, the awareness of the novel's intertextuality counteracted the image of Austen as an amateur and unconscious novelist.[25] However, in what kind of relationship to these predecessors did Austen's novel stand?

The most uncomplicated, and prevailing, view saw the 'charming burlesque' of *Northanger Abbey* as delivering the *coup de grâce* to the 'ridiculous sensationalism' inherited by the Gothic of Walpole and Radcliffe.[26] Reginald Farrer argued that two conflicting modes interweave in *Northanger Abbey*: parody and serious drama. Catherine is suspended between these poles so that much of the narrator's efforts go to keeping her there at the expense of characterization:

■ She is really our most delightful of all *ingénues*, but her story is kept so constantly comic that one has no time to concentrate on its chief figure. Fun, too, tends to overshadow the emotional skill with which the movement is developed.[27] □

The idea of double movement between parody and drama received a different approach from Annette Hopkins. In her carefully researched essay 'Jane Austen the Critic' (1925), Hopkins comments on Austen's numerous references to contemporary authors and works in the letters, and particularly in *Northanger Abbey* and *Persuasion*, concluding that they testify to Austen's critical independence and irreverence towards 'inferior novelists' and an 'undiscriminating reading public' alike. Moreover, Austen understood that inflated sentimentalism enfeebled the novel, and her service to the genre was to ground it within a discourse of common sense.[28] Hopkins's article is worth remembering not only for being among the first text-oriented essays to argue for Austen as a moralist of common sense, but also for linking the practice of reading in *Northanger Abbey* to that of the author. Hopkins praises Austen for her deep knowledge of the genre's effect upon the reader (as Henry Tilney's *impromptu* on the way to the abbey shows) and for 'abandoning herself to the spirit of a story at the same time that she is observing it from a critical angle'.[29] The simultaneous occupying of the position of the absorbed reader and that of the discerning critic produces the humorous 'incongruity between the ideal and the actual', which is an incongruity typical of Cervantean satire.[30]

Intertextuality is also Mary Lascelles's lens for understanding the pattern of burlesque in *Northanger Abbey*. In *Jane Austen and Her Art* (1939), the first book-length study of the novels, Lascelles shows Austen's indebtedness to less likely and less-discussed authors such as Charlotte Smith, giving full weight to the education of Catherine in the eighteenth-century tradition of a girl's entrance into the world (in the vein of Fanny Burney's *Evelina, or The History of a Young Lady's Entrance into the World* (1778)). Two forces vie for Catherine's education: Isabella, who inflames Catherine's imagination, and Henry Tilney, who is given the 'office of interpreter' by the narrator.[31] Henry appears here as the reliable educator who wisely leads Catherine on her passage from puberty to adulthood. Lascelles locates the mildness of Austen's burlesque in the instructive power of courtship. While other novelists entrust to characters of authority the task of awakening the delusional heroines, Catherine is cured by her lover and future husband.[32] Austen's gentle burlesque that Lascelles seeks to preserve remains curiously untroubled by the General's calculations. Yet Lascelles notes that Austen modifies the stock burlesque of the age, by refusing to attribute the General's vulgarity to Catherine's fancy. Nonetheless, Catherine's final unremitting condemnation of her future father-in-law does not square with Lascelles's benign burlesque. Although Lascelles's scholarly monograph represented a departure from the Janeites' (at times) unqualified encomia, there are incongruities which her study failed to address.

Significant interventions came from other quarters. First, the Canadian literary critic and theorist Northrop Frye categorized romance as one of the four forms of prose that feature in the title of his essay 'Four Forms of Prose Fiction' (1950). He mentions *Northanger Abbey* as a specimen of the parody of romance that originated with *Don Quixote* (1605):

> ■ a novel that looks at a romantic situation from its own point of view so that the conventions of two forms make up an ironic compound instead of a sentimental mixture.[33] □

Despite his reliance on structural characteristics, Frye has something to say about the socio-cultural history of this form's idealized characters and 'untamable' tendency. Romance, he argues, is affiliated with aristocracy, while its revival in the Romantic period coincides with the cult of the hero. In this time, the parody of romance ideals appears as a preferred theme of the bourgeois novel.[34] Many before Frye had observed that Austen distrusted romance ideals, but Frye is among the first to align this distrust with a bourgeois rebellion against the values of the landed class.

Marvin Mudrick's book *Jane Austen: Irony as Defense and Discovery* (1952) engaged with both generic and stylistic questions, firmly arguing for an even more subversive Austen than Harding had in 1940. Mudrick maintained that *Northanger Abbey* represents Austen's unlimited rejection of the values of both romance and realistic fiction. Drawing on Farrer's distinction between parody and serious drama, he recognizes two coexisting forms: the domestic novel and parody. Her experience with the juvenilia taught Austen that straightforward parody fails to satisfy the sophisticated ironist, so she challenges herself with the paradoxical task of writing simultaneously a Gothic and a realistic novel that proves the former absurd, while securing the reader's approval of the latter. Irony, which is both attitude and instrument in Austen, vibrates in the very decision she makes to solve this problem. Her novel responds and corresponds to Radcliffe's Gothic through domestic antitypes. The two modes, Gothic and realistic, concentrate within the consciousness of the heroine:

> ■ There is irony even in its internal point of view: in the fact that its two worlds must originate, converge, and be finally discriminated in the limited consciousness of that most ingenuous and domestic heroine, Catherine Morland. The double burden seems almost too much for so lightweight a mind.[35] □

Catherine, awkward, not beautiful, with no particular skills, is the very opposite of Radcliffe's heroines; Mrs. Allen's negligence contrasts starkly with the wicked, vigilant Gothic chaperone; no mystery whatsoever surrounds Henry, who like his author has no patience with sentimental nonsense; John Thorpe is a weak though importunate equivalent to the sinister intruding Gothic suitor; and selfish Isabella is the reverse of the good-hearted and virtuous confidante.

These antitypes fulfil the function of invalidating the Gothic, that is, of showing that the Gothic cannot to be trusted as a guide when it comes to grasping human nature as Catherine experiences it in Bath. Yet the antitypes also dismantle the world of Bath as being neither more agreeable nor more trustworthy than Radcliffe's Gothic. Agreeing with Lascelles, Mudrick praises Henry as the only character who perceives the inadequacies of each world, and consequently observes them with detached irony, as if he were a spectator. Being the one who detects their shortcomings and reversed correspondences, Henry acts as the spectator-character who helps reconcile them from within. However, Henry's figure also manifests the narrator's rather intrusive presence and her sometimes excessive irony in the novel.

Although Mudrick's view of Henry has been the most commented upon, his analysis of Catherine seems more crucial to his thesis about the novel's wholesale rejection of both the Gothic and realism. In Mudrick's account, Catherine's characterization suggests that Austen feels so compelled to detachment that she must reject even 'personality'.[36] Catherine does not qualify as a heroine of either world, of the Gothic or the realist novel: she is neither fully burlesque, nor is she allowed a degree of selfhood that awakens the reader's interest in a realistic context. Thus, Austen's rejection of romance entails the rejection of 'personality' *per se*. The resolution of the suspense around the figure of the General that the narrator allows Catherine to build up falls flat due to Austen's lack of commitment to the kind of development that the Gothic villain exacts. She instead limits her irony to the character's function as a mere antitype, for which reason she must cut him down to size. Finally, in the conclusion, this lack of commitment pulls the narrator back to parody and to the antitypes who, in the process of dismantling the Gothic, have come to embody mere 'faceless inconsequence' and end up rejecting not only the illusionary world but also the 'realistic basis of the novel'. This double demolition justifies Mudrick's claim of 'rejection unlimited'.[37]

Mudrick's analysis of 'personality' seems influenced by Reginald Farrer, who viewed *Northanger Abbey* as a hyphen between the teenage parodies, where farcical plots dominate, and the mature fiction of interiority. Already in *Northanger Abbey*, Farrer argues, character is a serious rival to the story, but in *Persuasion*, there is almost no story and everything is about the characters.[38] According to Farrer, the narrator's 'intensified tenderness' and 'glacial contempt', attitudes conveyed without recourse to irony, crystallize in the characters.

Echoing Farrer's comment about the novel's 'glacial contempt', Virginia Woolf writes of the harsh satire and crude comedy directed at characters like Sir Walter or Elizabeth Elliot. She claims that it is almost as if Austen were bored and less capable of deriving pleasure from chastisement and that the insistence on nature, its autumnal beauty and melancholy, compensates for the rawness of the comic aspect.[39] This refined sensibility towards nature hints at a new attitude towards life as less factual and more emotional. Appropriately, *Persuasion* evinces heightened readiness to dispense with dialogue in favour of interiority, which Woolf believes is the new path Austen paves for her future fiction. Elizabeth Bowen, too, thinks that Austen accomplishes here the double feat of breaking with earlier self-imposed limitations, while exploring the depth and maturity of restraint in the character of Anne Elliot.[40]

There is a sense in Woolf's piece that *Persuasion* departs from the youthful homely comedy and confronts the serious, or, as Bowen puts it, 'the more searching experiences of life'.[41] However, according to Lascelles, Austen never leaves the reader in the dark as to the genre she has opted for. With close-reading strategies similar to Harding's, Lascelles shows that the narrator bursts the tragic bubble at its climax in the Lyme scene:

> ■ By this time the report of the accident had spread among the workmen and boatmen about the Cobb, and many were collected near them, to be useful if wanted, at any rate, to enjoy the sight of a dead young lady, nay, two dead young ladies, for it proved twice as fine as the first report. (*P* 93) □

The clause 'nay, two dead young ladies' culminating in 'as fine as the first report' signals the tragic illusion and the narrator's 'civil unwillingness' to let the readers suffer under the misapprehension of the nature of the catastrophe.[42] Consequently, unlike Farrer who discerns no irony, or Mudrick, for whom irony is muted by pervading feeling, Lascelles concludes that dismissing such details leads to overlooking the fact that irony is the very idiom of *Persuasion*.

The Value of Fiction

Without mentioning the word 'irony' in his article 'Fiction and the "Matrix of Analogy"' (1949), Mark Schorer laid bare *Persuasion*'s implication in the language of commerce, an unsuspected and ironic discovery, considering that most critics summed up the novelty of the novel as residing in its emphasis on feeling.

Schorer is among the first to apply to novels the analytical lens hitherto employed by the New Critics to interpret poems. It is a lens that examines the structure of the images that dominate in a novel which, like a poem, is not life itself but a representation of it. Schorer selects the metaphorical quality as his image of examination in *Persuasion*, *Wuthering Heights* (1847) and *Middlemarch* (1874). In *Persuasion*, he is particularly drawn to the associations invited by explicit and dead metaphors pertaining to the concept of value. Whether personal, moral, professional or economic, the concept of value is persistently conveyed through recourse to words of commerce and property:

> ■ In this context certain colorless words, words of the lightest intention, take on a special weight. The words *account* and *interest* are used hundreds of times in their homeliest sense, yet when we begin to observe that every narration is an account, and at least one 'an account ... of the negation', we are reminded that they have more special meanings. When Anne's blighted romance is called 'this little history of sorrowful interest', we hardly forget that a lack of money was the blight. Is a 'man of principle' by any chance a man of substance?[43] □

The context is that of a material world, where all kinds of changes are referred to as *'material* alterings'; where faces are not *'materially* disfigured', Anne's hopes cannot be 'highly *rated*', *'funds* of enjoyment' can be scarce; and where Captain Wentworth says, 'I have *valued* myself on honourable toils and just *rewards*' – the final reward being Anne, who has become *'fixed* on his mind as perfection itself'. For Schorer, the word 'fixed' in Wentworth's final assessment describes Anne as 'a currency that has been stabilized' after a long period of 'lowness', which primarily refers to Anne's low spirits and slighted position, but at the level of style borrows from the language of the stock market to suggest that marriage itself is treated as a market and women as marketable stocks.[44] Hence, Schorer confidently concludes that *Persuasion* is a novel in which 'sensibility is subdued to property'. The point is not to argue that this represents the characters', narrator's or author's ethos, but that it is woven into the fabric of the text. Indeed, Schorer takes the crossing of the 'social sentiment' professed by the characters and the 'social fact' contained in the texture of Austen's style to be the very essence of the novel's comedy.[45]

Thinking about misrecognized aspects, John K. Mathison asserts, against the current of contemporary criticism, that Austen's defence of the novel in *Northanger Abbey* has been undervalued.[46] In disagreement with critics such as Lascelles and Andrew Wright (whose contribution is discussed in the next section), Mathison encourages readers to take Austen's eulogy seriously. Her occasional fun at the expense of Catherine as a naïve novel reader does not equate to a dismissal of the genre. Instead, Catherine's tendency to misread novels is concomitant with her misreading of people, in that both result from deficient education and parenting. Thus, the novel understands the maturity that shapes a character into an individual as a development despite and beyond imposed limitations. In Catherine's case, she must outgrow the entrapment of her sheltered life as well as an exclusively literal understanding of the fictional world. Hence, much of Mathison's interpretation revisits Lascelles's analysis of *Northanger Abbey* as a *Bildungsroman*. For Mathison, unlike Lascelles, novel-reading rather than Henry Tilney is the chief source of Catherine's education. Her maturation as a reader culminates in the encounter with General Tilney. With an inquisitive spirit (the very opposite of Mrs. Allen's yawning apathy), Catherine constructs a narrative that could account for the General's disturbing character. Although her narrative turns out to be wrong, the Gothic has prepared Catherine to expect villainy in the world, an expectation that the end of the novel confirms. Thus, the value of the novels that Catherine reads and Austen defends does not consist in them being fragments of real life but illuminations of it.[47]

Mathison elaborates on Lionel Trilling's claim in *The Opposing Self* (1955) that *Northanger Abbey* alerts readers to the fact that the novel's best-disguised lesson is reserved for the reader: the events of the story corroborate Catherine's vision of life as violent and unpredictable and it is the reader who must be weaned from the false security that 'life is sane and orderly'.[48] It is noteworthy that Trilling's and Mathison's validations of Catherine accord less instructive and authoritative power to Henry Tilney, who for most critics of the first half of the twentieth century embodies the narrator's own voice of common sense.

Morality and Modernity

Discussions about the value of fiction more often than not turned on the genre's moral import. Between Harding's subversive or Mudrick's wholesale rejection of morality, critics fascinated and dismayed by an amoral Austen undertake to demonstrate that irony in her fiction is an 'instrument of moral vision'.[49] Andrew Wright explains that Kierkegaard's definition of irony as the juxtaposition of two mutually exclusive views of life allows for the exploration of the novels' ironic themes. Thus, irony appears as a structural device of Austen's stories, characters and narrators and not merely as an element of phraseology. In the case of *Northanger Abbey*, Wright admits that the burlesque pervades, making parody the chief source of entertainment. However, when back home a rejected Catherine thinks that 'there are some situations of the human mind in which good sense has very little power' (*NA* 177), the limitations of common sense impress themselves upon the reader:

> ■ [The] indication that there is more on earth than mere common sense gives the book an ironic dimension of enduring value.⁵⁰ ☐

In *Persuasion*, the tension arises from two mutually exclusive sets of demands: those of prudence and those of love. The reconciliation between Anne and Captain Wentworth leaves the core tension unresolved (Anne reiterates to Wentworth that yielding to Lady Russell eight years ago was the right decision). Coupled with the comment on the limitations of common sense, this discussion of irony leads Wright to argue for Austen as a novelist deeply invested in the complexities of moral life:

> ■ [she] examines humanity closely, but the more she perceives the less she understands – or perhaps one had better say, the more she understands the more she is perplexed by the contradictions she finds.⁵¹ ☐

Stylistically, her investigations of humanity comprehend many shifts of viewpoints, from 'objective accounts', 'direct or indirect comment' to 'interior disclosures' that convey the narrator's involvement and detachment (which Wright conjectures to be Austen's reason for abandoning the original epistolary form of some of the novels, including *Northanger Abbey*). The moral lesson to be learned from these stylistic choices is that no single point of view can convey completeness. With this recognition of narrative technique, Wright responds to R. W. Chapman, for whom Austen was not 'conscious of having a style' and whose only mark of individuality can be found in dialogues.⁵²

The absence of any exhaustive point of view resonates in Ronald S. Crane's 'Jane Austen: *Persuasion*' (1957), which sees in the novel 'a serious work – serious ethically no less than artistically'.⁵³ Crane maintained that the novel represents a special case of being thoroughly concerned with morality but having no particular moral thesis. Although our interest in Anne and Wentworth's love story springs primarily from their happiness as reunited lovers, the deeper and lasting response is engaged by the newfound happiness of two moral individuals. If earlier critics had asserted that Austen's last novel celebrates love for another 'as the light of life' that overcomes egotism, suffers patiently and prevails even in the absence of hope of reward, Crane seeks to understand how the narrative structure enhances the morality of this goal.⁵⁴ For him, the relevance of *Persuasion* as a 'serious comedy' pivots not so much on interesting events and entertaining playfulness as on the fact that 'they happen to persons for whom we have a special concern by reason of their merits as individuals'.⁵⁵ Austen manages to elicit this response by aligning our concerns fully with Anne's: we take an interest in Wentworth to the extent that Anne does. She is the moral and emotional crux upon which depends the entire suspense of the story. Hence, the artistic value of *Persuasion* consists in the internal actions unfolding in Anne's perception and it is our attachment to her as an individual that the narrator must secure in order for love to be morally and emotionally powerful. But how does one depict vividly and appealingly a character with self-effacing manners? How does one rescue a passive and neglected heroine from dreariness and insipidity? And how can the interest of a much-courted and successful young man like Wentworth in such a heroine be sustained plausibly?

Crane identifies three devices: the narrator's insights into Anne's consciousness, the insertion of events and conversations peripheral to the romance, and the juxtaposition of Anne with other characters. The narrator's insights convey with efficient brevity and in well-chosen intervals Anne's pain, without making it appear excessive or monotonous:

■ in a fashion that suggests a certain amount of rational control and objectivity on her part, while keeping us aware that she is feeling as well as thinking.[56] □

Peripheral events and conversations provide windows into Anne's worthiness as a moral subject, her sound principles, her judgement of others and herself, her 'capacity for happiness' and, not least, 'her quiet sense of the ridiculous' visible in her frequent smiles even in hours of dejection.[57] Lastly, affinity with the Crofts and juxtaposition with her family and the Musgrove sisters round off her superiority, suggesting that she is best understood and appreciated by the Crofts and Harvilles and, therefore, belongs with them.

Yet Austen understood that the value of rapturous and rational love, as she wanted to evoke it in this novel, hinges upon the moral worth of both lovers (*P* 210). Hence, the final difficulty remained, namely to demonstrate (and not simply expect readers to take Anne's insights for it) that Wentworth deserves the value Anne confers on him. Tacitly influenced by T. S. Eliot's notion of the 'objective correlative' in his discussion of *Hamlet*, Crane reads the scene of Wentworth's letter and his last speech as delivering the 'objective evidence' that no illusions or excessive praise clouds Anne's judgement and that Wentworth is her moral equal.[58] Until then, other characters like the Crofts have spoken for, and indirectly bolstered Anne's unwavering attachment to, him.

Morality as described by Wright or Crane appears as an abstract and universal concept, and, indeed, there is general agreement in the period that Austen was timeless in the sense that Shakespeare was. Lionel Trilling, however, argued that the treatment of morality in her novels was profoundly modern. In *The Opposing Self* (1955), a study that focused on the literature of the nineteenth century, Trilling describes the relation between the modern self and modern culture. Drawing on Friedrich Hegel's idea of 'alienation' as a phenomenon that arises from the self's desire for fulfilment and the pain incurred by this aspiration, Trilling enlists Austen among authors like Shelley, Dickens, Flaubert and Tolstoy. He attributes to Austen the merit of introducing the category of 'personality', which Hegel held to be the structural element of modern culture. Indeed, Hegel distinguished between 'character' and 'personality', maintaining that the first was concerned with acts, deeds, facts to be seen and judged, whereas the second was derived from the personal quality of the doer and the manner in which it is performed.[59] The movement from 'character' to 'personality' entails a shift from action to the 'manner and style' of moral action as inextricably linked to the quality and entire identity of the agent. Austen, Trilling argues, is the first to capture this shift:

> ■ It was Jane Austen who first represented the specifically modern personality and the culture in which it had its being. Never before had the moral life been shown as she shows it to be, never before had it been conceived to be so complex and difficult and exhausting. Hegel speaks of the 'secularization of spirituality' as a prime characteristic of the modern epoch, and Jane Austen is the first to tell us what this involves. [...] She is the first to be aware of the Terror which rules our moral situation, the ubiquitous anonymous judgment to which we respond, the necessity we feel to demonstrate the purity of our secular spirituality, whose dark and dubious places are more numerous and obscure than those of religious spirituality, to put our lives and styles to the question, making sure that not only in deeds but in *décor* they exhibit the signs of our belonging to the number of the secular-spiritual elect.[60] □

Austen understands the profound requirements of modern personality and, in *Persuasion*, penetrates the extremes of this 'Terror' through the merciless ridicule to which she submits Mrs. Musgrove's 'large, fat sighings' over her late intractable son (*P* 59). Admitting Austen's unique 'aesthetical-spiritual snobbery' in this passage, Trilling regards it also as deeply symptomatic of her mode of judgement, an illustration of Hegel's 'secularization of spirituality', which demands that we scrutinize not merely the moral act, but also the quality of its agent. This double attention to the compound act-agent signals the emergence of the idea of personality from that of character and attends the process of secularization. The quality of the agent also comprises the unconscious intentions of the agent (Mrs. Musgrove's unconscious self-indulgence in belated sorrow and the narrator's and viewer's irrepressible urge to mock what taste cannot tolerate). This dimension, the quality of being at the centre of moral life, defines the novelty of modern personality and Austen's modernity. Trilling may be influenced by D. H. Lawrence, who described the 'technique of personality' as the 'sharp knowing in apartness' which creates 'the feeling of individualism' and 'existence in isolation'.[61] For Lawrence, it is both a moment of loss and modernity that he first encountered in Austen.

Unlike earlier critics, Trilling stresses the moral rather than humorous effect which performs the double task of entertainment and moral recognition. The probing into the subtleties of modern personality provides readers with pleasure, but, at the same time, it also awakens them to the demands of personality (which only the likes of Mrs. Allen and Sir Walter escape), of the labours of self-awareness and sensitivity to others which can transmute into exhaustion and disgust. Trilling's discussion of modern personality offers a new answer to the question of realism and Austen's (for some, puzzling) success with very diverse modern readerships.

'Inaugurator of the great tradition'

The proliferation of interpretations that examine the moral importance of Austen's novels stands in close connection to discussions of the development of English fiction, whose genesis most critics located in the beginning of the eighteenth century. In the nineteenth century, there had been several attempts to compile a canon of the new genre, the first being Anna Laetitia Barbauld's fifty-volume *British Novelists* (1810). Later in the century, Austen had appeared in numerous critical accounts and compilations. William Dean Howells, for example, in his brief mention of Austen in *Criticism and Fiction* (1891), declares that Austen's realism, 'the truthful treatment of material', is unequalled.[62] However, the study that firmly placed Austen at the head of the modern novel was F. R. Leavis's *The Great Tradition: George Eliot, Henry James and Joseph Conrad* (1948). Here, Leavis confidently claims that the three authors featured in the title of his book could not have written their masterpieces without Austen. She was the first of the greatest novelists, the 'inaugurator of the great tradition of the English novel'.[63] Impatient with overly broad definitions that failed to distinguish the truly great from good, commonplace or downright unreadable novelists, Leavis detects three criteria of greatness: originality, reconciliation of form and content and serious morality transform a work of prose fiction into a classic appealing to many generations of readers. On the heels of formative experimentations throughout the eighteenth century, Austen's *oeuvre* fulfils all three criteria. These were refined and transported into educated life by Fanny Burney, before reaching perfect harmony in Austen.

However, this aesthetic harmony has done Austen considerable disservice, Leavis argues, so that critics and readers speak of her greatest merit as residing in the crafting of delightful characters and enclaves of escape and carefree enjoyment. This is precisely the reasoning behind accounts that do not confer on Austen the title of the 'first modern novelist'. Against these, Leavis counters:

> ■ Jane Austen's plots, and her novels in general, were put together 'very deliberately and calculatedly' (if not 'like a building'). But her interest in composition is not something to be put over against her interest in life; nor does she offer an 'aesthetic' value that is separable from moral significance. The principle of organization, and the principle of development, in her work is an intense moral interest of her own in life that is in the first place a preoccupation with certain problems that life compels on her as personal ones.[64] □

Like Eliot, James and Conrad, she promotes 'awareness of the possibilities of life'.[65]

Austen is superior to her predecessors and only equalled by a few successors because she understood the mastery of form to be a conveyor of moral concerns: 'formal perfection [...] can be appreciated only in terms of the moral preoccupations that characterize the novelist's peculiar interest in life'.[66] Even her much-praised irony and impersonalized style draw their poignancy from the serious background of moral tensions without which she would not be great.[67] Arguing the case of Austen as a moralist invested in the life of the individual in modern society, Leavis seeks to prove that her work has the seriousness that Victorian literary critic Matthew Arnold had singled out as the watermark of great literature.[68]

Leavis greatly influenced the monograph that cemented Austen's prominence: Ian Watt's *The Rise of the Novel: Studies in Defoe, Richardson and Fielding* (1957). Watt, like Leavis, does not engage with Austen closely but treats her nonetheless as his point of reference. If Leavis sees the development of the great English novel take off under her pen, Watt investigates the fiction of the century that made possible her novelistic maturity as well as the solutions that she brought to her predecessor's unsolved problems. Her key influences were Richardson and Fielding, who together with Defoe explored the potential of a new kind of writing that departed from the old-fashioned romances, by aiming at authenticity not so much through the kind of life and human experience it represented, but by the way it represented it.[69] The novel, whether written by Defoe, Richardson, Fielding or Austen, concerns itself more than any other literary genre with the correspondence between literature and reality. Hence, a claim to realism (a persistent topic in Austen criticism before and after Watt's study) emerges as the lowest common denominator of the eighteenth-century novel.

This claim accounts for several new techniques: first, the novel genre repudiates traditional plots and borrowings from mythology or previous literature. Second, emphasis on particular and individual experience, hence originality, replaces generalizing tendencies and classical preferences. Particularity is foregrounded through the individualization of the characters' interiority and the detailed rendering of their environment.[70] Third, the novel (and its characters) shows awareness of time and space: Freudian before Freud; the novel is the first literary form to reveal a causal connection between past experience and present action, which is nothing less than a modern sense of time. Space, inseparable from time, is often concretely described as a correlative to the particular situation of the characters. Lastly, the novel's language favoured the closeness and immediacy of the situation lived by real-life people over stylistic elegance.[71]

It becomes clear that the particularity of any human experience represented by the novel necessitates a double focus on the subjects who experience it and their spatio-temporal surroundings. Richardson and Fielding attend to this double focus differently: Richardson, with his minute explorations of the psyche, individual characteristics and motivations, closely approaches the internal life of the experiencing self, whereas Fielding is more bent on representing external influences and objects of consciousness. Watt conceives of these different emphases as responses to the dualism between the ego and the material world that impresses on the self. Richardson relates his stories through an introspective lens and Fielding through a more detached viewpoint. What about Austen? Watt asserts that she borrows from both and avoids each master's pitfalls:

> ■ She was able to combine into harmonious unity the advantages both of realism of presentation and realism of assessment, of the internal and of the external approaches to characters; her novels have authenticity without diffuseness or trickery, wisdom of social comment without a garrulous essayist, and a sense of social order which is not achieved at the expense of the individuality and autonomy of the characters.[72] □

She adopts Fielding's omniscient narrator but is more restrained (less of a digressive and 'garrulous essayist'), more impersonal and less dependent on plot. To Richardson, she owed psychological closeness and the privileging of individual consciousness, but, unlike him, she kept a removed and comic stance towards her creations. In other than technical aspects, too, Austen refines the works of her predecessors: Defoe's treatment of economic individualism, Richardson's centrality of the marriage plot in women's social existence and Fielding's shrewd pictures of manners and norms.

Watt's account of the emergence of the novel, with Austen featuring at its apex, outlines a critical trend that would come to fruition in the second part of the twentieth century: the theorizing of a historical Austen, as a novelist strongly shaped by the social, political and cultural currents of her time. While giving credit to the novels' formal qualities and moral insights, this trend deepens the significance of form and content, by exploring them as responses to the intellectual milieu in which the novels originated. Both the novels and their cultural backdrop receive ample attention in the second half of the century, as Chapters 5 and 6 show. In Chapter 5, we turn to interpretations that plumb the novels' textual strategies and innovations and their relations to human psychic experience and an emerging capitalist modernity.

CHAPTER FIVE

The Text, the Unconscious and Commodity, 1950s–1990s

In the second half of the twentieth century, literary studies benefited from a burgeoning range of methodologies that drew attention not only to literature as a field of human experimentation and a reservoir of ideas about our identity, culture and society, but also to the ways these ideas came into being and created meaning in and beyond the literary realm. The investigation of the cultural production and communication of meaning prompted a variety of questions which in turn determined the perspectives from which to approach a text. This chapter discusses interpretations of *Northanger Abbey* and *Persuasion* that deploy some of the most productive critical approaches, ranging from formalist and deconstructionist to psychoanalytic and Marxist. Feminist interpretations do not appear here because, more often than not, they assimilate other critical approaches for the purpose of exposing the text's engagement with contemporary aesthetics and conceptions of gender identity. Thus, they contribute more directly to the picture of a historical and political Austen that will be the focus of Chapter 6.

Narrative Strategies

Until the 1950s, one area that had received more praise than systematic examination was Austen's style. For example, D. W. Harding's, Mark Schorer's and Ronald Crane's studies (see Chapter 4) had been stimulating explorations of the lexical and narrative patterns underlying *Persuasion*'s style. Schorer's and Crane's analysis was followed up by Joseph M. Duffy's 'Structure and Idea in Jane Austen's *Persuasion*' (1954).[1] Duffy revisits Harding's comment on *Persuasion*'s affinity with the fairy tale of the motherless, neglected but exceptionally good heroine, who, after a period of dreary isolation, finds a worthy companion (and compensation) in the heroic lover who values her as she properly deserves.

Duffy's point, however, differs from Harding's. He mentions the fairy tale only to demonstrate the lack of sophistication in Austen's choice of a story. Yet he maintains that *Persuasion* does not fall short of being 'a miraculous event in the history of English fiction'.[2] The miracle consists in the crafting of such a complicated and ambiguous novel out of a simple story. Indeed, the fairy tale is only the 'vestigial element', whereas the complexity of the novel rests on its organization of character, action and reaction in three concentric circles corresponding to a cosmic, social and personal force: time, the outer circle (and cosmic force), presses itself through pervasive symbols of decay, such as the passing of seasons, crumbling of cliffs, a long list of deaths, illnesses and accidents; the decline of the hereditary landed class and the rise of the navy represent the social force of the second circle; and while the inner circle, the personal force, revolves around Anne. The cosmic and the social prey on the protagonist constantly so that hers becomes the consciousness through which decay is experienced, whether natural like the autumnal surroundings of Kellynch Hall or social like the autumn of the aristocracy. Building on this structural arrangement, Duffy writes of the novel's metaphoric indirection in its evocation of nature imagery as complementing the social and personal forces that concentrate upon Anne: the threat of decline and hope of rejuvenation. With such emphasis on the personal, *Persuasion* moves away from neoclassic ideas of restrained feeling towards romantic celebration of emotive power.[3] Hence:

> ■ The whole moral direction of the novel is towards an embracing of energetic life and rejection of the life of leisure.[4] □

Sir Walter's life of leisure, which seems to lead to atrophy and homelessness, weighs more acutely on Anne than on anybody else. The reappearance of Captain Wentworth, strengthened by the Crofts' renting of Kellynch Hall, aligns the regenerating powers of emotive energy with the active life of the naval class. Accordingly, Duffy considers *Persuasion* to be Austen's most radical novel, but its radicalism promotes no ruthless dismissal of tradition. The novel's balanced resolution testifies to Austen's prudent radicalism, since romantic felicity comes to full bloom only after Lady Russell, the beloved mother-surrogate, representative of aristocratic pride, and Wentworth, the self-made professional, Anne's first and only love, recognize each other's worth.[5]

Similarly, Howard Babb, in his *Jane Austen's Novels: The Fabric of Dialogue* (1962), recognized metaphoric indirection as one of Austen's preferred narrative techniques. However, while Duffy speaks of metaphorical indirection in the use of nature imagery, Babb applies the term to dialogue in the novels, describing it as the kind of exchange in which:

> ■ the speakers can keep up an appearance of decorum by pretending to talk of the literal situation, while indeed they treat it metaphorically, thus betraying their most intense feelings.[6] □

Accordingly, in *Persuasion*, three dialogues obliquely refer to ideas that Wentworth and Anne cannot communicate directly to each other: first, the dialogue between Wentworth and the Crofts on the appropriateness of wives' accompanying their husbands at sea (*P* 60–1); second, Wentworth and Louisa's exchange on the firmness of character during the walk to Winthrop (*P* 72–5); and, third, Anne's indirect appeal to Wentworth mediated by the conversation with Captain Harville on women's constancy (*P* 186–8). The metaphoric indirection of dialogues creates a story that moves the reader's interest not through its succession of events, but through the accumulation of overwhelming impressions on the protagonist.[7]

This technique, although quite central in Austen's mature fiction, already appears in *Northanger Abbey*. Here, it is employed to dramatize Henry's immediate interest in Catherine Morland during the encounter in which Henry compares dancing to marriage. Babb considers this a crucial moment that must be present to complement other dialogues in which Henry readily assumes the role of the tutor. It, indeed, prepares Catherine (and the reader) to view him as a potential husband, while Henry acquires the double life of the mentor-lover.[8] Arguably, there is more reason to speak of metaphoric indirection in *Persuasion* than *Northanger Abbey*, since Henry's speech on the literal (dance) and the metaphoric (marriage) has little indirectness about it and hardly provokes more than Catherine's bewilderment. Nor are there any other instances of metaphoric indirections to sustain his life as Catherine's lover. Nonetheless, these are valid examples that demonstrate the claim of earlier critics that Austen's characters reveal themselves in conversation, or, as Babb puts it, 'the clues to their behavior lie in the deeds of their language'.[9]

Only a year after Babb's study of dialogue, A. Walton Litz in his *Jane Austen: A Study of Her Artistic Achievement* (1963), among other important points, expanded Babb's analysis, maintaining that, while her prose evinces literary traces of Johnsonian language and the novel of sensibility, the conversations are true to life. He singles out the conversation between Catherine, Henry and Eleanor on the newest book expected in London to show that 'a straightforward contrast between Gothic nonsense' and 'the common feelings of common life' erase Austen's irony (*NA* 81–3).[10] While the narrative builds on the subplot of Catherine's reading of Gothic novels and its impact on the main plot of her life in Bath and at the abbey, the novel pursues no sense-conquers-sensibility theme. Rather,

> ■ Jane Austen's irony is not directed at Catherine's sympathetic imagination, but at her misuse of it; and the novel's deepest criticism is reserved for the average reader's complacent reaction to the exposure of Catherine's 'folly'.[11] □

Catherine's education aims at the sophistication of imagination by grounding it in judgement. While the novel contains narrative inconsistencies such as the intrusions of the heterodiegetic narrator in her defence of the novel genre or in the concluding paragraphs, we also find in *Northanger Abbey* the first signs of the balance between dramatic action and psychological exposition that establishes itself as the distinguishing trait of Austen's best works. As a specimen of this balance, Litz mentions the scene in which Catherine observes the inappropriate growing intimacy between Isabella and Captain Tilney.

Litz's claim that Austen consistently masters narrative viewpoint in her mature work, culminating in *Persuasion*'s heroine, who carries the story's entire interest, is refined by Thomas F. Wolfe's 'The Achievement of *Persuasion*' (1971). Wolfe considers the novel's achievement to be the distinct dramatization of Anne's consciousness. Technically, the narrator's perspective is aligned with Anne's so that we develop a sense of identification with her thoughts and experiences. Thematically, the novel presents a profound antagonism between personal and social values. The personal values, associated with reflection and acute remembering of the past, can be conveyed only inadequately through public activity. Hence, Wolfe argues for a discontinuity between the first and second half of the book, in which Anne's public visibility increases. Striving to bring Anne and Wentworth together, the narrator's voice becomes dissociated from Anne. In unconventional (and at times more intuitive than analytical) close readings of Book I, Wolfe suggests that Anne's consciousness, her values and attitudes, penetrate the language used by the narrator to describe other characters. For example, the exposition of Elizabeth acting as the mistress of Kellynch Hall for thirteen years (a number repeated four times in an exposition of six sentences) conjures a melancholy revisiting of the past that elsewhere in the novel springs from Anne's rather than Elizabeth's consciousness.[12] Even dialogue, scarce as it is in Book I, matters primarily as chatter overheard by Anne and interwoven with her deeper and unspoken intimations. So do small gestures, like Wentworth's lifting of the Musgrove boy from Anne's neck.

The technique of Book I, argues Wolfe, is unprecedented in Austen's fiction and not as scrupulously executed in Book II. The weight and omnipresence it allows to Anne's personal experience speak for a kind of autonomy of sensibility that is toned down in Book II by the emphasis on social values.[13] In Book II, Anne's connections to the present are strengthened. She is less of an outsider, as she participates in the subplot that writes off Mr. Elliot through Mrs. Smith's intervention and seals Wentworth's desirability, who is now free and humbled by the consequences of his mindless flirtations. The autonomy of the sensibility of a separate and silent figure that permeates Book I reappears in the conversation between Harville and Anne, leading up to the climatic reunion and the lovers' anticipation of happy things to come (*P* 193). Wolfe abstains from discussing the implications of such an ending for the antagonism between personal and social values crucial to his argument. After all, Anne marries into the socially vibrant naval class, leaving behind characters like Sir Walter and Elizabeth whom the narrative reduces to merely social beings. It is hard to shake off the impression that Wolfe likes *Persuasion*'s aesthetics best when it lingers in the past so that steps towards future felicity come with a tinge of loss.

Perhaps Cheryl Ann Weissman's article 'Doubleness and Refrain in Jane Austen's *Persuasion*' (1988) helps explicate this residual melancholy. Weissman speaks of the novel's 'wistful tone' that replicates 'the stylized and gloomy milieu' of the fairy tales, in which the happy ending is 'a miraculous, precarious rescue'.[14] For all the narrative focalization that Anne receives in the novel, there is a residual mystery about her personality that escapes both narrator and reader. Weissman is not the only one to suggest this. Already in 1974, Karl Kroeber had argued that the transparency that is distinctive of Austen's language is transgressed in *Persuasion* by complex sentence structures that convey the 'extreme fineness of the discriminations' necessary for the rendering of personal feeling.[15] And about a decade after Weissman, Deidre Lynch, in *The Economy of Character* (1999), writes of Anne as a character whose roundedness hinders her from being seen completely and immediately.[16]

While Lynch locates the reason for obscurity in the constellation of characters, that is, their oblivion and neglect of Anne, Weissman attributes it to the novel's insistence on a past outside the narrative frame, a past that can only be reminisced about over and over again but never recovered completely:

> ■ Presented from its outset as a sequel to an implicitly meaningful, unwritten earlier story, this novel is a puzzling play on the notion of doubleness.[17] □

Weissman identifies doubleness at the level of plot and style. At the level of plot, two accidents have an impact on Anne and Wentworth's reconciliation: first, the injury of little Charles Musgrove brings Wentworth into Anne's presence after eight years of separation, and Louisa's fall reanimates their relationship. In addition, there is a dazzling doubling of names: William Walter Elliot, Sir Walter Elliot, Charles Musgrove, little Charles Musgrove, Charles Smith, Charles Hayter and the Marys and Elizabeths of the Elliot family listed in the *Baronetage*. Anne's usefulness and not-belonging at Uppercross is doubled by the old nursery-maid who had brought up all the Musgrove children and who, like Anne in Lyme, would see to Louisa's recovery back home. In the description of the nursery, Weissman recognizes the monotonous rhythm of a nursery rhyme, a doubling of diction that Weissman calls 'refrain', mirroring the doubleness of time. The reigning refrain is that of returns so that the reader is always kept in suspense wondering whether any return will lead to the protagonists' reunion. Consequently, if in other Austen novels, the happy ending is heralded by pleasing anticipation, *Persuasion*'s aura of apprehension never relaxes.

Words, Innovation and Deconstruction

Among other attempts to delve into the fabric of Austen's prose, Norman Page's *The Language of Jane Austen* (1972) and Lloyd Brown's *Bits of Ivory* (1973) are two important and complementary studies. In the series of enlightening chapters on style, vocabulary, syntax, narrative mode and letter writing, Page shows that Austen is as much a traditionalist as an innovator. In matters of vocabulary, her novels draw on the eighteenth-century tradition, but her syntax continually acquires the flexibility of a more conversational style that characterizes the later development of the novel genre. *Northanger Abbey* stands as the best example of Austen's preoccupation with the ways her characters use and manipulate language, with Henry's corrective response to Catherine's use of 'nice' being a case in point. Imprecise linguistic usage and language in excess of the subject treated make ambiguity the novel's marked feature.[18] Brown supports this conclusion by observing that the novel abounds in words with contrasting meanings such as 'amiable', which in the eighteenth century meant 'pleasing', 'lovely' as well as 'pretending or showing love'.[19]

Another example discussed by Page is the conversation between Henry, Catherine and Eleanor on the misunderstanding regarding the awaited Gothic novel that Eleanor confuses with a riot. Parallel to the comic effect of the *quiproquo* of talking at cross-purposes runs the more serious concern about words (and by extension acts and appearances) that invite more than one interpretation. The incident illustrates the theme of the novel:

> ■ It is, indeed, a foreshadowing of the more extensive misinterpretations of Catherine when she visits Northanger Abbey.[20] □

In *Persuasion*, Austen adapts her technique to the difficult task of registering 'the delicate fluctuations of mood and emotional response'.[21] Her syntax often blends the narrative and dramatic style so that boundaries between dialogue and narrative prose become almost imperceptible. For example, the dramatic soliloquy used to convey the speech of characters is replaced by free indirect speech as in the following passage:

> ■ Jealousy of Mr. Elliot! It was the only intelligible motive. Captain Wentworth jealous of her affection! Could she have believed it a week ago; three hours ago! (*P* 154) □

Unobtrusively, and without the apparatus of direct speech, the narrator slides into the character's perception to record her spontaneous thoughts, as if we were witnessing them in a theatre of the mind.[22] This is a technique, according to Page, that Austen perfects in the course of her career and for which she must be called an innovator. Her traditionalist roots can be seen in the influence that Samuel Johnson's language plays on her syntax. Well-balanced and symmetrical sentences like the ending of *Northanger Abbey*, 'I leave it to be settled, by whomsoever it may concern, whether the tendency of this work be altogether to *recommend parental tyranny*, or *reward filial disobedience*', have a Johnsonian ring that can still be found in *Persuasion* (*NA* 187, emphasis added), such as 'The manoeuvres of *selfishness* and *duplicity* must ever be revolting' (*P* 167, emphasis added). However, in *Persuasion*, more prominently than in Austen's other novels, such pairing serves to enhance an emotional rather than a logical or moral climax.

Kenneth C. Phillipps points out a further element of innovation at the level of sentence structure. In all Austen's novels, Phillipps identifies a wide use of expanded tenses as illustrated by these examples:

> ■ A question of force and interest to rise over every other, *to be* never *ceasing*, alternately *irritating* and *soothing*. (*NA* 171, emphasis added)
>
> Soon, however, she began to reason with herself, and try *to be feeling* less. Eight years, almost eight years had passed, since all had been given up. How absurd *to be resuming* the agitation which such an interval had banished into distance and indistinctness! (*P* 53, emphasis added) □

Phillipps attributes this usage entirely to Austen's linguistic sensibility. It is a new emphasis on temporality that he has not encountered in writers such as Samuel Johnson or Fanny Burney, to whom Austen's prose owes much. The construction gives 'increased actuality' to emotions, thoughts and states of mind, which explains its extensive appearance in *Persuasion*. In the example quoted above from this novel, the expanded tense supports Anne's steadiness as well as the slow and reluctant change of mature feelings.[23]

Brown, more explicitly than Page, insists that the investigation of technique be treated 'as the discovery of meaning', a credo he borrows from Schorer. Hence, our investment in any technical exploration is rewarding when it expands our understanding of the text. True to his conviction, when discussing *Northanger Abbey*, Brown makes two important discoveries: first, it has been wrongly assumed that Austen's language is unmetaphorical, as Krober argues (although Krober admits that *Persuasion*'s autumnal mode gestures towards the metaphorical). Symbolism already appears in Austen's early novel. First, the abbey is the architectural representation of Catherine's fantasies and of the General's self-aggrandizement.[24] Second, it is a constant reminder of the fact that the novel yokes together two narrative viewpoints: literature as escape and literature as the reflection of life. While Catherine (and the common reader) is weaned from the seductive powers of escapist reading, the likes of Isabella and the General remain the same. Hence, symbolism engenders the novel's parody. Brown also explicates *Persuasion*'s symbolism, by identifying with 'autumn' two contesting kinds of maturity: Anne's seasoned gentle awareness and self-knowledge and Wentworth's 'specious' maturity expressed through his headstrong pride.[25] The very title of the novel repeatedly reflects this tension through its use of the word 'persuasion' in a 'double meaning integral to Anne Elliot's character and experience': persuasion as 'exertion of moral and intellectual influence on a weak or indecisive will' and persuasion as 'a form of independent but flexible self-criticism'.[26] Both connotations were in use in the eighteenth century. Brown seems to suggest that these connotations do not simply coexist but that there is a shift of emphasis from the first, which evokes Anne's youthful past submission to Lady Russell's advice, to the second connotation that appears in Anne's mature reflections and her paradoxical defence at the end of the novel.

It is important at this point to mention another discussion of *Persuasion*'s title that dwells on the double meaning of the word with a different outcome. James Phelan's *Worlds from Words* (1981) takes the deconstructionist approach, which argues that the meaning of a text is derived from language alone, but since language is an unstable medium it can convey no fixed meaning. Phelan draws on J. Hillis Miller's literary application of the philosophical work of Jacques Derrida.

Phelan starts out with the assumption that 'persuasion' has a univocal meaning in the novel. Anne Elliot, led by mistaken advice ('persuaded') to reject her first love, strives at a mature stage to persuade her returned lover to propose again. Without any reference to Brown's analysis, Phelan first argues that the meaning is not indeterminate but ambiguous. In a sentence like 'Anne's persuasion', Anne can be the agent (the one who persuades) or the object upon whom the power of persuasion is worked. To be the persuader means to exert power and to be the one persuaded means to yield power, to be 'a moveable figure'. However, because the persuadable person is a moveable figure, the power of persuasion is an illusion. Wentworth himself recognizes the infinite positions that a persuadable character can occupy when he says 'that no influence over it can be depended on [...] everybody may sway it' (*P* 74). In addition, the persuader must be flexible and adopt his strategies to the dispositions of the one he/she would like to persuade. In this, Phelan recognizes a shifting power relationship and a reversal: in his/her obsessive desire to persuade, the persuader has become himself/herself moveable. Hence, the different connotations of the word 'persuade': cajole, coax, plead, influence, induce, convince, convert, etc.

We see how the relationship between persuader and persuaded is not one of clear dissimilarities and the 'more we try to pin down their relations the more indeterminate their meanings become'.[27] Thus, 'persuasion' leads to *aporia* or perpetual doubt about its meaning and ends up deconstructing both itself and *Persuasion*. However, Phelan's analysis does not end in *aporia*. He believes that the novel's success does not depend entirely on language. Other elements of construction, such as plot, characters, emotions and thoughts, although emerging from words, cannot be reduced to merely linguistic elements. For example, Anne's speech in defence of constancy must be there as an opportunity to persuade the proudly, unpersuadable Wentworth (which is why Austen revised it):

> ■ Regardless of the language in which Anne makes her speech, she must be given this chance. The action itself is crucial. Then, in order for us to be moved by the speech and in order for us to find it plausible that Wentworth is moved to propose, the language of speech itself must be carefully crafted. Austen, of course, is equal to the task.[28] □

Phelan recovers, and indeed is among the few to do so, the importance of the story. Compare Phelan's position to Sheldon Sacks', who maintains that Austen in her last novel transcends the plot tradition, paving the way for the techniques of the stream-of-consciousness novel.[29] Whatever plot there is in *Persuasion*, according to Sack, it only hampers the novel's lyricism. By contrast, Phelan insists that plot and action matter. They are not simple, trivial or subordinate to language and style. *Persuasion* is a masterpiece that does ample justice to linguistic and non-linguistic elements of the narrative.

Genre Criticism

When seeking to decode Austen's exceptional mastery, critics attempt to discover how her enduring narrative strategies and her innovations compare to those of other novelists, in particular to her eighteenth-century influences. For example, in continuance of some of the studies of *Persuasion* mentioned above, Michael Boardman argues that its place in the tradition of the eighteenth-century novel resembles a farewell, in so far as it disavows a Richardsonian correlation between virtue and reward.[30] Structural irony makes *Persuasion* Austen's most sceptical and most romantic novel. Like Weissman, Boardman considers the happy ending as precarious and dependent on the narrative's determination to make a virtue of misery. The comedy of earlier novels survives in *Persuasion*, but it is a survival by a hair's breadth, all the more fragile and powerful because it comes so close to not happening.[31]

With regard to language, John Dussinger furthers discussions about the novel's free indirect discourse. The narratological effect of this device is the reduction of the gap between narrator and character, a process that creates the illusion of psychological depth.[32] As such, free indirect discourse enhances the notion of identity and the perception of a space rooted in identity ('inner' space) and another surrounding identity ('outer' space). Hence, in novels abounding in free indirect speech, the narrator allots a high degree of responsibility to the character. Storytelling seems to flow from the workings of the mind of the character and not from the narrator. We have here, then, a plausible explanation for Austen being repeatedly perceived as a detached narrator. But despite the newness of the effect, Dussinger is able to show that the impetus behind this technique originates with the eighteenth-century epistolary mode of 'writing-to-the-moment', which reduces the distance between a thinking and writing subject.[33] Indeed, as other critics have argued for the epistolary mode, so does Dussinger for Austen's novels being polyvocal, that is, in them the narrator incorporates another's speech without completely merging with it. As an example of the immediacy of such incorporation, consider the confusion of voices following Louisa's fall in *Persuasion*:

> ■ Charles, Henrietta, and Captain Wentworth were the three in consultation, and for a little while it was only an interchange of perplexity and terror. 'Uppercross, the necessity of some one's going to Uppercross; the news to

> be conveyed; how it could be broken to Mr. and Mrs. Musgrove; the lateness of the morning; an hour already gone since they ought to have been off; the impossibility of being in tolerable time.' At first, they were capable of nothing more to the purpose than such exclamations; but, after a while, Captain Wentworth, exerting himself, said –. (*P* 95, emphasis added) □

To this coexistence of different speeches, Russian literary critic Mikhail Bakhtin gave the name 'heteroglossia', which he saw as an essential characteristic of the novel.

Another important generic aspect was Austen's treatment of the comic legacy of the eighteenth century. *Northanger Abbey* lent itself particularly well to this exploration. Frank J. Kearful was the first to unravel the entanglement between novel and satire in the text. The tension between the two, he argues, is due to their aims to create two different worlds: the novel, an imaginatively self-contained world, and satire, a world that exists only through indirect references to the world outside its own. This incongruity is *Northanger Abbey*'s organizing principle. The novel starts as a satiric parasite of the sentimental novel, when it evokes conventions of sentimental fiction only to abort them. Similarly, during her stay in Bath, Catherine becomes an avid Gothic reader and, at Northanger, tests out Gothic scenarios only to find out that reading and experience do not match squarely. However, according to Kearful, this is an essentially novelistic and not satirical method that we find in works like Fielding's *Joseph Andrews* (and not, for example, in Swift's or Pope's works). While satire magnifies absurdity in order to ridicule and reject it, the novel dissolves it by putting excesses into an ample context to provide a seemingly more realistic substitute.[34] However, the ending of the novel, with its *deus ex machina* resolution enforced by the intruding narrator, finally dissolves the illusion of the Gothic only to replace it with another illusion.

The alternation between a satiric and novelistic mode in *Northanger Abbey* enables the integration of satire within the world of the novel. It is telling that the General is the most unintegrated figure:

> ■ The General's peremptory manners and genuinely unpleasant behavior remain quite outside the range of burlesque diminution. Also, the main concern of his adventure, Mrs. Tilney's death, is unquestionably real: here our starting-point is not merely the projection of an obviously over-active imagination. A real death from unexplained causes is naturally more a subject for our concern than imaginary trap-doors. Furthermore, Austen never quite dissolves this second adventure in a comic or satiric solution.[35] □

This residual element of mystery about the General's past persists, because, as George Levine argues, the General stands for the force that wants to keep Catherine from rising in class. Levine reads Catherine as the bearer of the monstrous energy that 'squeezes past Jane Austen's ironies into the world that pretends monstrosity does not exist'.[36] It is an energy that parody must accommodate, as it does in the end. Nonetheless, Levine insists that Austen deems ambition like Catherine's to be attractive and dangerous so that she must parody it without dismissing it.[37]

If Levine argues that *Northanger Abbey*'s parody translates social aspiration into the novel, Tara Ghoshal Wallace makes a case for the narrative's obsession with the parodic discourse being grounded in Austen's concern with the act of reading. The ideal reader seems to be more actively involved in meaning-making than the naïve reader who accepts the sentimental or Gothic artifice of the novel or the sophisticated reader who cannot be fooled by romance. The ideal reader becomes a participant and even 'struggles with the narrator for control over the text'.[38] This struggle is best illustrated in Wallace's discussion of Henry Tilney's character. Austen's imagined reader is allowed to believe at first that Henry is her spokesperson. Had this belief been sustained throughout the narrative, the novel would have produced the sophisticated reader who knows a parody when he/she sees one. However, Wallace demonstrates through careful comparison of dialogues that Austen undermines Henry's parodic censure. For example, Henry's first performance as a parodist of the emptiness of Bath's social rites is followed and contrasted by Catherine's and Eleanor's first conversation, which the narrator considers as conventional as it is 'being spoken with simplicity and truth' (*NA* 51). The juxtaposition of these exchanges exposes the limitations and falsities of 'parodic discourse' and casts doubt over the narrator's commitment to parody.[39] Yet there would hardly be place to speak of struggle, if the narrator's stance could be so decidedly settled. Even the uncomplicated world of the Morlands, deployed to chastise the family of the sentimental novels in the opening chapter, appears gloomy, insensitive and unworthy of the disenchanted Catherine. The parody of *Northanger Abbey* can therefore hardly be dismissed, but as Wallace astutely concludes:

> ■ Parody is itself revealed as shallow and manipulative in its choice of targets and methods, while the putative ideal – the reality-oriented viewpoint – is shown to be dull and insensitive. Each stance is trapped within its own self-created limitations.[40] □

The difficult task of the kind of reader that participates in narrative control is to be alert to the self-serving 'targets and methods' of each stance. However, alertness does not ensure resolution. In the spirit of deconstruction, Wallace believes that *Northanger Abbey* refuses to endorse a stable vision and expects readers to disentangle it without the hope of deciphering its determinate meaning.

Psyche and the Unconscious

Questions about the meaning(s) of a given text, representations of the psyche and their relationship to human experience have fuelled interpretations that seek to recover the unconscious life of a literary work. Sigmund Freud's ideas as the founder of psychoanalysis stand behind most of these interpretations. Before looking at psychoanalytical readings of *Northanger Abbey* and *Persuasion*, however, it is useful to keep in mind some key tenets.

Freud postulates that childhood plays a central role in the formation of the mature individual and that every individual is inhabited by rational and irrational drives. The latter refers to the realm of the unconscious, that is, experiences, yearnings, fears and losses of which the self is not aware. Often the unconscious harbours materials that the psyche has repressed in order to defend itself from them. However, repressed material has a way of resurfacing in new attire, often causing physical and mental discomfort. The return of something familiar in an unfamiliar form was described by Freud as the uncanny. The goal of psychoanalytic therapy is to master the anxiety of the uncanny by reintegrating it into the realm of the conscious. The most effective way of freeing pieces of the self from the murky waters of the unconscious is the interpretation of dreams, in particular, the interpretation of the techniques of 'dramatization' that we use to make our dreams intelligible for others.[41] Hence, dreams and the unconscious that generates them function similarly to texts, whose threads can be unravelled and images decoded.

Let us now turn to *Northanger Abbey*. Due to its affiliation to Gothic themes and their re-enactment in Catherine's theatre of the mind, many critics view *Northanger Abbey* as a rite-of-passage novel: a narrative of transition from unheroic childhood through adolescent illusions to the ordered and rational reality of a future wife.[42] In these readings, Henry Tilney appears as both the catalyst and enlightened tutor of Catherine's excesses. One contribution that undermines such certainty about Henry's function, by bringing into play Freud's notion of the uncanny, is Paul Morrison's article 'Enclosed in Openness: *Northanger Abbey* and the Domestic Carceral' (1991).[43]

Morrison relies on Freud's ingenious etymological analysis of the German *unheimlich* (uncanny) to demonstrate that in *Northanger Abbey* the opposition between the dark, inscrutable closeness of the Gothic and the visible openness of Austen's novel has collapsed. The dark and the visible, the enclosed and the open, coincide: 'And from the collapse of this opposition is born the Gothic *unheimlich*.'[44] This operation in which two apparently opposite attributes or systems end up in a relationship of resemblance is itself an *unheimlich* (uncanny) movement already present in etymology. Freud explains that the German word *heimlich* (meaning 'homely or familiar') follows an ambivalent development until it becomes identical with its opposite *unheimlich* (meaning 'concealed, kept out of sight'). Morrison argues that Henry's view of a country 'where roads and newspapers lay everything open' stands for an ideology of the *heimlich* (the familiar) that is present everywhere in the novel. However, unlike Henry, the novel does not posit this ideology of the *heimlich* as the opposite of Gothic closeness and incarceration (or the concealed *unheimlich*). In fact, they are both means of surveillance, disciplining and subordination, in which Henry and General Tilney are implicated:

> ■ The point here is not simply that General Tilney recovers romance villainy in the realm of manners; rather, the realm of manners, the domestic parlor, reinscribes Gothic incarceration in and as a generalized economy of surveillance.[45] □

Furthermore, it is an economy of surveillance that Henry Tilney celebrates as an effective obstacle to crime and social injustice and that he himself deploys to control Catherine in her function as a female reading subject. Indeed, as Michel Foucault's research on eighteenth-century models of prison demonstrates, Henry's world of complete openness replicates the vision of Jeremy Bentham, eighteenth-century philosopher and social reformer, for a Panopticon, the all-seeing prison that enforces discipline not through the principle of obscure incarceration, but through compulsory visibility. Foucault emphasizes that the validity of the principle exceeds the walls of disciplinary institutions and permeates the whole fabric of social life. As Morrison explains, its success lies in the very uncanny operation that covers the traces of incarceration through visibility:

> ■ The parlor reinscribes Gothic claustration in the mode of light or visibility, all the more effectively for eschewing the obvious mechanisms and paraphernalia of Gothic enclosure.[46] □

Hence, critical blindness towards Henry Tilney's chastisement of Catherine in the name of a transparent reality matches his blindness towards the panoptic power that wishes to see without being seen. Morrison, then, regards Henry as an unwitting accomplice of his father's, a view expressed by earlier critics who observed that the son's jocose parody always skirts the paternal figure.

The myriad of comments on *Persuasion*'s autumnal mood and symbolism did not go unnoticed by scholars trained in psychoanalytic theory. In particular, two essays concerned with the novel's atmosphere of mourning add unexpected layers to the meaning of romance in literature. We need to start with Anita Sokolsky's 'The Melancholy *Persuasion*' (1994) in order to understand the modifications proposed some years later by Frances L. Restuccia's 'Mortification: Beyond the *Persuasion* Principle' (2000). Both pieces are inspired by Freud's and Julia Kristeva's work on melancholia. Freud wrote in 'Mourning and Melancholia' (1917) that the ego identifies with the lost beloved object and, in order to preserve it, incorporates it within the self (like the infant that takes possession of things by trying to devour them). The melancholy ego is overwhelmed by this identification and moves towards death, wanting to destroy indirectly the object that overwhelms it from within.

For Sokolsky, *Persuasion* foregrounds reading as a therapeutic act. At times, this act tends to be overshadowed by Anne's attachment to melancholy narratives such as the loss of her mother, her own social insignificance and more importantly the mortification caused by Wentworth's indifference. Yet Anne's tendency finds its therapeutic cure in the novel's commitment to 'melioration'.[47] Anne herself overcomes melancholy when she heeds 'her educable' impulses. Paradoxically, Louisa's fall, in itself a violent act, tips the scales in favour of melioration. There, at the sight of her injured and humiliated rival, melancholic Anne triumphs over unpersuadable Louisa after tasting the acid medicine of revenge. Here, Anne recoups her losses and, gradually, the narrative approaches the happy ending. Interestingly enough, happiness renders her elusive, as if the narrative wanted to suggest that it is 'exquisite sensibility which makes [Anne], finally, melancholy at the loss of melancholy'.[48]

For Sokolsky, Louisa's accident hurtles events towards a happy resolution, because it rewards Anne's and the novel's belief in persuasion as the ameliorative energy. Francesca Restuccia believes that such an optimistic conclusion sits ill with the violent climax. After all, why should 'a poor corpse-like figure' help a melancholic subdue melancholia (*P* 92)? Taking a cue from Julia Kristeva, who writes about depressed people remaining riveted to the lost subject which they cannot shed, Restuccia argues that after Louisa's near-death experience, Anne clings to loss more faithfully and more masochistically:

> ■ Eight years later, however, marriage to Frederick becomes a possibility – this is a turning point – not because there has been a break in Anne's melancholia (on the contrary I am arguing that Anne's melancholia intensifies

at this point), but because through this brush with death, Frederick has been sucked in, smeared with the enjoyment/*jouissance* of Louisa's 'poor corpse-like figure'.[49] □

Death haunts Wentworth's appearance in the story (in the figures of Dick Musgrove and Fanny Harville, whose passing away only Wentworth can communicate to Captain Benwick, and in the constant dangers of his profession anticipated in the last sentence of the book). Death (*thanatos*) and not love (*eros*) attracts Anne to Wentworth, because Anne is in love with the loss that has entered her life with her mother's death. Wentworth is only a blank slate on to which Anne transfers the loss of her mother. Hence, *Persuasion* 'renders the absent maternal figure amorphously present'.[50] This sophisticated though somewhat jargon-happy essay exemplifies the centrality allotted to the mother by feminist theory (as opposed to a father-fixated Freudian psychology). Restuccia then demonstrates that the mother is the lost and mourned object that *Persuasion*'s text (like the infant) has devoured, swallowed and re-presented.

The psyche intrigued Austen, particularly, in conjunction with the experience of reading. It remains, argues Adela Pinch, a constant concern, addressed not only by *Northanger Abbey*'s direct reference to Gothic novels, but also by *Persuasion*'s intense exploration of what it feels like to be a reader. The influence of reading haunts the narrative from the humorous opening on Sir Walter's coveted *Baronetage* to the power and influence of 'one person's mind over another':[51]

■ The question of 'persuasion', of the pressures that one mind can put on another, assumes at the phenomenal level less gentle, or at least, more physical forms. The novel repeatedly figures an acute awareness of others, an exaggerated sense of the contingency of the mind.[52] □

Pinch attributes to the rendering of these pressures *Persuasion*'s lyricism and the pleasures we derive from it as readers. However, if we were to redirect our attention to the reading taste and motivations of the characters, we would discover that the novel does not impart unbounded faith in reading as an indicator of taste or an unfailing remedy for loss. Wentworth wrongly believes that a reader of Byron like Benwick will live up to ideals of long-suffering and undying constancy. Nor can Anne distract herself by falling into poetical quotations after overhearing the conversation between Wentworth and Louisa during the autumnal walk. Pinch concludes that the only characters who have a satisfying relationship to books are men: Sir Walter, from his *Baronetage*, and Wentworth, from the *Navy List*, receive what they expect, namely their social existences recorded there.[53] Hence, Anne's feisty refusal to allow quotations as proof of women's moral unworthiness in her discussion with Harville is a repudiation of a long-standing, male-dominated, tradition. However, as Daniel Cottom notices, this argument is in itself a quotation from *The Spectator*.[54] Here, Pinch believes, Austen draws attention to herself as a writer, but also to a literature that since the publication of *The Spectator* abounded in deserted and loving women. This is also Anne's story: 'her early experience is like a text that she is repeating with renewed feeling'.[55] The temporal gap of eight years adds a certain literariness that makes Anne function as a reader who is crowded by a multitude of sensations as she revisits her past in her present, an activity that imitates our experience as (re)readers of *Persuasion*.

The Realities of Capital

Other roads can be taken to explain the bleakness of *Persuasion*, and, as critics influenced by a Marxist legacy insist, these roads necessitate a foray into the social and economic grounds from which literature grows. This appears most true for the time in which Austen lived and composed her novels, which Raymond Williams in his *English Novel from Dickens to Lawrence* (1970) finds

> ■ the most difficult to describe, in English social history: an acquisitive high bourgeois society at the point of its most evident interlocking with an agrarian capitalism that is itself mediated by inherited titles and by the making of family names.[56] □

Austen's world underwent the transition from an aristocratic order dependent on land, rents and accumulated wealth to a market society founded on capital, speculation and commodities. It is a transition that ends in the nineteenth century during which money, the medium of exchange of the professional classes, has not only replaced land but also metamorphosed into an object of desire.

This process, argues John Vernon in his study *Money and Fiction* (1984), fragments *Persuasion*. His analysis is a development of Schorer's sobering revelation of the novel's economic subtext (see Chapter 4) and a response to Alistair Duckworth, who dismisses any subversive subtext, as will be discussed in more detail in Chapter 6. Duckworth allows for the possibility of 'the improvement of the landed order by the infusion of new naval blood', whereas Vernon demonstrates that the novel registers the looming future in which the estate will be broken up by the likes of Mr. Elliot, for whom Kellynch Hall is a mere commodity and the absorption of land by money only a matter of time.[57] Vernon understands the term 'money' in its physical appearance as the circulating object that mobilizes 'larger economic forces – the Industrial Revolution in particular – and "smaller" psychological ones: desire, need, ambition'.[58]

Larger and smaller forces are felt and rendered through the character of Anne. Her initial refusal happens in a time of flux and her dilemma represents the double bind of an inherited code that pursues moral improvement but must also secure its financial survival through transmission of wealth. According to Vernon, Anne must perform the hardest task Austen has ever put to a heroine: 'to reconcile the morality of self-sacrifice with self-interest'.[59] Hence, her invisibility or 'blankness' as a character that mediates between conflicting exigencies and difficult antinomies, such as prudence and romantic love, rural and naval life, birth privileges and merit.[60] Not even Anne, or perhaps she less than anyone, can escape sordid economic considerations. Surely, her decision and standing before her own family is facilitated by Wentworth's money.

Materiality bogs down optimistic readings of *Persuasion*. The material world creeps through the many falls (Louisa's, little Charles's, Anne's falling in love) and cripples of the story (Mrs. Smith, Captain Harville and Louisa) and never relinquishes its hold on landed property. Unlike *Pride and Prejudice,* where Bingley, the merchant's son, is on the lookout for a suitable estate, in *Persuasion,* we hear the hammer of the auctioneer in Mr. Elliot's letter to Mrs. Smith. In Vernon's words:

> ■ Mr. Elliot will divide and sell the estate, which is thus for him merely a commodity. But the hammer also conjures up images of a more brutal division, of the reduction of all that an estate represents – tranquillity, security, the conservation of the past – to mere raw material, to wood, stone, dirt. Mr. Elliot's hammer threatens to knock Kellynch Hall from the feudal world into the world of high capitalism: out of society – at least society as Jane Austen knew it – into the world of matter.[61] □

Even commentators who hail the novelty of 'a luminous individual woman' like Anne Elliot must concede that rural England is abandoned in *Persuasion*. This is Anne's loss as much as her incorporation in the naval class is a loss to rural communal life.[62] As Judith Weissman remarks, by fully identifying with the life of a sailor's wife, an activity to which she herself has no economic connection, Anne has given up the economic power that heroines like Emma wield in the agrarian world.[63]

Vernon's understanding of money as a medium of exchange that affects economic, psychological and social phenomena underlies James Thompson's book-length study of Austen's fiction, *Between Self and*

World (1988).⁶⁴ Both critics owe this fundamental understanding to the Marxist theorist Georg Lukács, who conceived of the emergence of the novel as the result of commodity production, that is, a capitalist mode of production in which products are not produced for direct consumption but for exchange. In his *Theory of the Novel* (1916), Lukács states that the rise of this mode that estranges consumers from the process of production parallels the all-pervading alienation and objectification embodied in the novel as a genre. The most telling signs of this estrangement are dualisms such as subject/object, freedom/necessity and individual/society.⁶⁵ Drawing on Lukács, Thompson goes on to argue that all of Austen's novels grapple with these antinomies. The 'personality' that critics since Trilling had described as modern stands under the pressures of a capitalist economy that endows individuality with power, while coercing and finally annihilating it.

According to Thompson, the novels react to these pressures with a belief in the authenticity of private experience and, therefore, must 'be related to the social history of privacy'.⁶⁶ For this, attention to Austen's theory of language is crucial. In her novels, the constant preoccupation with a proper linguistic medium that communicates real feeling betrays the unsettling disjunction between expression and feeling. How can the self clothe perceptions, thoughts and emotions in words? Thompson selects the semantic metaphor of 'language-as-clothing' as a running theme that interconnects the six novels and their author to the tradition of the long eighteenth century, maintaining that Austen is close to Wordsworth and quite removed from predecessors like Pope:

> ■ Unlike earlier eighteenth-century conceptions of language, this Romantic or Wordsworthian notion of language acknowledges limits past which language cannot go, insisting that thought and feeling are finite.⁶⁷ □

Northanger Abbey, too, treats words-clothing-thought as an explicit 'figure of denial' that intervenes only when the narrative ability has broken down:⁶⁸

> ■ The General, accustomed on every ordinary occasion to give the law in his family, prepared for no reluctance but of feeling, no opposing desire that should dare to clothe itself in words, could ill brook the opposition of his son, steady as the sanction of reason and the dictate of conscience could make it. (*NA* 183) □

Austen's sensitivity about the inadequacies of language is revealed in the revisions of *Persuasion*. In the first draft of the last chapters, the narrator reports Wentworth's words that Anne 'had *gained* inexpressibly in personal Loveliness' (*P* 208), whereas the final version locates ineffability not in Anne's appearance but in her feelings about Wentworth's perception of her:

> ■ It is something for a woman to be assured, in her eight-and-twentieth year, that she has not lost one charm of earlier youth; but the value of such homage was inexpressibly increased to Anne, by comparing it with former words, and feeling it to be the result, not the cause of a revival of his warm attachment. (P 196) □

Wentworth's speech replicates the formulaic inexpressibility of heroes and heroines of late-eighteenth-century sentimental novels, but the final version engages in the work of describing interiority while registering its opacity.

A comparison of proposal scenes in Austen and her predecessors shows that opacity is Austen's way of preserving her characters' privacy and individuality.[69] For instance, in the closing chapters of *Persuasion*, Anne and Wentworth walk among 'sauntering politicians, bustling housekeepers, flirting girls' and must be shielded from the prying ears of the crowd (*P* 194). At this moment, we the readers have become part of the crowd, too, and are refused access to the intimacy shared by these characters we have come to know intimately.[70] There is a sense that, for the first time in the novel, Anne is not alone in a crowd and we may be dismissed. This allows Thompson to valorize the courtship plot as a vehicle through which Austen integrates the privatization of human relations (Mary Poovey contradicts this view – see Chapter 6).

Thompson's study, which treats the courtship novel as a formal and social choice dictated just as much by the reality of commodity culture as women's reduced opportunities in it, prepares us to address the gender dimension of Austen criticism during the second half of the twentieth century. In the next chapter, we turn to interpretations that read *Northanger Abbey* and *Persuasion* in light of the contemporary social, political and aesthetic conditions that affected, in particular, women as writers and readers of the novel.

CHAPTER SIX

Political and Historical Austen, 1950s–1990s

An important achievement of the second half of the twentieth century was the determination to historicize literature, that is, to explore the social, cultural and aesthetic conditions in which literature is produced. This approach does not treat texts in isolation but places them in a historical context, attempting to recover the textual influences, social phenomena and cultural ideas absorbed by literary texts. In this chapter, I have selected from the abundant criticism of the second half of the twentieth-century interpretations that question the image of an ahistorical Austen or unconscious artist. These interpretations examine the novels' grappling with hotly debated issues such as class, gender and political revolutions, as well as contemporary philosophical and aesthetic influences.

Class and Politics

In the previous chapters, we encountered Marxist analysis of the novels' engagement with the culture of commodity but also rather unqualified comments on Austen's loyalty to the values of the gentry, which sometimes led critics to claim that Austen was oblivious to social change and conflict and, therefore, promoted the endorsement of the *status quo* confirmed in the power of the landed class. An important study that shed some light on this issue, without repudiating the image of a conservative Austen, was Alistair Duckworth's *The Improvement of the Estate* (1971). Here, Duckworth proposes reading *Northanger Abbey* and *Persuasion* as two works that bracket a persistent preoccupation in Austen's career: the precarious stability of the home, which for Duckworth signifies the '"grounds" of being and action'.[1] In both novels, the heroines are excluded from home and submitted to an experience of loss. If Catherine's exclusion from the Abbey is nothing less than a literal expulsion, the severing of the ties that bind Anne Elliot to Kellynch Hall and to her inherited social position is combined with, and exacerbated by, the absence of any 'pattern of order and continuity' in all the places that Anne visits. *Persuasion*, then, finally faces the unstoppable loss of 'traditional grounds of selfhood', which is already present, albeit less explicit, in all of Austen's novels.[2] However, Duckworth is far from arguing that Austen, who pulls the rug of inherited assurances from under the reader's feet, champions irony and moral individualism. In fact, he has a bone to pick with the very proponents of a subversive Austen, such as Harding and Mudrick (see Chapter 4).

Duckworth's study positions Austen's novels at the point of transition between two centuries. Her novels draw on the favourite scheme of eighteenth-century fiction, in which the disruption of the protagonist's initial social embedment, followed by isolation and drifting, is resolved through final reintegration. At the same time, the novels also anticipate the burden of a world unfit to be lived in according to a Christian narrative of togetherness, isolation and reinstatement.[3] Although 'a latent possibility', the apprehension that 'society may not always provide a secure place, even for its worthy members' is nowhere as strong as in *Persuasion*.[4]

Duckworth interprets the final marriage as lacking any assurance of stability or unifying function, since Anne's union with Wentworth launches her on the existential uncertainties of the life of a sailor's wife rather than returning her to the familiar grounds of Kellynch Hall. This uncertainty harkens back to the temporal awareness of the novel, the eight years within which Anne and Wentworth have been apart and Sir Walter has seen his power decline. However, again, Duckworth insists that these elements of modernity, which align the novel with the fiction of the nineteenth century, should not be interpreted as signs of Austen's moral subjectivism or proof of her rejection of 'an inherited social morality':

> ■ What is no longer present as a substantial 'estate' remains present in Anne's inner thoughts and social actions. Unlike Mansfield Park, Kellynch Hall is in effect abandoned – Anne cannot preserve, much less 'improve' her estate – but Anne does not reject with the loss of her home a whole moral inheritance.[5] □

While urging the reader not to overemphasize modernity, Duckworth stresses Anne's selflessness, social orientation and surviving 'moral inheritance'. It is safe to argue that, despite its nuanced reading, Duckworth's analysis prefers to see Anne as a preserver rather than a reformer, hence, as a figure looking backward to a world in ruins rather than ahead to one of possibilities, the kinds of possibilities that

Nina Auerbach, for example, in her article 'O Brave New World' (1972), celebrates as powerful signs of Austen's 'new utopianism'.[6] The sea is the locus of utopian renewal represented by the professional class of the navy that shifts financial and moral power from the land to the sea. Indeed, Auerbach speaks of nothing less than 'the enormous revolutionary potential' inherent in *Persuasion*'s endorsement of mobility within a static society.[7]

David Monoghan's intervention, in his 'The Decline of the Gentry' (1975), tempers Auerbach's optimism (or Joseph Duffy's – see Chapter 5) and, by extension, Austen's radicalism, by throwing light on the novel's treatment of mobility. There are two elements that circumscribe progressive politics: first, although the decline of the Elliot family is undeniable, it does not appear to be the result of 'emerging industrial forces'; second, Kellynch Hall passes to Admiral Croft, not a mere bourgeois, but a reputable public character and 'a rising gentleman'.[8] Another similarly sceptical pronouncement comes from the historian David Spring, who argues that fiscally irresponsible landowners, being no novelty in English social history or in Austen's time, should not be perceived as heralds of social change.[9] Consequently, Spring predicts that after the retrenchments, Sir Walter will recuperate his earlier standing and then bestow the estate upon William Elliot.

However, Monoghan admits that the decline of the gentry stands for a novelty, albeit of a different kind than merely financial. *Persuasion* evinces a new awareness of the disrupted correlation between manners and rank. Moreover, this out-of-joint correlation cannot be readjusted by the professional representatives. If in Austen's earlier novels, the Burkean belief that rank vouches for manners as 'a medium for moral communication' prevails, in *Persuasion* the manners of the ruling class have become mere surface and an end in themselves. This is a degeneration that can be rectified only inadequately by the Musgroves or the navy representatives, who lack 'a mature comprehension of the importance of formal behaviour', despite being governed by 'a basic sense of duty and obligation toward others'.[10] Monoghan conceives of Anne's loss of a home in terms of Jane Austen's loss of faith in the very kind of close-knit society that she had cherished and beautifully depicted in the pages of her earlier novels.

Marilyn Butler comes to a similar conclusion in her study *Jane Austen and the War of Ideas* (1975). Butler, who evaluates Austen's novels in the context of the French Revolution and the literature it produced, organizes her study around two antagonistic camps: Jacobin fiction, the promoter of revolutionary ideas, and anti-Jacobin fiction, the defender of 'old ethical certainties'.[11] *Persuasion*, argues Butler, leaves the reader in a 'muddle'.[12] Formally, the novel's strong association with interiority is jarred by the treatment of exteriority, visible in the peripheral and unenlightening treatment of dialogue. Ideologically, Butler argues against critics like Duffy or Auerbach, who praise the novel's burgeoning individualism perceptible in its social critique of the ruling classes. For Butler, such critique fails to prove Austen's progressivism. On the contrary, it aligns her novel with evangelical and utilitarian ideas that not only condemned aristocratic idleness but also sought to counteract it with examples of active usefulness of which Anne Elliot is a perfect embodiment. This is not the moral inheritance on which the radicals drew, Butler insists, but rather the one espoused and disseminated by middle-class conservatives.[13]

Butler's study, strong for its textual analysis as well as its wealth of historical engagement, proved influential in fostering the view of a conservative Austen. It finally met a worthy match in Claudia L. Johnson's *Jane Austen: Women, Politics and the Novel* (1988). Here, too, the moment of the novels is crucial, but rather than conceiving of temporality as a threshold between the old and new century (as Duckworth or Monoghan had), Johnson's study, like Butler's, concerned itself with the impact of the French Revolution on fiction. Johnson speaks of the 'novel of crisis', among which Austen's work emerges as invested in the 'discourse rather than the representation of politics'.[14] Signposts of political discourse include absent or arbitrary fathers, self-important brothers and dubious mentors; in other words, those pillars of patriarchal moral rectitude and reliability venerated in the anti-Jacobin novel. Johnson demonstrates that suspicion towards such figures not only is present in all Austen's novels, but is also as disturbing as in the more direct and declamatory writing of the most radical contemporary female writers. In contrast to Duckworth's emphasis on the survival of 'moral inheritance', or Monoghan's nostalgic reading of a lost world of manners, Johnson writes:

■ But if in *Persuasion* the landed classes have not lost their power, they have lost their prestige and their moral authority for the heroine.[15] □

Less wary than Duckworth of countering Austen's 'moral subjectivism', Johnson describes Anne as an 'independent' and 'autonomous' heroine, whose allegiances lie less with inherited ideas than with new ones, such as Mrs. Croft's Wollstonecraftian vindication of women as 'rational creatures' rather than as subjects of filial or marital obedience.[16]

Johnson demonstrates that the *tour de force* characterization of Mrs. Croft comes from Austen's lifelong preoccupation with power relations between 'those who have what Eleanor [Tilney] calls "real power" and the constraints of those who do not'.[17] *Northanger Abbey* is a novel about bullying power, exercised by John Thorpe, James Morland, the archetypal bully General Tilney, and even Henry Tilney, all characters who refuse to accept a 'no' from a woman. Hence, the novel also investigates the feminine power of refusing men who set the boundaries of mileage (John Thorpe), time (General Tilney) or words (Henry Tilney). Particularly enlightening is Henry's posturing as the arbiter of the meaning of Gothic fiction, as entertainment of either absurd or mistaken mimetic value. For Johnson, Henry shares the claim of the privileged classes, which, upon finding themselves and their hegemony on language challenged during the 1790s, insisted that their superior linguistic expertise provided them with exclusive access to public discourse. Not surprisingly, the Gothic spoken about by Henry, or imagined and experienced by Catherine, allows the narrator to delineate the characters' differing political outlooks. Catherine identifies with the powerless characters of the Gothic and learns from them to distrust paternal power and to confront Henry's 'conservative tendency to be Pollyannaish about the *status quo*'.[18]

Hence, Johnson reads *Northanger Abbey* as a political novel that responds to the political upheavals of the 1790s by evoking riots, enclosure, pamphlets and anti-treason laws, and, more covertly, by variations on the theme of promise. This proved a dividing topic in contemporary discourse. William Godwin, radical thinker and writer, found promise-keeping coercive to the individual's freedom of choice. On the other hand, conservative readers saw social cohesion endangered by such attacks on promise-keeping. In this divide, Henry Tilney sides with the conservative camp when lecturing Catherine on the contract that underlies a country dance and, by metaphorical extension, marriage. Yet Henry's honouring of promises is trumped by his loyalty to his brother Frederick, who intrudes on the engagement of Isabella and James Morland. The point, here, is not that the novel devalues promises but that it denounces the arbitrary misuse of the rhetoric of promise by its most ardent promoters. What the novel critiques is promise turned into a tool of power. General Tilney's shocking eviction of Catherine in the middle of her stay is not only a casual example of individual cruelty, but also an act of political transgression.

■ Depicting the guardians of national, domestic, and even religious authority as socially destabilizing figures, *Northanger Abbey* has indeed appropriated the gothic, in a distinctively progressive way.[19] □

According to Johnson, Austen writes within the frame of conservative fiction but only to persistently subject 'its most cherished mythologies to interrogations from which it could not recover'.[20]

Johnson's comment can be seen as a direct response to Butler's interpretation of *Northanger Abbey*. This is because Butler vehemently dismisses any revolutionary impulse, categorizing the novel's satire as a 'very clear statement of the anti-Jacobin position'.[21] The clarity resides in Austen's condemnation of characters like Isabella Thorpe, spokesperson of the 'modern creed of self'; in General Tilney, whose acts of Gothic villainy are reduced to mere acts of rudeness; and in Henry Tilney's speech on England and its laws of probability, a much-needed admonition that brings Catherine 'at last to an understanding of the "real" world of long-lasting social and religious institutions'.[22] However, as we have seen, this 'real' world builds on the mythologies that the novel puts under investigation.

It is important to mention at this point Robert Hopkins's article 'General Tilney and the Affairs of State: The Political Gothic of *Northanger Abbey*' (1978). This article, by returning to the historical context, sought to achieve nothing short of beating Butler's argument at its own game 'once and for all'.[23] Hopkins's point of departure is the Beechen Cliff scene, where Henry, at the risk of boring Catherine, dares a 'short disquisition on the state of the nation' (*NA* 81). Hopkins discovers behind 'disquisition' the polemics around enclosure in the 1790s, a time in which laws were issued to implement acts of enclosure until then performed privately. Even enclosure proponents who offered rural workers cottages could not appease the pressing necessity to compensate the loss endured by the latter. These are also the years in which grain shortage exacerbated the effects of enclosure, leading to famine and 'food riots', possibly the very riots to which Eleanor unwittingly alludes. Read against this backdrop of food scarcity and enclosure laws, General Tilney's boasting about the pineapples produced in his hothouses, or his taste for lavish dinners, would have incurred the contemporary reader's disapproval of such a callous character. We see, here, Hopkins's attempt to demonstrate General Tilney's real social villainy rather than mere incivility, as Butler has it. However, the more damning proof hides in the 'duties' of the General, which Hopkins places in the context of the repressive activities, trials and laws undertaken by the government of William Pitt against sympathizers of the French Revolution. Associations created to intercept seditious writing, such as pamphlets, were part and parcel of the censorship. As Hopkins puts it, these were years in which 'The habit of local citizens volunteering to spy and to survey pamphlet literature was established.'[24] Austen offers hints that link the novel to censorship, when the General tells Catherine:

■ 'I have many pamphlets to finish', said he to Catherine, 'before I can close my eyes; and perhaps may be poring over the affairs of the nation for hours after you are asleep.' (*NA* 138) □

Hence, it is historically plausible to regard General Tilney as an 'inquisitor surveying possibly seditious pamphlets', rather than to treat his nightly business as the boast of a pompous man.[25] This contextualization also adds poignancy to Henry's comment on 'a neighbourhood of voluntary spies' beyond what Harding had suggested to be a slippage of unregulated hatred on Austen's part (see Chapter 4). For Hopkins, there is no slippage but only a beautifully crafted scene upon which the General appears as one of the 'voluntary spies' and, therefore, one of the very real villains of the 'nightmarish political world of the 1790s'.[26]

Gender

Considerations of Austen's political orientation during a pivotal moment of European history that saw the first public articulations of the concept of human rights soon also included inquiries into the novels' attitude towards women's place and status. One of the first critics to use the word 'feminism' in a study of Jane Austen's novels was Margaret Kirkham in her *Jane Austen, Feminism and Fiction* (1983), which extends the political nightmare of the French Revolution to the domestic affairs of *Northanger Abbey* and its imprisoned former mistress, Mrs. Tilney.[27] For Kirkham, the novel never dispels the charge of tyranny levelled by Catherine's Gothic misgivings about General Tilney. Nor does it treat the questions about the laws of England as mere rhetorical moves. It may be true that a wife cannot be murdered on English soil as easily as in the remote Catholic countries of Radcliffe's romances. However, Kirkham suggests that Austen's social criticism gains currency by implying that the much-praised civilized laws or manners of the age 'do little to protect' wives and daughters as equal citizens. How could it be different in a country where the wife is the husband's property?[28]

The problem of (in)equality, which is tackled in *Northanger Abbey*, receives more direct treatment in *Persuasion*. Here, Austen assumes the moral equality of men and women and rebukes prejudices that cripple women:

■ Men have had every advantage of us telling their own story. Education has been theirs in so much higher a degree; the pen has been in their hands. I will not allow books to prove anything. (*P* 188) □

In similar terms, in *A Vindication of the Rights of Woman* (1792), Mary Wollstonecraft had taken to task several male authors, among them giants like Rousseau, to show that no innate qualities justified the subordination of women. Kirkham shows parallelisms between *Persuasion* and Wollstonecraft's *Rights of Woman*. The same Wollstonecraft that condemns parental tyranny (as Austen does in *Northanger Abbey*) impels her readers to grant to a loving, educating and responsible parent 'all the rights of the most sacred friendship, and his advice, even when the child is advanced in life, demands serious consideration'.[29] In *Persuasion*, Lady Russell stands for this kind of parent entitled to Anne's 'most sacred friendship'. Kirkham convincingly demonstrates that:

> ■ Austen establishes her heroine's behaviour as in accordance with what Wollstonecraft had laid down as proper in a dutiful child of a 'solicitous' and affectionate, even though mistaken, parent.[30] □

Kirkham thus re-contextualizes Anne's prudence and obedience within the most radical feminist programme of her time. In this context, filial obedience, growing out of gratitude for a reciprocal relationship of care and affection, ceases to be a parental right *per se*. Wollstonecraft's influence also emerges in the new female prototype embodied by Sophia Croft, whose name signals Austen's endorsement of Wollstonecraft's critique of 'Sophie', Rousseau's virtuous but docile female ideal.[31]

Only a year after Kirkham's study, Mary Poovey published her much-cited monograph *The Proper Lady and the Woman Writer* (1984). Here, the works of Wollstonecraft and Mary Shelley offer the main context for reading Jane Austen in terms of female propriety and social duty, inhibition and desire. Poovey has little to say about *Northanger Abbey*, so we will immediately turn to her analysis of *Persuasion*. In this novel, she claims, Austen depicts women's disadvantageous position unequivocally. Anne Elliot voices her rejection of an essentialist definition of the Proper Lady, reiterating Wollstonecraft's conviction that education inscribes women's submission to this ideology. The presence and importance of characters like Mrs. Smith illustrate women's precarious social status and their emotional resilience, or, in Austen's words, 'elasticity of mind' (*P* 125).[32] For Poovey, unlike Duckworth, who distrusts Mrs. Smith's gossiping and self-interestedness, Mrs. Smith's power 'epitomizes female indirection', which significantly triggers the encounter between the novel's public life and Anne's privately nourished desire.

Uniquely in Austen's work, *Persuasion* permits a private sphere that can gratify personal desire and gesture towards moral reform but also reproduces through the concept of romantic love, in itself an individual matter, a separation of the public from the private.[33] This separation protects the illusion of romantic love from the bare facts of public reality, and only through this separation can romantic love stand for personal autonomy or reform. Poovey calls 'romantic love' an illusion with no power to 'materially affect society'. Precisely this premise, argues Laura Mooneyham White, is a blind spot in Poovey's analysis, because the social role of romantic love is something to be investigated rather than dismissed matter-of-factly as Poovey does.[34]

In a conclusion that juxtaposes Austen and Wollstonecraft, Poovey argues that these two writers propose similar solutions to opposed questions. While Wollstonecraft asks how an individual raised in a corrupted society can escape its influence and initiate reform, Austen asks how 'potentially anarchic' feelings can be put to the service of social reform. Both writers' solution is a separate sphere, where cherished individual values survive and assume mimetic power for the reader.[35] It is important to note that, although Poovey takes Austen's conservatism as a given, it does not hinder her from speaking of Austen's critique of gender bias and women's restricted desire and autonomy.

Because individual desire in all of Austen's novels flares up only to be channelled through the socially sanctioned institution of marriage, critics wishing for a less conservative Austen have found fault with her compulsory marriage resolutions. White argues that *Persuasion* should not leave such critics unsatisfied. Indeed, relying on Stanley Cavell's *The Pursuit of Happiness* (1981), a study of the marriage plot in Hollywood films, White demonstrates *Persuasion*'s modernity. The novel's innovation consists in conceiving of happiness as a getting back together again of the protagonists after a first failure. This would be the same formula of remarriage after separation or divorce that Cavell identifies as an innovation of twentieth-century film comedy.[36] White adds that the threat of separation does not lose its grip even in a novel ending with marriage:

> ■ *Persuasion* demonstrates, at any rate, Austen's surety that the achievement of the marriage plot is an act of faith, in the future and in the achievement of narrative.[37] □

Thinking more urgently on Austen's influence upon the Victorian novel, Julia Prewitt Brown writes that *Persuasion* ushers in marriage as a solution to a desperate situation. In all Austen's novels, marriage, being a form of participation in society, registers the functions of land in society. However, Anne and Wentworth's marriage draws its strength uniquely from the thoughts, feelings, values, friends and assets the two of them attach to it. They are its creators and sustainers, while marriage becomes a necessity. Hence, their marriage faces the immense and huge burden of the lonely modern couple. Brown's analysis stresses the estranged consciousness that Anne and Wentworth carry as alienated individuals confronted with the impermanence and uncertainty of the very things they have come to embrace such as their marriage and the navy.[38] It is a consciousness that inhabits the novels of George Eliot, Charles Dickens, Henry James and E. M. Forster. As such, although reminiscent of Percy Shelley's fragile hope in the spring to come in 'Ode to a West Wind', Austen's desire and determination for Anne 'to have Spring again' pivots on the sense of lost time as well as the fearful happiness and 'full consciousness of the fate of marriage in the following century'.[39]

Discussing desire in connection to the place of the body in *Persuasion*, John Wiltshire notices that the capacity of the male and female body to match each other's signs externalizes their untold thoughts and wishes. For example, Anne's utility within her family but also her desirability for Wentworth materializes in her skills in nursing the fragile body, when she nurses her nephew or Louisa Musgrove after the fall. Nursing in the novel, argues Wiltshire, is associated with 'the sexually and socially subordinate', with Anne, but also with Mary Musgrove's nurse, Jemima, or Mrs. Smith's nurse, Rooke. Initially, nursing implies not simply femaleness, but also femaleness without desire or bodily needs.[40] Nonetheless, the novel infuses desire by first linking the most desirable male of the novel, Wentworth, with nursing (it is he who takes care of Dick Musgrove and alleviates Benwick's grief-induced ailing) and then deploying nursing as a vehicle of desire. Thus, Wentworth can express publicly and without sexual equivocation his wish to have Anne nurse Louisa. But as Wiltshire argues:

> Whilst the relation is actually one of desire, it is conducted here, once more, according to the canons of solicitude. Wentworth's feeling for Anne can thus be masked by its ideological vehicle.[41]

The notion of ideological vehicle also fits interpretations of *Northanger Abbey*. Maria Jencic treats the novel's Gothicism as a misrecognized ideological vehicle. While more often than not the novel's Gothic affiliations are explained as being parodic, Jencic contends that Gothic references, whether stylistic or intertextual, convey women's relationship to reading, regardless of genre. *Northanger Abbey* ponders the freedom and hermeneutical skills of female readers, who were considered to be most vulnerable to the influences of print culture. Indeed, Jencic argues, characters (dis)qualify themselves in Catherine's and our eyes primarily as readers. Isabella and John Thorpe are corrupted readers; Mrs. Allen, her husband and General Tilney are not readers at all; and Henry Tilney and Eleanor become central for the narrative, because they reciprocate Catherine's love of reading and conversing about books.[42] Henry's influence or Catherine's initial inability to read him, however, harbour the true danger that many critics have attributed to the Gothic. It is Henry's impromptu that incites Catherine's imagination and not Radcliffe's *The Mysteries of Udolpho*, which Catherine had read during her stay in Bath without losing sleep or her grip of reality. On the one hand, Austen permits her heroine more freedom to read books of her choice, unlike Radcliffe who has Emily read texts selected by her father. Yet

Catherine's interpretative powers come to a halt and turn against her when she adopts Henry's assessment of the situation. Hence Austen's target, insists Jencic, is first and foremost reading men, who manipulate texts, construct 'romance visions' and dictate to women how to read them. As we see, Jencic redefines women's vulnerability to print culture not in terms of their inferior reading skills but their subjection to men who posture as cultural arbiters.[43] This redirection, believes Jencic, motivates *Northanger Abbey*'s satiric ending on 'parental tyranny' and 'filial disobedience'.

Growing research on Gothic literature proved fertile for innovative readings of *Northanger Abbey*, particularly in relationship to the new junction of Gothic feminism. For example, Diane Hoeveler argued that 'Gothic feminism is not about being equal to men; it's about being morally superior to men. It's about being a victim'.[44] Persecuted women would earn the readers' sympathy through the combination of powerlessness and virtue under patriarchal siege. The dead Mrs. Tilney, her oppressed daughter Eleanor and later the abused and disillusioned Catherine embody the psychology of female victimage to which no one had so poignantly given the name of social injustice as Wollstonecraft. Austen enters the genre explored by Wollstonecraft, inheriting and playing with both its melodrama and Gothicism. Her novel raises awareness that in a society where genders are polarized (as in Rousseau's *Émile*, to name a famous text), victimage represents the articulation and limit of women's resistance.[45] Moreover, Austen herself resists polarization. A good reader of John Locke's and George Berkeley's empiricism, Austen treats Catherine as a blank slate, raw material, 'on which Wollstonecraft's theories about female education and socialization can be tested and proved'.[46] It is part and parcel of this intention that the structural polarization of the feminine artifice of Bath and the masculine imprisonment of *Northanger Abbey* breaks down: equally instructive and dangerous for the heroine's socialization, both worlds fail Catherine.

Contemporary Influences

Interest in the social and political dimension of literature, not least as championed by the New Historicists, led to contextualizing approaches that linked *Northanger Abbey* and *Persuasion* to the philosophical and aesthetic ideas of the long eighteenth century. Jan Fergus noticed in her *Jane Austen and the Didactic Novel* (1983) that Austen (like E. M. Forster) started her career by writing novels about the novels that she herself had first experienced as a reader. In *Northanger Abbey*, she exploited sentimental and Gothic conventions, delighting in 'their absurdity and power to engross the imagination', without having a distinct interest in the ways that these conventions could be subordinated to more complex designs.[47]

For Fergus, Austen's engagement with her contemporaries in this early novel has not ripened yet, just like her Catherine, who does not achieve maturity in the course of the novel.[48] However, as Miranda Burgess reminds us in 'Domesticating Gothic: Ann Radcliffe, Jane Austen, National Romance' (1998), Austen's disclaimers of her uninformed and anti-heroic heroine do not tell all the tale. When it comes to aesthetic acumen, Catherine's appreciation of sublime landscapes puts her ahead of Radcliffe's heroine. Considering that, on the heels of the American and French Revolution, the sublime functioned as a marker of masculine experience, unlike the feminine beautiful, the scene where Catherine is struck by the magnificence of the city of Bath conveys the kind of development from which, as Wollstonecraft lamented, Edmund Burke had excluded women in his *A Philosophical Enquiry into the Origin of Our Ideas of the Sublime and Beautiful* (1757).[49]

Other critics, too, emphasized the intertextual subtlety of *Northanger Abbey* over deficient maturity. In *Jane Austen and the Fiction of her Time* (1999), Mary Waldron drew attention to the quixotic character that Austen borrowed from Charlotte Lennox's *The Female Quixote* (1752), a novel centred on a heroine absorbed by the plots and conventions of the French romance. If Lennox's heroine, Arabella, must defend herself from unruly lovers, Austen surrounds her protagonist with characters who foist their 'reconstructions of everyday life' on her. Unlike Arabella, whose amusing romantic fantasies Waldron deems to be relatively straightforward, Catherine starts as 'a burlesque of a burlesque' because she finds life exciting without the pursuit of romantic fantasies.[50] Similarly, the idea of the male and mature mentor resonates with *The Female Quixote*, where a Doctor of Divinity disabuses Arabella of all her romantic notions. However, Henry Tilney is 'too personally involved to function as the good doctor does', although he reiterates the latter's lesson on testing her judgment against probability.[51]

Admittedly, Waldron's interpretation of *The Female Quixote* verges on being too straightforward, if not reductive. Yet there is more to take from her intertextual analysis, especially when discussing Austen's revision of Radcliffian rhetoric. Waldron discovers parallels between *The Mysteries of Udolpho* and *Northanger Abbey* in their closing paragraphs. These are Radcliffe's parting words to the readers:

> ■ O! useful may it be to have shewn, that, though the vicious can sometimes pour affliction upon the good, their power is transient and their punishment certain; and that innocence, though oppressed by injustice, shall, supported by patience, finally triumph over misfortune![52] □

In contrast to Radcliffe's unequivocal moral tendency, Austen appeals to the readers to interpret the tension between 'parental tyranny' and 'filial disobedience', leaving the ending open to the jarring probabilities which can be deduced from a domestic future that includes General Tilney.[53]

The notion of 'probability', a favourite word of Henry Tilney's, has prompted valuable discussions of *Northanger Abbey*. Mark Loveridge's article '*Northanger Abbey*; Or, Nature and Probability' offers an in-depth contextualized reading of probability. In eighteenth-century usage, probability stands for (a) a sense of naturalness with the real world as its point of reference and (b) a term applied to literary works to convey 'internal self-consistency and homogeneity of tone'.[54] This second meaning makes it possible for a Gothic novel to be perceived as probable as long as it is so coherently and harmoniously organized that it appears a consistent alternative world. At the same time, probability requires the reading mind to make an inference from the narrative to the moral that the fable disguises. Hence, probability bears on morality. Loveridge argues that *Northanger Abbey* is caught in between these demands: first, it wants to achieve structural cohesion; second, it aims to bolster a sense of naturalness, that is, Catherine's sense of probability; and, third, it must also cater for Henry's moral inference. From these tensions, the novel derives its uneasy combination of the natural and the absurd, the realistic and the burlesque. Consequently, the very same passages that, when read casually, attract attention as credible renderings of intense experience also emerge as pieces of burlesque under the analytical lens. John Thorpe's 'abduction' of Catherine and Henry's Gothic description of the room that awaits her in the abbey are two such slippery scenes. While we seem to experience primarily Catherine's education, we also witness Henry's recognition of Catherine's natural goodness and of the limits of probabilism.[55] As Loveridge aptly puts it,

> ■ If others have hijacked probability to the cause of providing the poetic rewards for those pictures that made Jane Austen feel so sick and wicked, then clearly she needs to cleanse and decontaminate the term of its unwanted associations, as she does here through dramatic comedy and burlesque.[56] □

Here, burlesque functions as an unstable but necessary antidote to a fiction that had idealized naturalness to an unrealistic extent.

The question of genre, or more precisely the kind of writing that *Northanger Abbey* proposed to be (and yet avoided being), is re-examined by Devoney Looser's '(Re)making History and Philosophy' (1993). Looser believes that in this early work Austen ponders the ongoing contemporary dialogue about the role of philosophy and history in the novel, a dialogue that increasingly hinged on women's access to education.[57] In *Northanger Abbey*, moral philosophy is revealed through the characters' access to taste and, consequently, to class. The Tilneys seem the primary spokespersons of taste, but the narrative's focus on Catherine implies that taste can be acquired by those who possess innate emotional responsiveness:

> ■ Austen's character serves as a 'vessel' through which philosophy is transformed into intense emotion and novels.[58] □

The emphasis on a natural propensity is important because it decouples taste from class and provides a wider basis for the appropriation of philosophy.

Looser notices a similar usurpation of the role of history. The novel's important rival in the eighteenth century was history, which educators recommended as the proper and useful reading where women could expand their knowledge and imaginary experience without being endangered by the doubtful morals of the novel. Towards the end of the century, however, the novel's subordination is no longer a matter of course. On the contrary, novels complying with the codes of the conduct book start supplanting history in its educational status. Looser sees Austen's endeavours invested in defining and validating the powers of the novel as a medium that 'can improve readers in the roles that philosophy and conduct books formerly might have taken'.[59] The narrator's famous defence of the novel, bolstered by scathing comments on the abridged *History of England*, or of the obsolete *Spectator*, presents the novel as a present-tense history, appropriate to address the needs of the living age.

Philosophy, conduct literature and print culture proved fruitful for the exploration of *Persuasion*'s engagement with the literary culture of the eighteenth century. I have selected three interpretations that trace eighteenth-century influences through the concepts of moral luck, persuasion and female perfection. Robert Hopkins's article 'Moral Luck and Judgment in Jane Austen's *Persuasion*' (1987) takes its cue from Anne's final assessment of her former decision to relinquish Wentworth as 'one of those cases in which advice is good or bad only as the event decides' (*P* 198).[60] Such a statement could easily summarize the core maxim of consequentialism, a theory maintaining that the moral validity of an action must be judged on the consequences of the action. Although a twentieth-century coinage, consequentialism occupies an important position in Adam Smith's *Theory of Moral Sentiments* (1759). Smith readily agrees that from a theoretical point of view unintended consequences should not be the moral yardstick of action. Yet he must concede that, in particular cases, consequences matter. Hopkins takes as a particular literary case Fielding's Squire Allworthy in *Tom Jones* (1749), a man of sound principle and goodness of heart and intentions, but, as the plot goes to show, of catastrophic moral judgement. Smith's dilemma (or ours as readers who judge characters) stems from the fact that the validity of moral judgement depends on aspects that are beyond the agent's control but nevertheless receive moral approval as if all aspects were to the agent's merit. Such approval can be conceived of as moral luck. Placed in this light, *Persuasion* has more axes to grind with moral philosophy than to simply deploy chance and luck, major elements in Wentworth's career, for plot contrivances.[61] Hopkins concludes that:

> ■ Clearly Jane Austen is struggling in *Persuasion* with the problem of moral judgment under uncertainty. I believe that she is also reconsidering the ethical implications of her earlier plots which too readily reward prudential moral judgment with fortunate resolutions.[62] □

'Struggling' seems the appropriate word in a novel in which cautionary examples of uncertain and tragic engagements, like Benwick's, coexist with the rash and successful marriage of the Crofts. Hopkins follows Poovey's lead in speaking of an 'epistemological relativism' that is grounded in Anne as the only authoritative voice (rather than in the omniscient narrator).[63] However, unlike Poovey, who explains the novel's epistemological uncertainty by the decline of the gentry, Hopkins sees *Persuasion*'s dilemma as moral rather than class related.[64] Moreover, it is a dilemma that qualifies Austen as a liberal and progressive novelist, because Anne's consequentialist verdict transcends the limitations of closed communitarian morality.

A more progressive Austen also emerges from Arthur Walzer's intriguing analysis of the title of *Persuasion* in light of influential rhetorical traditions of the eighteenth century. Illuminating the theories of philosophers like George Campbell and Hugh Blair, Walzer states that these theorists distinguished between conviction and persuasion. Conviction implied the development of the hearer's understanding through critical reasoning, whereas persuasion appealed to the hearer's imaginative power (or passions) in order to compel him to action. Because persuasion aims at the hearer's actions, it is intimately linked with the desire to move or influence the hearer's will. It follows, as Walzer explains, that 'persuadability becomes synonymous with a weak understanding and pliable will'.[65] Darcy's retort to Elizabeth in *Pride and Prejudice*, 'To yield without conviction is no compliment to the understanding of either', suggests that this distinction was not utterly unfamiliar to Austen.[66] Whether in the philosophical writings of the eighteenth century or in the dialogue containing Darcy's retort, persuadability was associated with the feminine and conviction with the masculine. Walzer demonstrates that Austen, however, reworks this gendered dichotomy in her last novel.

To begin with, persuadability is grounded in reason as shown by Anne's and Lady Russell's attempts to persuade Sir Walter to retrench. Their attempts fail because this kind of persuasion thwarts Sir Walter's ruling passion, his vanity. Lady Russell's strategy when talking Anne into marrying Mr. Elliot, a union that will restore to Anne her dead mother's position, appeals to one of Anne's ruling passions in order to move her desire to action. However, this is a point on which Anne hesitates only briefly before the idea of Mr. Elliot supplanting Wentworth snaps her out of the reveries involving her mother and the estate. Fittingly, Anne and Wentworth's relationship is the most contested battleground of persuadability and conviction, with Anne propounding the value of (feminine) resiliency/weakness and Wentworth that of (masculine) resolve/strength.[67] The narrative's organizing irony pivots on the reversal of these expectations, from which Anne emerges as the strong one in possession of a sympathetic and moral imagination. Hence, Walzer infers that in her last novel Austen revises 'the confidence the theorists express in reason as a remedy to persuasion's problematic psychology'.[68]

Mary Waldron, too, offers a positive reading of Anne as a reformulation of the female stereotypes disseminated by contemporary novels and, in particular, conduct literature. Although Anne may invite readings of her character as an embodiment of the 'Woman of Feeling', it is equally central to state that the novel refuses to build upon the reason-feeling dichotomy. In many senses, Anne skirts the conventions of female perfection: flawless, tender-hearted and musically talented, and, as this inventory intimates, predictable and flat. Austen takes this unpromising and worn-out model in a new direction by first foregrounding Anne's loss and isolation and later her initiative 'against all heroinely modesty and reticence'.[69] From Fanny Burney's *Camilla* (1796) and Sarah Burney's *Clarentine* (1796), two novels that she mentions in her letters, Austen borrowed the motif of difficulties that keep lovers apart. However, she took care to introduce these difficulties as integral parts of character and plot:

> ■ In *Persuasion* conduct is to be natural, the difficulties will derive predictably from common rather than extraordinary situations, and the outcome will be satisfactory but quite independent of anyone's deserts.[70] □

The difficulties, of course, arise from Anne's decision to reject Wentworth (although she thinks of it more in terms of relinquishing him for his own sake). Anne may regret her decision, but the narrative suggests, through the examples of the disabled and on half-pay Harville, or the death of Fanny Harville during the absence of Captain Benwick, that anything could have happened and the unfraught happiness of the Crofts may be a matter of luck. Austen couples this instability of meaning with the difficulties that emanate from Wentworth's 'version of a contemporary expectation of female conduct'. In the beginning, Wentworth appears as a faithful reader of Hannah More's *Coelebs in Search of a Wife* (1809) – a novel that provoked Austen's discontent – featuring a self-effacing and firm heroine.[71] He expects his future wife to be both meek and rebellious, a contradiction that tugs at Anne throughout the narrative. Waldron approaches Wentworth's transformation rather sceptically, since, when pronouncing Anne as 'maintaining the medium of fortitude and gentleness', Wentworth has lost none of the vehemence of the unrealistic lover.[72] Consequently, Anne's moral emancipation exceeds Wentworth's.

Romantic Austen

The wealth of cultural and intertextual references discovered in the novels led to assessments of the position that Austen occupied in what has been retrospectively dubbed the Romantic period. Crudely put, the question was whether Austen's novels were linked to Romanticism temporally (by a mere coincidence in time) or ideologically (through a set of common concerns and techniques). For a long time Charlotte Brontë's dismissal of Austen as an unromantic writer held sway. However, with the reconceptualization and expansion of the field of Romantic studies, prompted largely by Feminist and New Historicist research, Austen's case became a favourite for those who argued that the period hosted a broader spectrum of writing than the Romanticism of the famous male poets, commonly referred to as the Big Six (Blake, Coleridge, Wordsworth, Shelley, Byron and Keats). Others, unimpressed by Brontë's authority, took on the challenge to prove her wrong by showing affinities between Austen and the major Romantic poets.

This is Susan Morgan's claim in 'Guessing for Ourselves in *Northanger Abbey*' (1980), which credits Austen's first novel with a new vision of fiction, 'specifically a new idea of character, one closer to the ideas of romantic poets than of previous novelists'.[73] According to Morgan, ingenious Catherine, an anti-heroine, resembles Don Juan, that other Byronic anti-hero. The new idea of character depends on the crucial role of education through perception and seeing from another's point of view. Morgan draws on Robert Kiely's *The Romantic Novel in England* (1972), which isolates the relationship between self and society as the main concern of Romantic literature. The heaviest charge brought against this literature – here Kiely includes not only the Big Six, but also Gothic novelists – was its antisocial propensity.[74] Solitary rambles (both literary and literal), seclusion, contemplation (and inaccessibility) of the sublime and the inadequacy of language to communicate the depths of human experience were perceived as the repertoire of a kind of literature that endeavoured to valorize the individual at the expense of the social.

Kiely deems the worlds of Bath and the abbey to translate this division into another related dichotomy of social conventions and subjective fancy roaming the dark prisons of its own making.[75] Kiely insists that Austen must be considered within Romantic ideology for choosing to construct her narrative upon this paradigm in the first place. To the question of her final verdict, Kiely answers:

> ■ The book is entertaining, and it was obviously Austen's purpose to ridicule the excesses of an untutored imagination. But though she shows us that Catherine's Gothic dreams are derived from false suspicions and inadequate information, Austen does not pretend that the collision of a susceptible mind with the world of hard reality is a false situation or even a wholly ludicrous one.[76] □

Kiely tones down the figure of General Tilney to a petulant, narrow-minded father against whom Catherine must arm herself with education rather than rebellion. Thus, education is Austen's answer to a period that produced radical and passionate literature.[77] This choice, according to Anne K. Mellor, defines the difference between masculine and feminine Romanticism, the latter being almost synonymous with Wollstonecraft's call for a revolution of female manners in *Rights of Woman* (1792). Austen pursues with Catherine the sharpening of women's ability to think rationally and outgrow youthful delusions.[78] Consequently, the novel responds directly to a 'Romantic culture of the self' committed to 'self-knowledge and self-mastery'.[79]

Emphasis on developmental identity, argues Clifford Siskin in *The Historicity of Romantic Discourse* (1988), represents the core Romantic reworking of earlier models of subjectivity. Siskin reads *Northanger Abbey* alongside Wordsworth's *Prelude* (1799; 1805) to make a case for the innovative contribution that Austen and Wordsworth bestowed on the literature of their time. His argument rests on a claim of novelty rather than continuity. Austen (like Wordsworth) perceived and made real in her works a changed picture of the thinking and feeling subject. Siskin calls the new aesthetics depicting this changed subject the 'lyrical turn' that renders the 'ordinary extraordinary'.[80]

The lyrical had more readily been applied to *Persuasion* even before the exploration of Austen's affiliations to Romantic poetry. However, when brought in connection to the latter, as A. Walton Litz argues, the necessity of a refined definition of the qualities of Romantic poetry imposes itself. In *'Persuasion*: Forms of Estrangement' (1975), Litz warned critics not to find proof of Romantic influences in Captain Benwick's rapturous praise of Scott and Byron. These are references to which Anne retorts ironically, recommending to Benwick 'a larger allowance of prose in his daily study' (*P* 85). Nevertheless, the most innovative poetry of the time permeates the narrative, particularly in the 'poetic use of nature as a structure of feeling'.[81] Anne's autumnal walk, 'that season of peculiar and inexhaustible influence on the mind of taste and tenderness', resonates with Wordsworth's view of nature mediated through the responsive ego (*P* 71). Yet sometimes Anne betrays a literary consciousness, as when she realizes that she has fallen into quotations that align her more with William Cowper (1731–1800), one of her favourite poets.[82] Litz also notes that Romanticism makes itself at home more in the first volume, where free indirect speech governs the readers' access to the heroine. Not surprisingly, in the first volume, a more 'rapid and nervous syntax' constructs the sensory assault on Anne's consciousness.[83] On the other hand, the ending of *Persuasion* assembles in a few paragraphs notions of modern sociology such as 'estrangement', 'alienation' and 'removals' – all words that register the awful power of time.[84] Litz stops before suggesting how such apprehension of time interacts with Romantic aestheticism, but this is a question which Peter Knox-Shaw answers with some different results.

There is more to say about Byron's presence in the novel. According to Peter Knox-Shaw, Byron is to *Persuasion* what the Gothic is to *Northanger Abbey*, 'the butt of criticism and an index to the novel's quick'.[85] Benwick's appropriation of Byron and the impact of his poetry on the novel's revisiting of loss indicate Austen's critical engagement and troubled kinship with her famous contemporary. *The Giaour* (1813), *The Bride of Abydos* (1814) and *The Corsair* (1814) left their imprint on *Persuasion*'s themes. *The Giaour* is the story of a young Venetian warrior pining for the loss of his love, a young slave, who is thrown alive into the sea by her owner, the vengeful Pasha. Time in both *The Giaour* and *Persuasion* is telescoped; the past is experienced as irrevocable and yet inescapable:

■ Anne's landscape is dominated, as severely as the Giaour's, by a single landmark, her renunciation of Wentworth in the distant summer of 1806. Jane Austen succeeds remarkably in winning assent to the claim that 'to retentive feelings eight years may be little more than nothing'.[86] (*P* 53) □

In addition, the suffering yet constant lovers in *The Bride of Abydos* match Benwick's initial constancy, a crucial theme in the novel and an ideal also in Byron's *Corsair*. At the same time, Anne leans towards forbearance, setting limits to Byronic gloom. Indeed, her advice may not be terribly different from that of *Sense and Sensibility*'s prudent Elinor Dashwood. However, in *Persuasion*, Austen adopts a new technique that juxtaposes Anne's immediate and sometimes raw perception with her expressed opinions. Hence, we hear her advice to Benwick but are more permanently struck by their shared 'hopeless agony' (*P* 84). The stuff of what Byron calls 'the indistinctness of the suffering of the human breast' runs through the lines of *The Corsair* and *Persuasion* as hardly categorizable, both invigorating and draining sensations: 'It was agitation, pain, pleasure, a something between delight and misery', writes Austen about Anne's silent endurance (*P* 142).[87]

The question of Romanticism and Austen's place in the literature of her time, as well as her status as a key representative of the modern novel, had sustained appeal for critics of the new millennium. The task called for rigorous historicization, revealing a broader picture of the philosophical, political and aesthetic currents absorbed and reworked in *Northanger Abbey* and *Persuasion*. In the following chapter, we will pursue these new directions.

CHAPTER SEVEN

New Millennium, New Directions

It would be fair to say that one of the novelties of twenty-first century criticism resides in a stronger convergence of text-oriented methods with historicizing ones. Historicization holds an unabated fascination in the revisiting of earlier ideas, but, as the following pages demonstrate, the combination of theory with historical perspectives yields fresh insights. The present chapter focuses on interpretations revolving around key concerns such as gender, aesthetics and history. Gender discussions, which continue to feature prominently and penetrate almost every other concern, are enriched by considerations of masculinity, an interest that coincides with the proliferation of theorizing and historicizing approaches in masculinity studies. Aesthetics matter in three distinct ways: in the ideological relationship to contemporary currents like the Gothic or Romantic aesthetics; in the narrative techniques that Austen borrows from these traditions and reinvents; and in the artistic decisions of the novelist at work, revealed in the writing and revising process. Lastly, history links the novels to the political and cultural climate of the long eighteenth century and their impact on the understanding of the role of the individual in human history, and history's role in the education of the individual. The chapter addresses these concerns by organizing them under six headings: masculinity, history, revisions and narration, the Gothic and professional sublime and romanticism reconsidered.

Masculinity

The enduring emphasis on women's representation in fiction; their education, role, duties and rights; fostered by interdisciplinary interest in issues of gender; brought to the fore the rather unexplored field of masculinity.
    The first monograph devoted to the question of male sexuality in Austen's novels and its relation to home and the nation was Michael Kramp's *Disciplining Love: Austen and the Modern Man* (2007). This study

addresses the anxiety of masculinity by making use of Michel Foucault's insights in *the History of Sexuality* (1976) and Giles Deleuze and Félix Guattari's conception of love. Kramp's analysis of *Northanger Abbey* aligns Henry Tilney with the male protagonists of Austen's juvenilia. Henry masters his anxiety through performances of the various male models available in the 1790s. Although different, all these performances are governed by the principles of Enlightenment rationality, which ultimately ensure Henry's success as a hero. However, as a lover, Henry flounders. He is a 'socially functional man' of restrained masculinity, subject to the kind of excessive self-disciplining that Foucault demonstrates to be a key formation of eighteenth-century civil society, but which is, as Kramp adds, also an ideal of Jacobin masculinity.[1] Self-monitored through the principles of reason, these are men unstirred by nascent desire and unperplexed by the power of the irrational and the sublime. Such a diet of masculine self-surveillance serves the existing hegemony of the nation but at the cost of the passionate love that Kramp calls a 'love of radical multiplicities',[2] a notion introduced by Giles Deleuze and Félix Guattari, for whom:

■ love destroys the singularity and security of the individual and compels each lover to embrace the diversity and complexity in both the self and the other.[3] □

Persuasion's Wentworth, argues Kramp, is a welcome exception to Austen's male lovers, precisely for his malleable masculinity. He suffers and accepts the challenges that loving Anne entails. Accordingly, his relationship to the nation has no precedent in Austen's fiction. The experience of radical love in all its complexity and destabilizing potential occurs (and becomes possible) during his service in the name of the nation, yet removed from the nation through a life at sea to which married heterosexuality does not put an end.

Addressing the bawdiness of gender performance in *Northanger Abbey*, Jill Heydt-Stevenson reads Henry Tilney's masculinity as the exaggerated mimesis of supposedly female manners. To critics who see in Henry the authoritative centre of the narrative, Heydt-Stevenson juxtaposes Henry the verbal cross-dresser, *connoisseur* and consumer of women's fashion and therefore 'a less stable version of the patriarchal police'.[4] Austen's preoccupation with male culture and its different models of masculinity becomes evident in her depiction of John Thorpe. No other male character strives so desperately to embody 'ultimate masculinity': his bragging about hunting, horse races and speedy rides complements his attraction to homosocial encounters. As Heydt-Stevenson notices, Thorpe's admiration relies much on appearances, not least on the physical appearance of men.[5] When he first sees Henry, he estimates his body as if it were that of an animal ('A good figure of a man; well put together. – Does he want a horse?' (*NA* 54)), and proposes immediately an exchange *à trois* between himself, Henry and Sam Fletcher, his future roommate. The homoeroticism of such fantasy underscores Thorpe's 'bombastic masculinity'.[6] Heydt-Stevenson believes that Austen's interest in the male body does not waver in the mature works and that a strong attachment like Anne's towards Wentworth is ratified by erotic desire. For Anne, Wentworth's heroic virility, unlike William Elliot's 'under-hung' physique, translates into indisputable erotic desirability, as shown in the passage where she conjectures Lady Russell's canvassing of Wentworth's beautiful body, while walking on the streets of Bath (*P* 114).[7]

These discussions of masculinity, in relation to the concept of love and the body, benefit from historical approaches that consider the gender ramifications of philosophical and aesthetic influences. For example, Christopher Miller's 'Jane Austen's Aesthetics and Ethics of Surprise' (2005) argues that the evolution from *Northanger Abbey* to *Persuasion* involves a gendered treatment of the aesthetics of surprise. Miller defines the eighteenth-century conception of surprise as an experience that jolts the subject from inattention to awareness.[8] Hence, surprise is of moral import. Catherine's ability to be surprised by the conventions of Bath, the novels she reads and the people that surround her should strike us not as proof of her girlish naïveté, but as signs of her alert moral sensibility. Austen contrasts Catherine's susceptibility to surprise with other characters' defence mechanisms. Henry Tilney's reliance on probability wards off surprise to the point that his stoic resistance epitomizes this masculine attribute. It is an attribute that befits also the narrator of *Northanger Abbey*, who insists on the ordinariness of her female protagonist and on the importance of probability. And yet Catherine's transformation into the heroine of the novel and Henry's gratitude – surprisingly for him, turned into affection – show also the shortcomings of the impulse to 'predict the unpredictable', mostly a pose of 'masculine control or superior omniscience'.[9]

Austen's flexibility with the aesthetics of surprise is fully fledged in *Persuasion*, which sets off on the opposite premise to *Northanger Abbey*. Not only does Anne Elliot have few things to be surprised by, but she has taught herself to assimilate surprise in consciousness. Hence, surprise here is a matter of interiorized expression. Under these circumstances, the language of surprise fails to be an indicator of moral responsiveness and is replaced by a phenomenology of surprise, that is, by the sensory and emotional experience of surprise:

> ■ We can even better appreciate the novel's phenomenology of surprise in counterpoint with the conventional, reflexive language of shock that so many of Austen's characters speak.[10] □

Significantly, this contrast also affects masculine stoicism: Wentworth's dropped pen during the conversation involving Anne and Captain Harville signals the strongest sensory and cognitive intrusion of surprise.

Other critics devote attention to Wentworth's involvement in the Napoleonic Wars and the ways in which military pursuits inflect masculinity. In *Mothers of the Nation* (2000), Anne Mellor speaks of Wentworth as a professional Prometheus figure, a self-made man, who takes risks and accumulates wealth.[11] For Mellor, who reads *Persuasion* as a who-will-rule-England novel, Wentworth's risk-taking masculinity requires the tempering guidance of rational and cautious Anne. Other studies persuasively demonstrate that the popular glorification of important military men such as the Duke of Wellington and Admiral Horatio Lord Nelson provided commanding paradigms of masculinity. Joseph Kestner's 'Jane Austen: Revolutionizing Masculinities' (1994) associates Wentworth's very name with the perseverance that Wellington's fortitude elevated to a cherished masculine trait.[12] Jocelyn Harris's *A Revolution beyond Expression* (2007) expands Kestner's insights, exploring Wentworth's character in light of Austen's ambivalent opinion of Nelson. Although Nelson fell at the Battle of Trafalgar in 1805 about ten years before the events of *Persuasion*, Harris believes that the famed Admiral, Napoleon's nemesis, informs Wentworth's masculinity. Wentworth's rapid success mimics Nelson's meteoric naval career. Indeed, after his death, Nelson was hailed as much for his allegedly meritorious rise as for his prowess. In addition, Austen invested Wentworth with Nelson's skill to master potentially disastrous weather. However, as Harris argues, association with Nelson would also imply the public ridicule that the latter endured upon abandoning his wife for Emma Hamilton, wife of Sir William Hamilton. Austen may be toying with the idea, but despite the dangerous flirtation with Louisa Musgrove, she rescues Wentworth from charges of fickleness through the novel's final praise of his domestic devotion.[13]

History

The exploration of Austen's reformulations of desirable masculinity in the face of contemporary models and expectations has been complemented by new critical interest in her engagement with historical phenomena, such as the role and impact of history itself.

The question of history as recorded and reported past is one that preoccupies *Northanger Abbey*, in particular. The story pivots on one of the most-cited frustrated readers of history, Catherine Morland, who, surprised by Eleanor Tilney's fondness of the subject, frets:

> ■ I read it a little as a duty, but it tells me nothing that does not either vex or weary me. The quarrels of popes and kings, with wars or pestilences, in every page; the men all so good for nothing, and hardly any women at all – it is very tiresome: and yet I often think it odd that it should be so dull, for a great deal of it must be invention. The speeches that are put into the heroes' mouths, their thoughts and designs – the chief of all this must be invention, and invention is what delights me in other books. (*NA* 79) ☐

Peter Knox-Shaw offers a balanced interpretation of the conflicted stances voiced in this passage by Catherine, Eleanor and Henry. In his *Jane Austen and the Enlightenment* (2004), Knox-Shaw, basing his findings on the books that Austen and her family owned and read, identifies Austen's allegiance with liberal historians.[14] Knox-Shaw stipulates that Henry admonishes and seeks to cure Catherine of her Gothic misconception by appealing to a public sphere sufficiently equipped to penetrate the privacy of its members, who have been inculcated to strive for the approval of impartial public spectators. Catherine humbly acknowledges the power of this truth and relegates domestic horror to Radcliffe's chosen southern regions of Catholicism. Yet Radcliffe's novels, despite their forced spatial and temporal distance, function as lessons in the 'apprehension of evil', in so far as they disabuse Catherine of the illusion of pure virtue or vice.[15] Austen, then, recognizes that Radcliffian historical distance may obfuscate the irrefutable fact that in civil society 'there was a general though unequal mixture of good and bad' (*NA* 147). This lesson owes a debt to the empiricist thought of liberal historians like David Hume, who conceive of the contradictory cultural and psychological propensities that play upon human action.[16]

Catherine may complain about the futility of history, but historical sense is precisely what Catherine lacks and needs. Knox-Shaw argues that David Hume's treatment of history lurks behind Catherine's and Eleanor's dialogue. In his essay 'Of the Study of History', Hume, addressing the relationship between history and female readers, endorses historians' invention of speeches. Such contextualization incapacitates claims about Austen's alleged disinterest or disdain for history. Far from it; Catherine's boredom courts the company of such influential thinkers as Voltaire, who, also tired of popes and kings, heralded a new kind of historiography in his preface to *Charles XII*, a book that Austen's family owned. William Robertson's *History of Scotland* (1759), a clear influence on Austen's juvenilia piece 'The History of England', is another example of this kind of historiography, where women feature prominently and story-telling is foregrounded, a technique that narrows the gap between history and the novel. Although subsequent historiography strikes another path, the closeness of history and the novel raises the question of invention and imagination. As Knox-Shaw puts it:

> ■ In choosing to centre the discussion of history in *Northanger Abbey* on the propriety of invented speeches, Austen points to the openly admitted role of fiction in a sister genre which was not only solemn, as Catherine has it, but had recently been canonized.[17] □

In a concluding remark, the relevance of which exceeds the distinctions between history and the novel, Knox-Shaw notes that the richness of Austen's work, as well as her indebtedness to liberal historiography, comes with a persistent scrupulosity that shuns dichotomies and revisits earlier positions critically.[18] This strategy epitomizes her vision of history and society; because no position can provide a view of the whole, history and society must be approached as dynamic composites of competing views.

If Knox-Shaw revises the misconception of a history-hostile Austen, Janine Barchas's *Matters of Fact in Jane Austen* (2012) discloses the extent to which the novels absorb contemporary circumstances, thus belying the myth of the socially aloof novelist. Barchas demonstrates that Austen's interest in the rises and falls of the great of her day, the circulation of novelty and scandal in high and low literature, flares up in the ironic reweaving of names and places. One of the major contributions of Barchas's research concerns the misunderstanding that propels Catherine Morland into the Gothic scenario, after John Thorpe takes her to be the heiress of Mr. Allen. Skilfully imputed to Thorpe's blather, the misunderstanding has historical foundation. The wealthy Ralph Allen (1693–1764), former mayor, entrepreneur and philanthropist, known publicly as 'the Man of Bath', must be behind John Thorpe's assumption, in particular because Ralph Allen's immense fortune was in transition at the time of *Northanger Abbey*'s composition. The fortune was held by his niece for three decades before returning to the Allen family. Hence, Thorpe's interest in the niece of Mr. Allen is not without ground.

Ralph Allen was also the proprietor of a folly (an ornamental building with no practical purpose) called Sham Castle, upon which was modelled a decade later Catherine's much-coveted Blaise Castle.[19] In addition, only seven miles in the opposite direction to Allen's folly, Bath offered the ruins of a real castle and abbey, Farleigh Hungerford Castle, at the time a tourist attraction. Built during the reign of Henry VIII, Farleigh Castle, with its long history of wife murdering and poisoning, would be the very site that Catherine expects to find at Northanger. The kitchen, mentioned half a dozen times in the novel as the space that separates the old from the new through its many improvements, emerges in the history of Farleigh castle as the crime scene *par excellence*. For Barchas, this historical backdrop validates earlier critics' claims that 'Austen finds the Gothic in genuine history, slyly demonstrating that real-world events can be as bizarre as gothic invention.'[20] This does not imply that local history delivers the final proof for the General's guilt, but it suggests it. A similar allusion is made by Claire Tomalin, who writes that the eighteenth-century British countryside provided its share of Gothic abnormality.[21] The macabre taste of landowners like Austen's neighbour Lord Portsmouth for slaughterhouses, staged funerals and the torturing of men and animals flies in the face of Henry Tilney's gullible confidence in the Christian sanity of the country house.

Revisiting the dialogue between Catherine and Eleanor, Barchas detects in Catherine's formulation of 'real solemn history' the pronouncement of Samuel Johnson on the utility of the study of history (*NA* 79). Johnson expressed doubt about the existence of real authentic history. While allowing for personages and events to have existed, he called the philosophy and embellishment involved in history writing a conjecture. At the same time, Austen echoes Radcliffe's *Sicilian Romance* (1790), which is introduced as 'a solemn history'.[22] The blending of Johnson's with Radcliffe's phrase mirrors the interweaving of Gothic stereotypes with the history of Bath, a mixture that draws history and novel writing closer together. More importantly, Barchas insists that Austen does not simply show affinities between the two, but she even reverses the techniques: while historians, as Catherine argues, invent the speeches of historical characters, Austen grounds her fiction on the historical facts of Bath, perhaps experimenting with her own construct of the historical novel. In this version of the genre, celebrity culture (and one might add here also tourism) appears as 'a type of glue between history and invention'.[23]

Revisions and Narration

To readers who turn away sceptically from the evidence that links Austen to the history, characters and culture of her time, wondering whether her choices of names, location and words were intentional, a study of her writing practice suggests that she left little to coincidence and was her own work's most meticulous critic.

Persuasion with its revised ending, the earlier version of which exists in manuscript form, provides telling insights. In *A Revolution beyond Expression*, Jocelyn Harris devoted detailed investigation to the revisions that MS Chapters 10 and 11 underwent before transmuting into Chapters X–XI and Chapter XII respectively. The manuscripts show a writer hard at work, striving and struggling for a satisfactory resolution to her tale. The published version comprises four modifications worth special attention: first, the final revision promotes Anne from a state of perplexed psychology to decisive eloquence; second, Wentworth's pronouncements alternate between direct and indirect speech, while in the manuscript chapters his elucidation reaches the reader solely in indirect speech; third, Austen opts for a resolution that negotiates more successfully between privacy and public life, as depicted in the dialogue unfolding on the streets of Bath; and fourth, many of the modifications combine to create an almost too good heroine by eliminating Anne's uncharitable thoughts towards Lady Russell and by bolstering her exculpation with Wentworth's insistence on his misguided pride.[24] To give an example of this last point, if in the manuscript version Wentworth explains his flirtations with Louisa petulantly as the 'attempts of Anger and Pique', in the published chapter he regrets more solemnly the 'attempts of angry Pride' (P 208, 195).[25]

The two versions handle the confrontation of the lovers very differently. Initially, Austen allotted to the Admiral the role of the mediator. Anne, who meets the Admiral accidentally, is invited by the latter to pay a visit to Mrs. Croft, who happens to be busy with her dressmaker. The reason for the Admiral's pressing invitation lies with the rumours of Anne's marriage to William Elliot, an event that would thwart the Crofts' lease of Kellynch Hall. When Anne enters the Crofts' drawing room, she finds there 'Nobody' but Captain Wentworth (P 205). In an awkward and brief *tête-à-tête* that Anne cannot help overhearing, the Admiral asks Wentworth to find out about the alleged match between Anne and William Elliot. This rather contrived situation leads to the *éclaircissement* of the unfounded rumours and the renewal of Wentworth's attachment to Anne, a scene in which Anne features mostly as a passive receiver. By contrast, in the published chapters, Anne and Wentworth are at the Musgroves' lodgings and in the presence of others. The motif of eavesdropping from the earlier version metamorphoses into a speech with two audiences: Anne speaks to Harville but encodes her defence of female constancy with cues meant to communicate to Wentworth her enduring love. In return, her powerful eloquence meets a worthy declaration in Wentworth's letter. Harris aptly concludes that:

> ■ Instead of keeping Anne mute, Austen engages her in a debate reaching back through time and literature; instead of resolving the plot through Admiral Croft and the Kellynch lease, she reveals Wentworth's mind through a passionate soliloquy. It is often said that Austen never shows men conferring together in the absence of women, but the Richardsonian device of a letter allows her exhibit his true feelings, just as Darcy's letter had proclaimed his.[26] □

The study of the manuscript chapters thus offers the clearest refutation of the myth of the unconscious artist.

In light of the self-critical and meticulous (re)-writing process, textual features like punctuation and capitalization deserve critical interpretation. Many of these features can be found only in the manuscripts. Although Austen uses capitalization to emphasize words, printers chose to cohere with the standardizing fashion of the day and omit them. Italics as well, another strategy of accentuation and urgency, disappear in the published novels. Similarly, dashes, a frequent device in Austen's letters and manuscripts, are often replaced by other punctuation. From Katherine Sutherland's study of *Mansfield Park*, we learn that the obliteration of dashes entails the silencing of an informal voice more often than not linked to female agency. Harris, too, believes that gender bias plays a role, since the 'Romantic dashes of Lord Byron were treated with more respect'.[27] Harris's comments on punctuation are deepened by Tandon Bharat, who observes that several of Anne's thoughts or speeches end in dashes, which Bharat associates with the silence typical of the wordless emotion simmering in Anne. The unexpected halt of sentences, such as 'Here Anne spoke –', reflects the 'notion of being prematurely cut off at twenty-seven' (*P* 21).[28]

While Bharat links the use of the dash with Anne's consciousness, D. A. Miller in *Jane Austen, or the Secret of Style* (2003) ascribes the novel's entire narration to it. Exceptionally, in *Persuasion*, the Austenian narrator breaks with the usual impersonality and 'contemplates the possibility of falling into personification'.[29] In the other novels, the style of narration preserves detachment from the characters, a position that prompts Miller to call the typical Austen narrator a 'No One'.[30] However, in *Persuasion*, the character of Anne absorbs the style, chastising the narrative of the ironical treatment or the 'slapping', to use Miller's term, that other protagonists like Emma endure at the hands of their creator. Mortification and self-scathing criticism, Anne Elliot's daily bread, preclude and assimilate the narrator's derision. In Miller's dry summary: 'The narration of *Persuasion*, then, can do little that Anne has not already done to herself.'[31] Miller considers the substitution of personification for impersonality to be a loss because it disables the superb irony that distinguishes Austen's style.

However, some critics find unprecedented virtues in *Persuasion*'s style, as Penny Gay does persuasively in her monograph *Jane Austen and the Theatre* (2002). Gay, who reads Austen's novels in the context of the theatrical performance and theory of the long eighteenth century, discovers a strong influence of the genre of melodrama in Austen's last novel. The revised scene of Anne and Wentworth's reconciliation, unfolding in the presence of the Musgroves and Captain Harville, invests the novel with unrivalled dramatic force. The early version, with the lovers confiding in each other in the Crofts' room, is the typical stuff of sentimental drama or the sentimental novel, in which the passive heroine is led to happiness by the intervention of a paternal figure and the words of her constant lover.[32] By contrast, the revised scene exudes dramatic intensity through its innovative use of performers, audience and the favourite eighteenth-century trope of eavesdropping. Austen had already deployed this device in the first volume during the walk to Winthrop, where Anne overhears Wentworth and Louisa discussing the importance of fortitude. After reversing the position, with Wentworth now the passive receiver, Austen provides her male protagonist with an outlet for accumulated repressed emotions. No genre capitalized on this experience of victory over repression as successfully as the emerging genre of melodrama. The style of Wentworth's letter, suffused with extreme words such as 'my soul', 'agony', 'precious feelings', 'pierce' and 'death' and with emphatic inversions such as 'Tell me not' or 'Unjust I may have been', has original exclamatory intensity (*P* 191).[33]

Austen's indebtedness to melodrama also affects the figure of Anne, the marginalized character in whose consciousness many of the narrative's tensions accumulate. It was characteristic of melodrama to provide a climactic release of speech and emotion through the marginalized figure. Austen bestows on her heroine the agency that corresponds to melodrama's fantasy that, despite disenfranchisement, the individual can take things into her own hands. Yet she also modifies the prescriptions of the genre; for example, the 'aesthetics of the visible' charted by the melodramatic climactic release.[34] First, not only is the coded exchange between Anne and Wentworth visible for the reader and not the Musgroves, but soon after the lovers meet in the presence of the unwitting Charles Musgrove, the curtain drops on their private exchange. Now the reader, like the Musgroves before, is excluded from the aesthetics of the visible. Second, Austen's ironic perspective on the melodramatic art of her time materializes in the ending, where an acute sense of real-life lacks and dangers supplants the poetic justice of the restorative resolutions of the melodrama.[35]

As for *Northanger Abbey*, although the act of revising must have been crucial for the completion of the novel, since we know that Austen reworked it at different points, the latest revision being in 1816, most critical insights amount to conjectures in the absence of the manuscript.[36] The latest alterations may have consisted in stylistic refinements without substantial changes to the narrative voice. Narelle Shaw argues that the presence of free indirect discourse marks the most mature passages of *Northanger Abbey*.[37] Unlike indirect speech, where the thoughts or words of a character are reported in the third person by the narrator, in free indirect discourse the narrator seems to disappear. This disappearance has a somewhat paradoxical effect: on one level, the distance between readers and a character's thoughts or words is reduced; at the same time, however, the vanishing of the narrator can entail detachment. An example of Austen's masterful play with free indirect discourse is Mrs. Allen's weather prediction: 'Mrs. Allen's opinion was more positive: "She had no doubt in the world of its being a very fine day, if the clouds would only go off, and the sun keep out"' (*NA* 58). The reader has access to Mrs. Allen's words without any introduction along the lines of 'She said she had no doubt'. Yet the narrator's retreat can signify a gesture that lets Mrs. Allen be condemned by her own foolishness; figuratively speaking, Austen steps back and mischievously enjoys seeing Mrs. Allen hang herself.

Shaw also notices that the speeches of General Tilney are most consistently reported in free indirect discourse. Ironically, his speeches are often representative of the misunderstandings that keep Catherine at the Abbey. When the General, misreading Catherine's interest, tries to impress her on the tour of his gardens, hothouses and modern kitchen, the free indirect speech reveals the opacity of their communication. Shaw is right to hold that:

> ■ The distancing effect contingent upon the substitution of third for first person pronoun technically dramatizes the lack of accord between the two characters.[38] □

Hence, self-aggrandizement conveyed in free indirect discourse marks the General as the villain of the story even before the Gothic adventure unfolds.

The study of free indirect discourse has yielded some valuable explorations of Austen's irony as well as her affinity to Gothic and Romantic aesthetics. In *Persuasion*, the capacity of free indirect discourse to establish intimacy between characters and readers but also opacity between narrator and reader has been associated with Romantic irony. As Caroline Franklin explains, Austen and Byron, in their treatment of romantic love, combine first- and third-person approaches to characters in order to create 'distancing portraits of individuals' who yearn for love as the thing closest to sublime spiritual human experience.[39] John Wiltshire explains the distancing effect of free indirect discourse in *Persuasion*, when holding that Anne's own feelings and their intrusion upon everything she experiences marginalize her. Not only does she keep her thoughts to herself, but she keeps them from the reader, conjuring up 'a kind of bank, or freight, of painful, unexpressed experience and emotion'.[40] Indeed, for Clara Tuite, to whose study we now turn, free indirect speech as deployed in *Persuasion* is the very device with which Austen realizes what Clifford Siskin has called the 'lyrical turn' that distinguishes Romanticism: 'The free indirect discourse is *the* strategy by which Austen lyricizes the novel.'[41] However, before addressing Romantic aesthetics, we must consider new interpretations of the Gothic sublime, which lead to the novels' appropriation of Romantic themes and motifs.

Gothic Sublime

The doubling of closeness and distance involved in free indirect discourse replicates the paradoxical tug of parody in *Northanger Abbey*. This is Clara Tuite's insightful claim in *Romantic Austen: Sexual Politics and the Literary Canon* (2002). Tuite does not celebrate Austen as the inventor of free indirect discourse. An avid reader, Austen encountered the device in the novels of Fanny Burney and Ann Radcliffe. Indeed, the latter's skilful handling of free indirect discourse inaugurates what critics call the 'female Gothic'. The gender distinction consists in the representation of female interiority crucial to Radcliffe's novels but not to the male Gothic, for example, the fiction of Matthew Lewis, which relies on 'a materialist aesthetic in the production of sensation and horror'.[42] The parody of *Northanger Abbey* entertains an ambivalent relationship to Radcliffe's female Gothic. Despite the burlesque, Austen's Gothic, like Radcliffe's, derives its energy from the 'heroine's interior apprehension and imaginative production of violence'.[43] Austen recognizes the potency of free indirect discourse to produce something like a Gothic theatre of the mind. Hence, Tuite argues that:

> ■ Austen's parody can be read as a drama of literary apprenticeship that turns on the identification of Radcliffe as the mistress of a certain form of interiority and negotiates the inheritance of this technique from Radcliffe.[44] □

In Tuite's analysis, 'drama' is the right word not only because it suggests the staging of interiority, but also because the relationship between apprentice (Austen) and teacher (Radcliffe) is fraught with tensions that erupt in parody.

When it comes to the representation of interiority, free indirect discourse makes it difficult for the reader to distinguish the character's thoughts from the narrator's. A similar doubling, or blurring, of positions generates a parody in which the parodied object, Radcliffe's novels, merges with the parodying subject, Austen's novel. In both, an approaching stance coexists and competes with a distancing one. Tuite draws on the definition of philosopher and sociologist Pierre Bourdieu, who conceives of certain forms of parody as a process of appropriation and emancipation. Following Bourdieu's lead, Austen's parody can be associated with that typical of:

> ■ newcomers [who] 'get beyond' [*dépassent*] the dominant mode of thought and expression not by explicitly denouncing it but by repeating and reproducing it in a sociologically non-congruent context, which has the effect of rendering it incongruous or even absurd, simply by making it perceptible as the arbitrary convention it is. This form of heretical break is particularly favoured by ex-believers, who use pastiche or parody as the indispensable means of objectifying, and thereby appropriating, the form of thought and expression by which they were formerly possessed.[45] □

Tuite believes that parody understood as belief and heresy fits Austen's act of 'appropriation'. If nothing else, the amount of evidence that critics have brought forward to demonstrate Austen's thorough knowledge of, and keen engagement with, Radcliffe's novels suggests implications that surpass both downright imitation and dismissal. For Tuite, an Augustan account of irony as detachment fails to explain the process of appropriation that 'desires to purge and also to imaginatively possess and reconfigure' the female Gothic in *Northanger Abbey*.[46] The use of free indirect discourse, which trained readers would have automatically identified with Radcliffe's style, develops in the later novels decoupled from its origins.

The female Gothic, as an interior dramatization of feelings of terror, demands a close investigation of the ways that Gothic aesthetics had an impact on the theatre culture of the long nineteenth century. Whole generations of scholars insisted on Austen's hostility to theatre. The reason for this stubborn, though unqualified, assumption was Fanny Price's reluctance to participate in the domestic theatricals at Mansfield Park. One study in particular, Gay's *Jane Austen and the Theatre*, debunks this misconception by tracing the influence of Gothic drama in the narrative of *Northanger Abbey*. Gay argues that Austen implants in the genre of the novel the mechanism of curiosity operating in spectators of Gothic drama. Several critics had insisted on the importance of reading and readers, but Gay deepens this claim, as she argues that Catherine's novelistic experience is a crossover with the gaze of the spectators of the Gothic stage, which at the time of the novel's composition was at the height of popularity.[47] Austen translates the communal Gothic encounter provided by the stage into the private experience of the theatre of the mind.

Theatricality permeates the novel, starting with Catherine's first appearance at the Upper Rooms in Bath, under the scrutinizing though not-so-enthusiastic gaze of men, to Henry's self-appointed role as master of ceremonies, to his little performance as *improvisatore* of the Gothic scene he conjures up for Catherine during their ride to Northanger and, finally, to Catherine's eagerly enacted role of the Gothic heroine, whose most mature realization is that 'she has been both audience and performer in her own private theatre'.[48] Descriptive details about space, light, darkness and bodily moves in conjunction with emotional responses replicate the stage of Gothic drama. However, to speak of replication would not do justice to Austen's originality and critique. While Gothic drama staged the male gaze projecting the fantasy of masculinity upon the distressed and passive heroine, the drama of *Northanger Abbey* is fuelled by the fantasy of an active and stereotype-defying heroine.[49] As for Henry, Gay reads the theatricals that appear to lend him superiority over the inexperienced Catherine as a strategy of sublimation that compensates for his subordination in his father's house. It is when he rebels against the paternal usurpation of agency, by joining Catherine at Fullerton, that Henry becomes an actor in the non-theatrical sense.[50]

Gay's study of the theatrical leanings and revisions that help create the Gothic theatre of the mind begs the question about the ideas that came to be associated with Gothic experience. The most influential discourse exploring Gothic sensations of shock and terror drew on the concept of the sublime. As already mentioned in Chapter 6, Edmund Burke's philosophical essay on the sublime and the beautiful was fundamental in that it led to many discussions and applications of the term. Natasha Duquette finds several accounts of the sublime mingling in *Northanger Abbey*, some of them satirizing Burkean sublime horror. In 'Motionless Wonder: Gothic Sublimity in *Northanger Abbey*' (2010), Duquette sees Burkean sublime – the terrifying experience resulting from confrontation with extraordinary manifestations of divine power or mystery – being counteracted by the 'contemplative sublime':

> ■ Jane Austen satirizes excessive aspects of the Gothic sublime arising from Burke's *Enquiry*, but she reveals her astute awareness of an expanded notion of sublimity operating within the works of her female contemporaries.[51] □

In particular, the notion of the 'contemplative sublime', proposed by the abolitionist theorist Mary Anne Schimmelpenninck and later espoused in the writings of the dramatist Joanna Baillie and the novelist Ann Radcliffe, offers more dynamic and flexible aesthetics.

Contemplative sublimity tones down the excessive emotional involvement of Burke's sublime. Indeed, Radcliffe's novels abound in moments of 'sublime repose', where reverential wonder has restorative powers. An amusing moment of Austen's treatment of awestruck and reverential response occurs upon Catherine's contemplation of the rooms of Bath. According to Burke and Radcliffe's aesthetic of the sublime, the view from a mountaintop provokes strong feelings in the human mind as it confronts its smallness. In a parodic gesture, after being taken by Mrs. Allen to a high point from which they can estimate the geography of the room and the size and movements of the crowd, Catherine is filled with 'utter amazement' as she 'enjoy[s] the repose of the eminence' (*NA* 11). The counterpart of this parodic sublimity occurs in the Abbey, where Catherine's expectations of an experience of the Burkean sublime dwindle into bathos. However, Duquette reminds us that the interplay of parodic sublimity should not obfuscate Austen's exploration of what the German philosopher Immanuel Kant called the 'noble sublime', an experience connected with the cultivation of social bonds and friendship, unlike Burke's terrible sublime that thrives on solitude. Such a notion of 'noble' sublimity is present in the works of Ann Radcliffe, Mary Wollstonecraft and, of course, Austen's *Northanger Abbey*, where Catherine and Eleanor find respite away from the intimidating General, as they commemorate the loss of Mrs. Tilney. Hence, Austen imagines the kind of intimate female friendship that Radcliffe envisages only between her male characters.

Nation and Professional Sublime

As a Gothic novel, *Northanger Abbey* has readily prompted investigations revolving around the moral implications of the aesthetics of sublimity, whereas *Persuasion* has drawn critical attention for imbuing the courtship plot with a Romantic sublime ethos. In works like *Persuasion* or *The Giaour*, as Caroline Franklin aptly summarizes it in the words of Byron's protagonist, this ethos is 'to die and know no second love'.[52] While Byron's Giaour makes no concession, Austen tests this ideal, wondering whether second attachments are not more natural in the face of the vicissitudes of life to which she subjects many of her characters. The novel teems with widows and widowers: Captain Benwick, William Elliot, who will soon marry for love or financial security, Sir Walter, Lady Russell, Mrs. Smith and Mrs. Clay. Indeed, considering the high rate of female mortality during childbirth and the age difference between husband and wife in arranged marriages in the early nineteenth century, first attachments seem to be the exception.[53] Franklin reminds us that pure contingency (Crofts' leasing of Kellynch and Wentworth's supervision of Dick Musgrove) has returned Wentworth into Anne's circle of acquaintances, while the unexpected romance between Louisa and Benwick, following the accident at Lyme, liberates him. Combined with the presence of an eligible and cunning suitor like William Elliot, the plot's reliance on contingent conditions intimates a different ending.[54]

Significantly, even in its optimistic resolution, which reconciles romantic constant love with marriage, the final sentence with its mentioning of the dangers of Wentworth's profession damps Anne's coveted idealism.

Recent research has insisted on the value of professions in Austen's last published novel. Anne Frey in 'Nation without Nationalism: The Reorganization of Feeling in Austen's *Persuasion*' (2005) offers an astute analysis. Her argument deserves particular attention because it not only formulates a new type of sublimity, but also goes against several influential claims about the function of the novel as a genre. Frey argues that reconceptualizing the 'Romantic sublime as a new professional context' is Austen's solution to the core concern of Romantic literature: how can the individual, from her particular situation and perspective, conceive and represent the wholeness of experience?[55] This question, which involves the status of perception and imagination, pertains to *Persuasion*'s representation of national community. Other critics have argued that, in this novel, Austen expands her fiction to encompass a vision of the nation, its future and its most reliable members, with Anne emerging as the most worthy representative.[56] Frey agrees that the novel foregrounds ideas about the nation, but she removes the power of representation from Anne or any character in particular, because the nation, corresponding to the whole in Romantic models of community, cannot be perceived and therefore represented by one particular consciousness. Austen does not believe that imagination mediates between individual perception and a community based on shared heritage, values and traits. As Frey puts it:

> ■ Austen rejects the synechdochal logic whereby one character stands in for an entire nation, because such a synecdoche would ignore the vast parts of the nation that this character does not represent. And an inability to represent the nation therefore presents a problem for the novel's resolution: if no individual can conceive the nation as a whole, how can a novel represent national citizenship, and the hero or heroine's place in the social order?[57] □

Persuasion's answer is not a particular character but the navy, the professional class, which interpellates its members as citizens of the nation. The navy, one state apparatus among other bureaucratic agencies on the rise in nineteenth-century imperial Britain, defines individuals as subjects with certain obligations towards the nation. Therefore, the visionary imaginative sublime translates into the sublime that operates through agencies which, like the navy, provide structures where individuals can be made aware of their membership in a nation. Frey calls this the 'professional sublime' that enables characters to perceive the otherwise 'sublimely inconceivable British nation'.[58]

Frey borrows the term 'interpellation' from the Marxist philosopher Louis Althusser, who developed it to describe individual consciousness as a product of ideological structures or apparatuses. The navy embodies and projects a consciousness of Britishness that competes with and, ultimately, conquers a Burkean ideal of the English nation as based on aristocratic landed inheritance. Not surprisingly, representatives of the navy step into the breach created by vain landlords of Sir Walter's ilk, or potential rapacious successors like Walter Elliot, assuming the role of mindful estate administrators and patricians, as happens in the case of the Crofts' management of Kellynch Hall and Wentworth's assistance of Dick Musgrove and Mrs. Smith. Hence, it would be wrong to argue that Austen rejects aristocratic values and obligations, whereas in fact she transfers them onto the new professional class.[59] One could argue that the odds are that members of the professional class, in the process of applying aristocratic values, also modify them precisely because of the state interpellation that distinguishes them from the aristocracy.

Several influential accounts are contested by Frey's formulation of 'the professional sublime'. First, by emphasizing the navy as a professional class that 'incorporate[s] disparate individuals or communities in one single nation', Frey departs from critics like Brian Southam who had argued that Austen's interest lay with the actual navy.[60] Second, 'the professional sublime' is offered as Austen's revision of the Romantic sublime. In the Romantic sublime, imagination mediates between the part (the self) and the whole (the community or nation) which cannot be perceived by the senses. Novels or poetry channel imagination. However, according to Frey, *Persuasion*'s 'professional sublime' deems individual imagination incapable of perceiving the nation. In its stead, the bureaucratic agencies like the navy assume a mediating role, a substitution that for Frey entails the incapability of the novel, and literature in general, to create the shared consciousness that links individuals together as members of the nation. When writing that '[l]iterature cannot cohere communities but only depict these communities',[61] Frey allows literature merely mimetic value, challenging previous critics who have attributed the rise of nationalism to people's shared consciousness, in which print culture and literacy played a performative role.[62] In addition, treating literature as being incapable of uniting communities contradicts the novels' cohesive power in the imagination of readers and writers. Reading Claudia L. Johnson's *Jane Austen's Cults and Cultures* (2012), one gains the impression that imaginative bonds sustain Austen readers as diverse as Rudyard Kipling's fictional Humberstall or real-life reader and critic Reginald Farrer. Humberstall, who owes his spiritual survival as a soldier in World War I to the little secret society of Austen readers, returns to the novels after the war not to find comfort in a past and gentle England but to recover the world of the trenches, its smells, sounds and bonds of brotherhood.[63] Similarly, Farrer's reports from the front, written during his service for the Foreign Office in World War I, frequently recollect Austenian snippets that 'establish a secret fellowship with a subset of readers'.[64]

More importantly, the pitching of the 'professional sublime' against literature encounters difficulty in a novel in which identities are firmly anchored in pieces of print culture, such as the *Baronetage* and the *Navy List*. The chief representatives of the novel's juxtaposed classes, Sir Walter and Captain Wentworth, draw the essence of their self-worth from the existence and dissemination of these two texts. It appears that interpellation through state structures relies on the dissemination of historical inventories like the *Navy List* which induce the desire and necessity of individuals to imagine themselves as part of the whole. Janine Barchas's *Matters of Fact* gives reason to put more weight on these two documents. Although the novel seems to endorse the rise of a new professional class, an investigation of the *Baronetage* and the navy lists in circulation at the time reveals less clear allegiances. This is because Austen bestows on her naval representatives names from the most ancient families of the English aristocracy, such as the Wentworths and Crofts, whereas names that in *Persuasion* are given to landed gentry, such as Dalrymple, Carteret and Elliot, belong to the navy greats recorded in the navy lists.[65] The real-life characters behind these names share a common denominator:

■ By focusing on names that have risen, through merit and controversy, to high positions in both the *Baronetage* and the *Navy List*, Austen may point out that both systems of rank allow for promotion and change. Both systems are equally meritorious and sometimes corrupt. [...] Some of the most ancient families in the *Baronetage*, most notably the homeless Crofts, and 'extinct' Russells and Wentworths, need renewal.[66] □

Thus, *Persuasion*'s modernity incorporates respect for rank and tradition. On the one hand, Barchas's conclusion corroborates Frey's observation about the survival of aristocratic values; on the other hand, it points to a shared sense of the past that implies continuity and an organic vision of the nation that is at odds with exclusively state-interpellated citizenship.

The idea that Austen recognizes the need for the renewal of the landed class already appears clear in *Northanger Abbey*, where the industrious General Tilney commands new methods of production and productivity. Katherine Kickel urges readers to view the character of the General and his obsession with time and improvement as a sign of Austen's awareness of the growing economic pressures that weighed on the gentry for the perpetuation of the landed economy. This is an anxiety that we need not overlook simply because it goes unnoticed by the novel's heroine. The authority of the clocks at *Northanger Abbey* announces an era of industrialist efficacy from which the landed gentry can escape as little as the labouring classes.[67] The General's strategy is to turn his estate into a site of agricultural and industrial modernization. If we can take his word, his semi-industrial establishment, with its gardens and expensive hothouses, employs an entire parish. However, as Kickel observes, this happens at the expense of leisure time and sociability, the very thing that the fiscally irresponsible Sir Walter has in abundance. The emotional distress produced by the chiming clocks at *Northanger Abbey* registers the changes that the gentry home would undergo, when coping with the economic imperatives that threatened its survival.[68]

Romanticism Reconsidered

General Tilney's pride in his hothouses is the cue that leads critics to Austen's engagement with two key Romantic tropes, nature and education, as argued by Deidre Lynch's '"Young ladies are delicate plants": Jane Austen and Greenhouse Romanticism' (2010). Lynch bases her claim that Austen participated in contemporary debates about nature, nurture and cultivation on *Northanger Abbey* and *Mansfield Park*. While the latter novel has been frequently associated with Romantic influences, *Northanger Abbey*'s Romanticism, beyond its Gothic resonances, seemed a less certain thing.

In particular, William Deresiewicz's monograph *Jane Austen and the Romantic Poets* (2004) locates *Northanger Abbey* at the watershed that separated *Sense and Sensibility* and *Pride and Prejudice* from the novels of the mature phase, *Mansfield Park*, *Emma* and *Persuasion*. Deresiewicz believes that only after *Northanger Abbey* did Austen's style benefit from reading Wordsworth, Coleridge, Byron and Sir Walter Scott. The clearest evidence for the impact of these writers consists of concerns like childhood, education, nature, time and memory that appear in more articulated shape in the later novels.[69] Consequently, Deresciewicz has more to say about *Persuasion*, in which widowhood, as both a metaphor and literal status, enhances explorations of loss and memory reminiscent of Byron's and Scott's poetics. On a larger scale, Austen found in Byron and Scott the language necessary to depict the story of bereavement that portrays the nation's mournful coping with twenty years of war and emotional exhaustion:

> ■ The story of widows, in other words, was written as a way of addressing the fact that England itself had been widowed – widowed thousands of times over – and was trying to understand, after twenty years of war, how to move forward.[70] □

Indisputably strong on the mature stage, Deresciewicz's study tends to oversimplify the relationship of Austen's early novels to Romantic literature, possibly, because he establishes a significant number of common themes among a restricted range of Romantic texts.

Lynch's article follows the opposite strategy: it investigates the botanical idiom of growth and reproduction in a variety of contemporary texts extending from science to literature. Lynch discovers in these texts a correlation between women's development and botany. The most famous example of the period is Wordsworth's poem 'Three years she grew in sun and shower', in which 'she' stands for a female child and a flower. Austen's women, suggests Lynch, in contrast to the raw education of Wordsworth's wild flower girl, grow naturally in 'artificial habitats', a phrase concocted by contemporary proponents of greenhouse gardening.[71] The paradox of an artificially produced and sustained cultivation complicates the period's approaches to nature and, more importantly, the understanding of an aesthetic and cultural movement like Romanticism, whose proto-ecological consciousness has earned it the name green Romanticism.[72] Were we to follow the history of green Romanticism, of the flower girls that live on rain and sun, none of Austen's heroines would fit in the picture. However, as Lynch's investigation of scientific and literary texts reveals, the period perceived plants, their growth and reproduction, in plural and contradictory manifestations that required a process of translation and experimentation. Strong interest in natural processes led to the somewhat paradoxical necessity of learning from and about nature through practices of artifice and exhibition, of which greenhouses and hothouses are the clearest expression.[73] Hence, if we expand the period's consciousness to include the cultivation of nature in artificially protected worlds, then we must also revise green Romanticism into greenhouse Romanticism and read General Tilney's hothouses as imprints of this very consciousness. They have emblematic importance for our understanding of Austen's position between realism and Romanticism and of the reasons that she has been deemed both a most natural (by Richard Simpson) and unnatural writer (by Charlotte Brontë – see Chapter 3 on Victorian responses).

Lynch argues that Austen confronted the oxymoronic expectation of writers like Wordsworth or Charles Lamb, whose advice to Coleridge was the 'cultivation of simplicity'.[74] For writers like Lamb, artificial cultivation undermined organicism and led to overculture that expressed itself in overheated aesthetic embellishments (as if grown in hothouse beds) or in the unhealthy precocity of modern children. *Northanger Abbey* registers the oxymoronic tenet of the Romantic project of 'the education in natural feeling' ambivalently, and tellingly enough, through the aesthetic experience of flowers.[75] This ambivalence arises in the scene where, after successfully lecturing Catherine on the picturesque, Henry determines that she has 'a great deal of natural taste' (*NA* 81). Similarly, Henry praises a rather horticulturally apathetic Catherine when she develops a taste for hyacinths – Catherine's own words are: 'I am naturally indifferent about flowers' (*NA* 127). Lynch's comment of this passage is worth quoting:

> ■ If with that loaded word 'natural' Austen pokes fun at the self-delusions of a pedagogue who confuses his own self-realization with another's, it is with characteristic gentleness. But such mockery may well mark Austen's dissent from the developmental vision on which her contemporaries drew as they reconceived education as a process in which the teacher fostered a natural, innate potential that the pupil possessed from birth. It might mark her suspicion of the facile manner in which the educationalists' appeal to Nature's authority promised a reconciliation of individual autonomy with political obedience.[76] □

Indeed, Austen warns her readers about the novelist's authority over claims of truthfulness, naturalness and realism through the metafictional intervention that ends her story: 'we [narrator, readers and characters] are all hastening together to perfect felicity' (*NA* 185). Such a revelation of narratorial power gives away the artful will that has brought about her protagonists' 'espousal', a term used for the bio-engineered plants of the hothouses.[77] However, as Sonia Hofkosh observes in 'The Illusionist: *Northanger Abbey* and Austen's Uses of Enchantment' (2009), Austen's play with the illusion of realism does not entail a juxtaposition, because 'illusion may be profoundly effective in producing real consequences', a recognition that aligns Austen with Coleridge's 'poetic faith'.[78] The narrator in her novels assumes the voices of both the 'magician' and 'natural historian',[79] resembling thus the most exquisite hybrids of horticultural experimentation.

More inclusive reconceptualizations like Lynch's green Romanticism or Anne K. Mellor's feminine romanticism (see Chapter 6) help us to understand the period's richness in interconnected ways that shape into a web of ideas rather than clear-cut categories.[80] A rethinking of Austen's place within this reconceptualized field demonstrates that her novels grew in the real-life soil of contemporary debate. It is in such a debate that *Persuasion*'s contribution gains relevance. As Enit K. Steiner writes in *Jane Austen's Civilized Women* (2012), the focalization of the narrative on Anne's consciousness and the abandonment of the impersonal style (which Miller regrets) foreground the ideas of partiality that Austen links to women's experience. Insistence on a mature heroine who is haunted and made wiser by experience echoes Wollstonecraft's attempts to reassess the features of the civilized women, who are kept behind not least by novelistic expectations.[81] For Wollstonecraft, the novels of her time provide a model of 'heroinism' that requires women, as she puts it in the preface to *The Wrongs of Woman, or Maria* (1798), 'to be born immaculate' and 'to act like goddesses of wisdom, just come forth highly finished Minervas from the head of Jove'.[82] Female readers encountered such pictures of immaculate innate wisdom in celebrated novels like Hannah More's *Coelebs in Search of a Wife* (1809). Hence, the portrayal of Anne Elliot vindicates female experience by endowing it with the particularities of an individualized life. At the same time, like Wollstonecraft's *Maria*, *Persuasion*, launched from Anne's particular experience, seeks to speak in the name of an entire group, of women as members assigned to a gender-defined rank. We encounter this group consciousness in Anne's defence of women's constancy, which she, however, does not consider the result of innate female virtue but the consequence of women's uneventful and home-bound life.[83] This has implications for Anne's understanding of partiality: while speaking for women's universal experience, she acknowledges the bias of her claim, reminding readers and herself of their own specific locations and the impossibility of impartiality, an important notion in the thought of Romantic philosopher and novelist William Godwin, Wollstonecraft's partner. Moreover, Anne's endorsement of partiality anticipates twentieth-century feminist models of public life that seek the inclusion of all persons and all groups not based on unified universality but on the acceptance of heterogeneity.[84]

Addressing women's social location in the Romantic period from a different angle, Melissa Sodeman's 'Domestic Mobility in *Persuasion* and *Sanditon*' (2005) makes a case for *Persuasion*'s modern treatment of the domestic sphere. Austen exploits domestic fiction and disrupts 'conservative conjunctions placing women at the center of the modern household'.[85] In *Persuasion* as well as in the unfinished *Sanditon*, she imposes displacements on the heroines, 'in order to envision them within domestic structures that more readily accommodate mobility'.[86] During the course of the novel, Anne Elliot dwells in five different residences, all of which are experienced as noisy if not oppressive. She voices her experience during her conversation with Captain Harville when she denounces the crippling effect of women's domestic confinement. However, the most efficient critique of a culture that binds women at home is *Persuasion*'s licensing of female mobility by associating it with virtue, as suggested in the heroine's relocation in a companionate marriage.[87] Sodeman's analysis softens the sting of Anne's lack of a fixed home that many critics have lamented, making a virtue of the expanded field of experience enabled by her attachment to the mobile life of a navy officer, as well as the reconfiguration of domestic bonds within this new more flexible structure. Hence, towards its close, with domesticity unmoored from fixed spaces, *Persuasion* adopts an inclusionary stance in which the national and the domestic have become indistinguishable.[88]

It is necessary to keep in mind the shift in Austen criticism from a view of her as an ahistorical ironist to a view of her as a socially engaged writer, because the story of the filmic adaptations discussed in the last chapter of this guide complements the trend of historical contextualization. As we shall see, the adaptations are not merely translations from one medium into another, but also adaptations to the critical engagement that culminated in an examination of the novels' attitudes towards contemporary social conditions and aesthetics as well as towards modernity.

CHAPTER EIGHT

From Words to Image and Sound

The 1980s and 1990s witnessed numerous adaptations of eighteenth- and nineteenth-century novels, to the extent that classical-novel adaptations became a recognizable film genre, which drew connections to the novels as well as to other filmic adaptations. Due to Austen's popularity, film adaptations of her novels came, by the end of the twentieth century, to epitomize the genre of the classical-novel adaptation.[1] Yet despite their iconic status, the adaptations have elicited mixed responses, especially from literary critics, who applaud the central place Austen's work enjoys within the repertoire of another medium, but often regret the loss that the visual and aural language of film inflicts upon the novel.

The dilemma of screen adaptation resides in the transfer of content from one medium to another, a transfer that necessarily involves a change of codes, whereby finding technical correspondences between two very different media becomes the main challenge. Before delving into the adaptations of *Northanger Abbey* and *Persuasion*, it is worth keeping in mind Kathryn Sutherland's elaboration of the difficulties faced by filmic adaptations of Austen's novels:

> ■ In moving from novel to film, how is an equivalent story told by means of non-equivalent codes? And, given their different codes, how can film, respecting the novel's difference, also occupy the same space in its own structural terms? Austen's novels are largely plotless (and film relishes action); Austen's text displays a weak dependence on metaphor and figurative language (and film's power lies in the manipulation of image and imagery); Austen's mature art (and risky word, her 'essence') is a sophisticated aural figuration in which, through free indirect discourse, voice is laid on voice to produce critical (specifically, ironic) connotative effects, and the blurring of character and narrator, which are almost impossible to achieve in film whose aural effects, however sophisticated, are subordinated to an immense visual rhetoric.[2] □

There are certain technological correspondences that directors can exploit; for example, the camera can shift from subjective viewpoint to distance, the way a camera is held can influence the intimacy created between characters and viewers and voice-over can convey subjective impressions or comments, while jump cuts and montage can render irony and juxtaposition. In addition, successful adaptations play upon qualities of the novels that lend themselves to filmic representations, such as scenes of dramatic quality (entrances and exits), emphasis on dialogues and methods of characterization. Clearly, even the most successful adaptation invites questions about the material preserved and lost during the transformation of written words into images and sound.

Mary Favret addresses the issue of fidelity, that is, of being true to the source, as a process that involves the dynamics 'of animation or mortality'.[3] Favret develops the idea of mortality from Fredric Jameson's observation about film being a medium that assimilates death and injects the past with the 'lively energy of radical difference'.[4] In adaptations, these two processes must intermingle in order to convey the novels' core characteristics, which in the case of *Northanger Abbey* is the heroine's absorption by Gothic haunting, and in *Persuasion* is a world constructed around and from the viewpoint of an astute but subdued protagonist shrouded in 'silent attentiveness'.[5] The present chapter discusses and compares two adaptations of *Northanger Abbey* (1987, 2007) and three of *Persuasion* (1971, 1995, 2007).

Northanger Abbey

The first cinematic adaptation of *Northanger Abbey*, also the first BBC and A&E production, appeared in 1987. Based on a screenplay by Maggie Wadey and directed by Giles Foster, it starred Katherine Schlesinger as Catherine Morland and Peter Firth as Henry Tilney. A second adaptation was announced in 1999, with a screenplay by Andrew Davies and directed by Jon Jones. This adaptation, with Felicity Jones as Catherine and JJ Feild as Henry, was about eight years in the making and was finally released in 2007.

The 1987 adaptation marks a point of departure from earlier Austen adaptations. It dispenses with the theatrical, indoor settings, benefiting from outdoor scenes in beautiful locations. The liberty it takes with the content shows less reverence for the issue of fidelity. Wadey's screen play recognizes the gendered psychological dimension that the Gothic plot highlights. The viewer's first encounter with Catherine involves Gothic novel reading rendered in voice-over and followed by scenes emerging out of the novel. In these scenes, Catherine either imagines a dead female body or herself being carried by powerful men. In one of these opening scenes, long before Catherine arrives in Bath, a gloomy General Tilney haunts Catherine's visions as the villain who will later appear in her real-life events as well as in her dreams. The screenplay quite forcefully identifies the General as the Gothic villain, making a connection for the viewer that materializes more gradually in the novel. Due to the frequent recurrence of waking and sleeping dreams, contemporary reviewers have found fault with the sensationalism of this adaptation, a notion which is also supported by fast cutting techniques, stark visuals and often overstated costumes that serve as an almost too obvious means of characterization.[6] As Sue Parrill cautiously suggests, the filmmakers' emphasis on Gothic material, sensationalism included, reflects a recent development in Gothic studies, in particular, the pivotal relationship between novels, women and sexual awakening. Hence, in the movie, Catherine's vivid fantasizing about persecuted and kidnapped women compensates for the dearth of real sexual experience.[7] Parrill, then, concludes that the butt of the joke is not Gothic fiction itself, but its 'unsophisticated' readers, of whom Catherine is one, because she refuses to learn from the lessons of the heroine of the *Mysteries of Udolpho*. The lesson to be learned is the use of reason and self-control, a conclusion, one might say, that ignores some of the most intriguing and complex literary analysis of the novel. To make its point, the film has a sober and rational Catherine burn her copy of *The Mysteries of Udolpho* in a rite of passage that should seal her emancipation from youthful illusions. Hence, the movie exorcizes with equal clarity the very visual fantasies it has conjured.

It is perhaps not surprising that this adaptation has met with disappointment. In '*Northanger Abbey* at the Movies' (1998), Bruce Stovel sees in it a cautionary tale, insisting that the failure can be salutary if future moviemakers keep in mind six qualities and challenges: the self-conscious narrator from which derives the reader's chief enjoyment; the comic disparity between the world as Catherine sees it and as it is; the lack of Gothic content in Catherine's daily life; the integration of the Thorpes even when Catherine is in Bath; the sharpening of Catherine's ability to think and choose for herself; and the lack of action in a novel that looks inwardly into the heroine's psychical development.[8] In particular, Stovel's point about the representation of Catherine's social world is telling about the ways that the novel and the movie orient their audiences. In the novel, the worlds of Bath, of Fullerton and even of the Abbey are less uncanny and disturbing than in the movie, where Gothic atmosphere pervades more or less every location. For this reason, the movie obfuscates the disparity between the world as it is and as Catherine increasingly perceives it through the Gothic lens. Consequently, much of the fun and irony that enliven and complicate the novel do not materialize in the film. This may be exacerbated by the fact that the adaptation never depicts a Catherine free of Gothic fancy: she is a

Gothic reader from the word go, whereas in the novel, she is introduced to the novels by the opportunist Isabella.[9]

Nor does Stovel find any praise for the contrived romantic ending of the 1987 *Northanger Abbey*. Unfolding on a misty field, where Catherine has gone riding, the scene focuses on Henry's arrival and his much-expected reaction, after learning about the cruel treatment Catherine has endured. The entire resolution is encapsulated in her question 'But he knows you are here?' and his answer 'Yes', followed by a kiss and the appearance of Catherine's younger brother who, at the start of the movie, interrupts Catherine's Gothic daydream. In view of such flatness, Stovel, albeit not hostile in principle to adaptations, wishes to remind moviemakers that a picture is not necessarily worth a thousand words, especially 'if the picture is not remarkable and the words are Jane Austen's'.[10] More ambiguously, Marilyn Roberts dubs the 1987 adaptation 'an interesting failure': its interest lies in the visualization of Catherine's sexual pleasure, which leads viewers to identify her absorption in Gothic fiction with a Freudian and Lacanian enjoyment (*jouissance*) of romance reading. However, the excessive, if not grotesque, visualization caters to viewers' voyeuristic appetites, without exploiting them.[11]

The 2007 adaptation, written by Andrew Davies (who had adapted *Pride and Prejudice* for the BBC in 1995) and directed by Jon Jones, has fared better with the critics. Felicity Jones starring as Catherine Morland and Carey Mulligan as Isabella Thorpe, and also the knowledgeable script and solid direction, garnered special praise. Felicity Jones made for a credible and likeable Catherine by embodying 'humility and humour with perfect aplomb'.[12] In the UK, this was the second most-watched of all Austen adaptations, with *Mansfield Park* leading the pack.

Two aspects may have proved particularly appealing to twenty-first-century audiences. As Tamara Wagner notices in 'Shopping Around for Fashion and Fashionable Fiction in Jane Austen Adaptations' (2012), the 2007 adaptation develops two distinct and competing social hermeneutics: Catherine's interpretation of the city of Bath through contemporary popular fiction and Mrs. Allen's investment in the paraphernalia of fashionable society, both linked to the contemporary taste for consumption. Isabella appears in between these trends: she shops for sensational novels and attires that will attract men. Mrs. Allen's devotion to fashion culminates in the scene where a string of servants loads a carriage with the parcels she has purchased.[13] Although such visual materialization and the omission of several dialogues between Mrs. Allen and Mrs. Thorpe tend to turn the former into a slapstick character, the adaptation does credible justice to the fact that no other Austen novel is as concerned with shopping and consumerist pleasure as *Northanger Abbey*.[14]

Pleasure, more precisely erotic pleasure, is also the focus of Jonathon Shears's '"Why Should I Hide My Regard?": Erotic Austen' (2012). Shears compares the adaptations of 1987 and 2007 through the lens of the erotic content that in the novel is organized around codes of courtship and recognizable Regency standards. In the movies, 'these codes are restructured in order to control erotic feelings in different ways, primarily to make them appear consistent throughout the story'.[15] This necessity motivates the opening scenes of the adaptations, both of which foreground Catherine's sexual desires through fiction-fuelled daydreaming. Thus, both adaptations confirm a recurring pattern:

> ■ whereby the desire to reveal, inspect and objectify private sexual feelings, particularly those held by women, leads to a corresponding movement through which they can be supervised and contained.[16] □

Erotic fantasy meets with disciplinary measures of punishment and retribution. The Wadey/Foster adaptation draws on images of bondage, obsession with rape and virginal sacrifices, intensified by the visual experience of Gothicized make-up and the auricular uncanniness of a heavy-metal music score. Both the 1987 and 2007 versions channel the autoerotic energy of the female adolescent as desire shaped through reading or writing. After zooming in and then moving across Catherine's body, the camera focuses on a book, before unfolding the sleeper's dream vision. However, in the Davies/Jones version, Catherine does not even appear as a participant in her own dreams, but as a spectator, for instance when viewing the fight between the two suitors, Henry Tilney and John Thorpe.

Containment as well as evasion of supervision reinforces autoeroticism: an adventure-hungry Catherine hides in order to read, write and, not least, consume the auto-erotic pleasure derived from these activities that Eve Sedgwick calls masturbatory in her seminal and controversial essay 'Jane Austen and the Masturbating Girl' (1991). The channelling of female sexuality into private autoerotic spaces, made explicit in the movies, signals a retreat from the possibility of a social figuring of female erotic life. Shears concludes that such withdrawal testifies to the 'understandable but substantial irony that the paternalistic anxieties that Austen satirized in *Northanger Abbey* are being reduplicated in her adaptation for television and film'.[17] However, Shears treats rather superficially the potential of the movies' blunt visuals to satirize the same anxieties with different means for a modern and uninitiated audience.

The erotic material prompted a *New York Times* critic to write that the 2007 adaptation offers 'innocent faces and heaving breasts, visual hyperboles of the sex that always lurks beneath the surface of Austen's astringent presence', adding that the movie re-enacts and decodes the novel's parodic engrossment with the experience of reading:

> ■ The movie visualizes these fantasies with full submission to their campiness, effectively conveying the novel's ideas about the way pop culture invades our psyches.[18] □

As this review demonstrates, the 2007 film of *Northanger Abbey* is acknowledged for translating a novel portraying a burgeoning nineteenth-century print society into terms recognizable and relevant for a twenty-first-century movie audience. If nothing else, this translation captures Austen's modern acumen and makes more palpable the transition of social constructs from print to pop culture.

Persuasion

Fidelity to the original text remains a contested ground: if a movie aims to be a faithful version of a text in a different medium, then the interest in such an undertaking cannot be about reproduced sameness. On the contrary, the difference and novelty gained by the transfer is the propelling reward. Yet the difference raises the question: what kind of difference is most serviceable? Is it the difference that illuminates details and renders them visible on screen or the difference that aims at reconstructing the spirit of the text in image, words and sound?

As a good example of the negotiation between freedom and fidelity let us take one scene from the 1995 adaptation of *Persuasion*, written by Nick Dear and directed by Roger Michell. This screenplay has Anne witness the servants covering the furniture of Kellynch Hall with white linen in preparation for the family's move to Bath. The house becomes a dead corpse and Anne almost a metonymical extension of it. The next scene sends Anne to the storeroom, where she finds an eight-year-old copy of the *Navy List*, containing a letter folded up into a boat, the visual cue that couples Anne's loss of a home with her loss of Wentworth. Although the connection between the lost home and the rediscovered boat-shaped letter visually conjures the ending of the novel, in which Anne's future home will predictably be a ship, critics have found the image a concentrated and 'a too potent associative testimony' for the 'inner voicing and the agony of private recall' that the narrative administers more slowly.[19]

Knowing and exploiting the medium's own means considerably affects the success of filmic adaptation. This, indeed, seems to define the contrast between the 1971 and 1995 versions of *Persuasion*; while the 1971 version draws on stage techniques, the latter, although less faithful, 'succeeds in finding substitute means' to parallel Anne's inner life. In the 1971 movie, the camera privileges a standpoint that takes in whole rooms, whereas Anne's thoughts (divulged in the novel in free indirect discourse) are communicated out loud as if spoken to the audience facing the stage. As John Wiltshire argues, the 1971 adaptation, written by Julian Mitchell and directed by Howard Baker, fails to transfer novelistic effects and techniques into cinematic ones. On the contrary, the novel's melodramatic affiliation is translated into staged melodrama.[20] It is worth mentioning, however, that these rather conservative aesthetics result greatly from the available technology in 1971. Heavy cameras make shooting outdoors expensive and the dynamic movement of camera and cables within the dramatic space of the set almost impossible. Indeed, the camera can most conveniently glide along the invisible fourth wall of the set, which in the end creates a static and staged picture.[21]

It is perhaps one of the greatest virtues of the 1995 version of *Persuasion* that it does not dismiss the theatricality of the earlier version but rather puts the new technology at its service by emphasizing the dramatic aspect. Roger Sales insists on the importance of a neat balance between dramatization and staging. The 1995 adaptation of *Persuasion* conveys the theatricality of the life of Regency landed gentry without being stagy. The movie offers a smarter use of camera angle, lighting and music. New screen proportions allow for a greater variation in shot size, alternating between close-ups and mid and long shots. In addition, lighter cameras and more advanced editing techniques allow for more dynamic aesthetics: hand-held cameras enable travelling shots, circling cameras provide a balance between the individual and communal, and music is used in sophisticated ways that enhance the story-telling.[22] These new techniques already interact in the opening scenes, where the inventiveness of the producers deserves particular praise. The movie opens with alternating images of the sea, oars moving in synchrony and sailors rowing to the shore, mirrored on land by carriages approaching the grounds of Kellynch Hall, carrying Mr. Shepherd and Lady Russell to the Elliots to discuss the latter's distressed finances.

Inventiveness is also effective in rendering both Anne's withdrawal and her need to confide in someone. For example, prompted to open up to Lady Russell by the boat-shaped letter found in the *Navy List*, after the latter summarizes Anne's life in Kellynch in terms of imprisonment, Anne seizes the moment with the words 'I have never said this –.' However, she is cut short by her godmother who, picking up a book, rambles on about 'these Romantics'. Faithful to the novel's protagonist, Anne, in the movie, withdraws from conversation, submitting to Lady Russell's reluctance to revisit the past. The camera focalized on her face recreates in the spectator the sensation of disheartened compliance that the novel realizes through free indirect speech.[23] Here, we encounter an effective translation of verbal into visual focalization. Appropriately, Wiltshire notes, Anne's face in the movie is pale, blank and reminiscent of the tabula rasa that relegates all significance to thoughts that the reader must conjecture intuitively.[24] Hence, in order to recreate interiority, the film must rely on the unsaid and a different kind of character knowledge from the novel's openings into consciousness. Indeed, reading and viewing the character of Anne does not yield an identical knowledge but a similar emotional response to the depth of subjectivity in which Austen excels.

Sales discusses the male characters in the 1995 version of *Persuasion*, finding their appearances in the movies too suggestive. Clues as to their suitability, made visible through 'transparent looks and mannerisms', undermine the suspense of romance.[25] Anne's acquaintance with Benwick as a potential romantic storyline flounders the moment the viewer sets eyes on an unkempt Benwick. William Elliot fares no better: his duplicity emerges as soon as he opens his mouth in Lyme. In addition, a slightly tilted camera that gives full view of Wentworth's stature when he enters Charles Musgrove's living room establishes him as the uncontested hero of romance, too exquisite for such lightweights as the Musgrove girls. Hence, the suspense of the film suffers from the combination of immediately recognizable male competitors with the absence of adequate females to rival Anne.

Sales offers another key observation: in the movie, we are made aware of the servants who wait upon the gentry but who go unnoticed in the novel, except for the character of Nurse Rooke. Sales notices that Anne and the servants share a blankness of expression (especially at the family table in Kellynch) and a similar treatment by Elizabeth Elliot. Only in the movie does the awareness sink in that Anne is not merely neglected, but through this neglect also humiliated in the presence of the servants. Hence, this public exposure sharpens the edge of her private loss.[26] Marxist-minded critics add that insistence on the presence of servants 'makes it impossible to ignore the fact that the indolence of the Elliots is purchased by the labour of numerous servants and dependents'.[27] Precisely due to this awareness, Tara Goshal Wallace, in 'Filming Romance: *Persuasion*' (2003), finds puzzling some important omissions in the movie such as Sir Walter Elliot's preparations of 'condescending bows for all the afflicted tenantry and cottagers who might have had a hint to show themselves' (*P* 34) or the fishermen who gather around Louisa's unresponsive body 'to be useful if wanted, at any rate, to enjoy the sight of a dead young lady, nay, two young ladies, for it proved twice as fine as the first report' (*P* 93). Yet careful and intelligible handling of intratextuality complements the depiction of class and family relations, for example, when Anne is taken to Uppercross in a farm-cart transporting pigs, while Sir Elliot, Elizabeth and Miss Clay travel to Bath in a carriage attended by liveried servants or when:

> ■ Elizabeth engineers a public announcement that Lady Dalrymple's carriage awaits her. The interweaving of transport and status enriches the spectator's understanding of how Regency society uses class markers.[28]

If Dear's screenplay shows sensitivity to class-based marginalization, it leaves unsatisfied some feminist expectations, so much so that Rebecca Dickson writes of 'a damage done' to the 'quiet feminist force' of the novel.[29] While Devoney Looser wonders why the adaptation, of which she generally approves, omits the scene in which Mrs. Croft takes over the reins from her husband, Dickson finds fault in Dear's decision to exaggerate Elizabeth's coarseness in order to provide a transparent foil for Anne.[30] The more that viewers stumble upon Elizabeth's selfishness, the readier they are to turn to Anne as the ideal character. Although a similar intention may motivate the novel's narrator, the movie sacrifices verisimilitude in its portrayal of women's position and social restrictions in the early nineteenth century. A slouching Elizabeth Elliot, with her legs sprawled on a chair and sucking her fingers after helping herself to a box of chocolate, misrepresents the formal and rank-conscious Elizabeth of the novel and misconstrues women's freedom, thus testifying to a glaring neglect of women's history.[31] Dickson assumes that this neglect results from market pressures in the industry to produce movies that sell by making crude representations on screen of what is subtle on the page. On the other hand, as Carol M. Dole notes, Dear's adaptation refuses the prettification of the costume drama that mainstream audiences are drilled to expect from an Austen-based movie.[32]

Indeed, the 1995 adaptation of *Persuasion* was warmly received by art-house devotees. Beyond this select group, it was reviled precisely for its ungainly cast and the bleak references to the historical context that some reviewers thought to be Brontë-like and, more grievously, a distortion of elegant and homely Austen who, next to Shakespeare, had become the literary icon of 'heritage' nostalgia and content.[33] Some attempts at prettification, as Amanda Collins astutely observes, are made on the poster and the cover of the video cassette of the 1995 *Persuasion*: on the poster, Amanda Root and Ciaran Hinds appear suspended in the moment before the kiss, framed by a blooming rose bower and flower beds, rather than the background of a travelling circus that is parading through Bath and intrudes as a marvellous moment which connects the idea of romantic fulfilment to a 'fantastic spectacle'.[34] Additionally, on the cover of the video cassette, an unknown and attractive couple substitute for the unconventional Root and Hinds. Collins explains this metamorphosis as a response to the reviewers' discomfort with this gritty adaptation. Such attempts at prettification betray a lingering 'disdain for the "real"' that lies at the root of the postmodern nostalgia for a past and an Austen that never existed.[35] The adaptation's final kiss on the streets of Bath provoked the Janeites' displeasure at such an obvious, erotic deviation. Yet before discarding Dear and Mitchell's decision as crowd-pleasing *kitsch*, we must be informed, by Penny Gay's study of theatrical influences in *Persuasion*, that the kiss adopts the 'aesthetics of visibility' of eighteenth-century melodrama, which are also skilfully at play during the scene of Wentworth's arrival at the Elliot's evening party.[36]

Discussing the final scene, Wallace finds no other fault with the lovers' quiet intimacy, offset with the carnivalesque parade, than the 'nervous quiverings' of the heroine played by Amanda Root. Seeing in Ciaran Hinds a mature and very good-looking Wentworth, Wallace doubts the chemistry between the protagonists: how could such a man be moved as profoundly as Wentworth in the novel by a jittery and overtly expressive Anne?[37] Amanda Root's girlish performance and her lack of control over her body (for example, when she cannot repress visible malaise at the mentioning of Wentworth or when she scampers across the Pump Room to seek the company of the Crofts with whom she seems on too familiar terms) would fit a Lydia Bennet in *Pride and Prejudice* or Marianne Dashwood in *Sense and Sensibility* rather than the self-composed Anne Elliot. Wallace could not have predicted that both Anne's 'nervousness' and impulsivity would be only exacerbated by the 2007 version of *Persuasion*. However, before addressing this point, it is worth saying a few words about the 2007 adaptation.

The 2007 adaptation of *Persuasion* was produced to be screened on ITV in the UK and as part of a 'Jane Austen' series within the *Masterpiece* prime time drama series in the US. Consequently, the team came from an experienced television drama background but also a more commercial one. The film was written by Simon Burke and directed by Adrian Shergold, starring Sally Hawkins as Anne and Rupert Penry-Jones as Captain Wentworth. From the beginning, the team envisioned a different version from the previous adaptations. The pressure to do something different and more audience-conscious arose from the changed context of British television. In 2007, television drama was facing a multi-channel and digital reality, which meant that, unlike its predecessors, this adaptation of *Persuasion* could not count on a popular time slot in the schedules and had to compete with business-minded channels. In addition, the co-production with the American WGBH only increased the pressure of producing a film that would sell across the US and worldwide.[38] In order to secure the sympathies of young viewers, the interpretative energies went into highlighting the love story between Anne and Wentworth.

As Sarah Cardwell emphasizes in her essay 'Persuaded? The Impact of Changing Production Contexts on Three Adaptations of *Persuasion*' (2014), the 2007 film benefits from a new technology that enabled unprecedented screen proportions. A wider screen, now standard in Europe, makes it possible to explore space in more creative ways, meaning that long shots of houses, grounds and landscapes provide a better sense of the world surrounding the lonely female protagonist.[39] The new proportions also allow for more natural distance between characters, as well as between characters and viewers, which leads to 'less "distanced" aesthetics' than in the 1971 and 1995 versions. Nonetheless, the 2007 adaptation would feel less 'choppy and disconnected' if the very long shots of landscapes and houses, to which the widescreen lends itself, were not mismatched by extreme close-ups that do not tally well with the new screen proportion, because either part of the human head must be left out or surrounded by a great deal of redundant space.[40] Perhaps Cardwell's strongest charge against this adaptation, however, is the mismatch between new technology and the antiquated narrating strategy of voice-over, compounded by the equally exhausted topos of journal-keeping, as when a stunned Anne relates the encounter with Wentworth in her journal. Cardwell finds this solution an unnecessary break not only with the novel's narrative choice but also with that of earlier adaptations of *Persuasion*:

> ■ This simplistic technique for expressing point of view lacks the sophistication of either the 1971 and 1995 versions, and implies little trust in the viewer's ability to draw inferences from the actor's performance and the programme's aesthetic choices.[41] □

Perhaps critics found an additional clash between the extreme close-ups conveying focalization and interiority and the movie's fast pace. Not surprisingly, a reviewer writes that the 'new' *Persuasion* 'is hurried and forgettable'.[42] As Cardwell puts it, in light of the oddly modern and old-fashioned 2007 version, the one from 1971, though stagy, stilted and dated, gives the drama of *Persuasion* time to breathe with its long shots, assured handling of the material, slow unfolding of the plot and the frequent absence of music or dialogue.[43]

The hurriedness, if not nervousness, of the 2007 adaptation is heightened by an extroverted Sally Hawkins as Anne Elliot, whose facial restlessness is accentuated by the adaptation's extreme close-ups.[44] Moreover, if the 1995 Anne Elliot is censured by critics for scampering around like a teenage girl, the final scene of the 2007 version, also culminating with a long-drawn kiss between the protagonists, has Anne Elliot sprint through Bath in search of Captain Wentworth.

John Wiltshire elaborates convincingly on this climax of the 2007 adaptation, raising it to a case study to tackle the question of fidelity. The choice for such a physical climax attempts to compensate for the poor use of two opportunities that are present in the novel and skilfully deployed in the 1995 *Persuasion*, to render Anne's grief and her movement from being an 'abjected listener' to a spokesperson of constancy.[45] The first moment reveals to the reader Anne's thoughts about Benwick's mourning of Phoebe Harville, envying his younger age and better prospects: 'he has not, perhaps, a more sorrowing heart than I have. [...] He is younger than I am, younger in feeling, if not in fact; younger as a man. He will rally again, and be happy with another' (*P* 82). The 1995 *Persuasion* converts this silent monologue into a dialogue between Anne and Captain Benwick, where Anne soothes the bereaved lover by saying 'You will rally again.' Benwick resists her optimism, assuring her that she cannot fathom the depths of his grief, to which she quietly counters: 'Yes, I can.' In the 2007 adaptation, this shared moment is bundled together in Anne's words to Benwick: 'You are still young, and I pray you may one day rally and be happy again.' The wording of the sequence evinces a double intertextuality, that is, between the movies and the novel, but also between the 1995 adaptation and its successor. Yet, as Wilshire argues, it also evinces the potentiality of intertextuality to improve or collapse its source:

> ■ Lifting the sentiment out of Anne's self-communings and inserting it into each dramatic scene minimizes the self-pity that threatens here to ambush Austen's conception of the character, and arguably improves on the novel. But the earlier film, by allowing Anne to listen to Benwick's 'You cannot know the depths of my despair' and responding softly that she can, makes Benwick's articulated sorrow the vehicle for Anne's unspoken grief. In the successor version, Anne appears to be merely making politely consolatory remarks.[46] □

Clearly, the 2007 *Persuasion* does not look back only to the novel but also to its powerful cinematic predecessor of 1995.

A second moment in which the 2007 adaptation strikes the knowledgeable viewer/reader as an unsatisfactory hybrid of the novel and the 1995 version is the dialogue in which Anne breaks her silence and defends her own (and women's) constancy when all hope is gone. The scene in 2007 involves Anne and Benwick, not Captain Harville. Spoken in the absence of Wentworth, the scene only attempts to live up to the intensity of Anne's identification with bereavement that had been portrayed in the above-mentioned dialogue between Anne and Benwick in the 1995 version. The greatest loss is the double audience (Harville and Wentworth) on which the scene builds in the novel and in the 1995 adaptation. Having lost the opportunity to portray a climax that Anne in the novel experiences as 'a revolution almost beyond expression', the 2007 adaptation must find another way to bring the events to a close. Its choice is then to send Anne running along the Royal Crescent, a decision that deprives her of the reversal of positions that we witness in the novel and in the 1995 movie. Anne, up to this moment a listener constantly invaded by all kinds of conversations, speaks and subjects Wentworth to a listening position. To rob Anne of the opportunity to effect the dénouement in her own words is to misread the narratological, political and emotional resolution of the story. Hence, Wiltshire asks critics who disparagingly circumvent the question of fidelity:

> ■ What can a criticism which responsibly takes the opportunities offered by these films to revisit and review the novels that are at their source, call it, but an act of infidelity?[47] □

Such meticulous comparative analysis of intertextuality between different filmic versions and the source text demonstrates, against critics who require that as moviegoers and critics we remain uninfluenced by the source text, that the informed novel reader can be an ideal reader of the film.[48]

CONCLUSION

In the course of nearly two hundred years since the publication of *Northanger Abbey* and *Persuasion*, a critical trajectory has emerged that reveals to readers the value of sustained criticism itself or, even better, the ways criticism enhances the reading experience. As this guide hopes to have shown by structuring the chapters diachronically and thematically, enhancement consists in the deepening of existing aspects and the investigation of new ones.

At the time of publication, *Northanger Abbey* drew attention for its treatment of the Gothic, the tension between the natural and the probable and the dramatic quality of its prose. In the centuries that followed, these themes were revisited, expanded and deepened in illuminating ways. The question of genre serves as a telling case. The first reviewers of the novel argued that *Northanger Abbey* wore its Gothic allusions too visibly: the experiment of an apprentice, the novel's parody lacked moral and formal sophistication. The biographies published in the second half of the century convinced even some otherwise perceptive readers that the novel, written in continuation of the author's juvenilia, could not compare with her mature work. However, later critics, spurred by the unbroken Austen hype and the rise of Gothic studies, went on to examine the novel's relationship with the most influential fiction of the day, in particular Ann Radcliffe's. Moreover, a key eighteenth-century concept like the sublime (first encountered in the work of Edmund Burke and later in that of women novelists and philosophers) opened up the novel to unprecedented discussions about moral judgement. Further unprecedented insights came from psychoanalytic critics: textual and etymological interpretations of the notion of the uncanny saw the Gothic parody blending the visible with the invisible, the familiar with the unfamiliar and the private with the public surveillance. It was a blend that, by reinscribing the Gothic into the British parlour, unsettled the very comforts that readers expected to find in the sphere of domestic familiarity. In addition, this merger reflected upon the importance of reading as a process of maturation in order to repudiate an understanding of the Gothic as mere entertainment through harmless parody. It was a narratorial strategy that posited a female reading subject striving for autonomy in the presence of male arbiters of taste and morality and an example of the (sometimes) unacknowledged dialogue that fiction seeks with the political events, philosophical concerns and cultural discourse of its time. In light of such a matrix of questions, it has become impossible to speak of the irony of *Northanger Abbey* in terms of a straightforward satire of naïve novel readers or of an uncomplicated endorsement of the Gothic genre.

The sprawling interpretations of the Gothic also bear on discussions of character. While in the nineteenth century the majority of critical voices endorse Catherine's playfulness and candour, so skilfully contrasted to Isabella Thorpe's cunning, some influential twentieth-century critics find Catherine a too sketchy and naïve character to master the yoking together of realist and Gothic impulses. Henry Tilney, for some readers a stick of a character, functions for others as the narrator's mouthpiece. In particular, his almost misanthropic commentary on a neighbourhood of spies seems to speak the language of acerbic irony redolent of Austen's letters. The role critics attribute to Henry Tilney appears to determine Austen's gender politics. If Henry is the reliable centre of the narrative, then Austen has rather faithfully adopted the eighteenth-century trope of the mentoring male lover who takes to heart the task of educating the young girl. However, as numerous critics insist, Henry's bias towards the male characters of his family (his father and his brother), detectable in his reluctance to submit them to the kind of parodic play that he jocosely reserves for Catherine and all other female characters, testifies to his moral blind spots. Such analyses have the double benefit of demonstrating a similar gender bias in the very critical apparatus that places irrefutable trust in a genderless idea of common sense. This reflects the main concern and practice of feminist criticism, which is to question the very basis of critical interpretation by reminding readers again and again that literature is not a gender-neutral product, nor is the criticism to which it gives rise.

Some of the most exciting interpretations occur when critics venture to demonstrate how Austen borrows and transforms existing ideas. For instance, few critics doubt Austen's preoccupation with education, but increasingly this theme is brought into connection with the role of reading. Hence, it is not Henry, but the novel, that is a vehicle of education. However, is it the only one? What about history? Where does the frontier lie between fiction and history? Read from this perspective, *Northanger Abbey* confronts us with complex questions to which no single character can offer conclusive answers. Contemporary attempts to define history and the novel pivot on the roles of imagination and invention. Austen absorbs these discursive attempts. She never relinquishes the urge to investigate available dichotomies in order to elevate the cultural labour accomplished by the novel, albeit without allotting to any single kind of writing the power to provide a comprehensive view.

The inquisitive spirit that we see Catherine develop through the confrontation of novel narratives (the persecutions of Radcliffean Gothic) and real-life narratives (the oppression of Eleanor Tilney and the lonely death of her mother) dramatizes one of the most oxymoronic expectations of Romanticism: education in natural feeling. If we consider Austen's choice to build her story around an inexperienced, simple-minded heroine in light of the long eighteenth century's educational and horticultural treatises, we understand that the novel grapples with the uneasy categories of naturalness and artificiality. Another blind spot related to the role of the educator surfaces in the era's ambition to cultivate presumed natural propensities. The conceptual delusion behind any educator who believes in good faith to be performing the work of nature is embodied by Henry Tilney, whose influence upon Catherine approximates that of the educationalist who regards cultivation as the execution of an innate blueprint. In a novel, where the naïve but stubborn heroine stumbles upon the educator's version of natural truth, cultivation in naturalness disguises the educator's desire for the pupil's (political) docility. When Henry believes that his instruction cultivates Catherine's innate taste, the novel not only ironizes self-congratulatory illusion, but also distrusts any recognizable boundaries between the real and the illusory. Not simply because they overlap, but because the illusory can very well provoke real consequences. Catherine's Gothic illusions lead her into a Gothic theatre of the mind where the psyche's emotional responses are lived as physical realities. Similarly, Henry's possible illusion that he is tapping into Catherine's innate resources creates and naturalizes its effects: Catherine truly develops a taste for the picturesque and hyacinths.

Persuasion has had an equally active afterlife. Not an indisputable favourite with contemporary readers who thought it to be less sparkling, less round in plot and character than the earlier novels, *Persuasion* has, in the course of two hundred years, proven a reassuring testimony for readers who seek traces of Austen's engagement with Romantic aesthetics and historical phenomena. Nowhere, it has been argued, does Austen tackle as openly the burden of history as in *Persuasion*, whereby history should be understood as gendered (his story/her story) and embodied (bearing markers of class and nationality). Neither *Persuasion*'s Romantic nor its historical leanings seemed so sure in the nineteenth century. On the contrary, even some of the most appreciative critics spoke in terms of a restrained imagination that underlay the restricted set of mostly unlikeable characters and selective realism. Both kinds of restraints implied the narrator's emotional coldness towards her characters and their historical circumstances. These are the years where the myth of an ahistorical Austen, germinating in the biographical note that her brother wrote, takes shape.

It was only in the last three decades of the twentieth century that critics recovered the intricate embedment of the plot of *Persuasion* in the reversals of the Napoleonic Wars. The chosen temporal frame demonstrates Austen's conscious decision to separate by almost a year the narrating time from the time of composition. The novel was begun after Napoleon Bonaparte's escape from Elba and his ultimate defeat at Waterloo in June 1815. *Persuasion*'s story starts to unfold in the summer of 1814, the summer of the Treaty of Paris, only a few months after Napoleon's exile to Elba in April 1814. A time of peace is interrupted by Napoleon's return in March 1815, a mere few weeks after the reconciliation of Anne and Wentworth at the White Hart, so that *Persuasion* ends just before the news of Napoleon's escape reaches British shores and war breaks out again. Such a tucking in of the romance between two anxiety-ridden moments in British history increases the precariousness of the happy ending.

The historical pulse of the novel matches the narrative's contemporary aesthetic awareness, particularly the magisterial reliance on Romantic themes such as the correspondence between the self, natural world and social environment. Already at the beginning of the twentieth century, critics recognized a pattern of mourning in Anne's relationship to her past, to the decline of the estate and to nature itself, so that melancholy becomes the common denominator of experiences of the self, nature and society. In the second half of the twentieth century, critics located the novel's Romantic aesthetics in the recurring motif of loss. A reassessment of Austen's position in the canon of Romantic literature has led to a convergence of historicizing and textual analysis. The analysis of Austen's use of free indirect speech exemplifies the power of such a combination of methodologies. In *Persuasion*, Austen foregrounds subjectivity through a rhetoric of estrangement: Anne's alienation within her family renders doubly painful her estrangement from Wentworth. This alienation weighs heavier in the first volume, where Anne's thoughts and perceptions often reach the reader in free indirect discourse, a device that she borrows from Ann Radcliffe's novels. Her Romantic affiliations seem the more complex when one realizes that the free indirect discourse highlights a conception of time similar to that in Byron's Turkish tales, where the past is telescoped and endured as something irrevocably lost and irreplaceable. Indeed, Anne's fixation on Wentworth, her staunch defence of constancy, resonates with key Romantic texts like Byron's *The Giaour, The Corsair* or *The Bride of Abydos*.

Yet if Byron genders constancy by celebrating it as an ideal of his male protagonists, Austen validates Anne's doubts, loss and risky commitment to Wentworth, thus aligning herself with another Romantic text: *The Wrongs of Woman, or Maria*, where Wollstonecraft vindicates women's right to live and mature through direct experience rather than inculcation. As one critic emphasizes, even in Anne's conviction that Lady Russell, an affectionate surrogate mother, deserved Anne's compliance, we can detect the influence of Wollstonecraft's groundbreaking *The Rights of Woman*, where a notion of moral autonomy is articulated that anticipates the revisionary work of twenty-first-century feminist thinkers. The very title of the novel, *Persuasion*, captures the coexistence of conviction and malleability, self-mastery and compliance. For Wollstonecraft, self-chosen compliance to a loving parent does not overwrite individual autonomy. In *Persuasion*, Lady Russell's entitlement to such daughterly compliance results from the central absence in Anne's life: her mother, the former prudent mistress of Kellynch Hall, whose death taints with melancholia even Anne's love for Wentworth. Anne mourns Wentworth with such constancy because she has transferred onto him the primeval loss of her mother. It is the process of coping with this loss that binds Anne both to Lady Russell and Wentworth.

For more text-minded critics of the twenty-first century, *Persuasion*'s indebtedness to Romantic aesthetics, expressed in the rhetoric of mourning and erotic fixation, ruins Austen's incomparable irony. Here, the narrator breaks with her usual impersonality (or the detachment that made Victorian reviewers uneasy and which was vehemently denied by Janeites until and after D. W. Harding wrote of Austen's 'regulated hatred'). With Anne at its centre, the narrative becomes personified by her perspective. Austen allows her protagonist to hijack the narrator's voice, erasing the distance that enables the kind of chastisement present in character-focalized novels, such as *Emma* or *Mansfield Park*. Anne's mortification precludes and assimilates the narrator's derision. Yet other critics disagree, maintaining that, although most events and characters interest us mainly because they provide us with access to Anne's inner world, not every word is the product of this world. Characters like Sir Walter Elliot or Elizabeth show that the stakes of Austen's irony are raised to encompass the parasitic lifestyle and moral bankruptcy of the ruling ranks.

Significantly, the landed class is shown to be in dire financial distress due to fiscal irresponsibility. The fate of the estate runs through all of Austen's novels; indeed, the estate appears as the seat of financial and cultural power. In *Northanger Abbey*, the anxiety about the survival of the estate in an industrial society echoes with every chiming of the clocks. Even though Catherine remains unimpressed by the General's agricultural and industrial modernization, the novel registers the pressures of a market striving for industrialist efficacy that will take its toll on a culture of leisure. This is a lesson that Sir Walter of Kellynch Hall refuses to learn and to prepare for.

In *Persuasion*, the estate emerges as an abandoned home. Critics have reached no consensus about the future of Kellynch Hall, a synecdoche for the position of the landed class. Between those who argue that the novel hails a meritorious age led by the professional class and others who soberly remind us that the beginning of the nineteenth century was not the first moment in history in which the aristocracy had to adapt to new economic conditions in order to survive – after all, Sir Walter is not the first prodigal baronet – more text-oriented interpretations remind us that the estate faces the constant danger of transmuting into a mere commodity of exchange. This awareness reverberates in the passing of the estate from one family to another but more importantly in the final sale contemplated by young William Elliot, who well before setting foot in Kellynch hears the auctioneer's hammer. Fittingly, the language of commerce and property permeates all kinds of sensibility. As such, language in *Persuasion* is experienced as inadequate to convey in words the authenticity of private experience. Linguistic expression can only give shape by clothing, hence covering, thoughts and feelings. Austen's acute awareness of the opacity of represented interiority characterizes the language chosen for the resolution of the romance and distinguishes the revised final chapters of the novel from the unpublished ones.

In view of such rich scholarship, the filmic adaptations face the double challenge of transferring the linguistic text of the novels into a medium of visual and auditory signs while absorbing the ever-growing critical interpretations and perspectives they have generated. Historicization and the examination of gender politics, two key tenets of recent criticism, also make themselves at home in the adaptations, particularly those produced in the last three decades. In the adaptations of *Northanger Abbey*, the relationship between Austen's parody and late-eighteenth-century Gothic translates onto the screen the seductive power of fiction, which is capable of conjuring a mental theatre. The uninitiated modern viewer, helped by at times exaggerated and explicit visuals, replicates Catherine Morland's reading experience of Gothic fiction. Highlighting reading as both a pleasurable and instructive activity, the adaptations recognize the social character of desire, especially female desire. Catherine appears as not only a reading but also a desiring subject, for whom Gothic novels represent a source of imitation, instruction and erotic enjoyment. Even in one adaptation, where the heroine, on the path to maturity, must exorcize Gothic novels as youthful delusions, the psychological exploration made possible by the Gothic casts maturity as the honing of the heroine's interpretative skills. Hence, the adaptations draw on the insights of literary criticism to convey the performative role that the novel played in the formation of modern subjectivity. In addition, the viewer is immersed in a world where novels can be consumed like mere commodities. In such a society, an inquisitive reading practice makes the difference between consumers and readers.

Historicization has been a core criterion in the evaluation of the film adaptations of *Persuasion*. With increasing emphasis, critics have praised or found lacking the adaptations' engagement with the Napoleonic Wars, representations of the estate and the portrayals of Anne and Wentworth. In particular, literary critics welcome adaptations that capture on screen the bleakness and fragile hope of the novel by attending to the period's precarious political and economic context. The 1995 adaptation by Dear and Michell, more than any other, fearlessly recreates the novel's romance without dipping into the repertoire of commercially oriented strategies. The hardship of a sailor's life materializes in the physical ruggedness of Wentworth, while Anne's helplessness in the face of the neglected and abandoned estate compounds her insignificance within her foolish family and in the presence of the servants. Admittedly, such directorial courage goes against the tide of the interminable Austenmania that draws on and contributes to the image of Austen as the author of happy endings and heritage nostalgia, encouraged also by filmic adaptations of her other novels.

The wealth of recent literary criticism, as discussed in Chapter 7 of this guide, demonstrates that the pressures of Austenmania continue to be confronted by scholarly criticism. Indeed, Chapter 7 owes its title to the international conference 'New Directions in Austen Studies', held in the summer of 2009 in Chawton, where Austen spent the last eight years of her life. These were prolific years in which she revised her early novels and wrote new ones. But, as Kathryn Sutherland remarked in her keynote speech at this conference, there are also silences among these years.[1] The most glaring is the two-year gap in Austen's letters following her arrival in Chawton in 1809. It remains to be discovered what lies behind this silence and what compelled Austen to start revising the novels that became *Sense and Sensibility*, *Pride and Prejudice* and *Northanger Abbey*. Other areas in need of further elaboration regard the novels' dialogue with the trends, events and concerns of their time. Equally important is the in-depth exploration of the impact that Austen's artistry had on the genre of the novel and not just on the realist novel. These explorations will benefit from Kathryn Sutherland's research on Austen's manuscripts, which are rare treasures, considering that 'Austen is the first novelist for whom we have a substantial body of manuscript remains.'[2] Textual research promises important insights about stylistic aspects such as the fluency of Austen's diction, her choice of punctuation and mastery of conversation. In an ever more interactive world, Austen's afterlives require sustained and interconnected criticism, in continuation of recent studies such as Claudia L. Johnson's *Jane Austen's Cults and Cultures* (2012), the collection of essays edited by Laurence Raw and Robert G. Dryden, *Global Jane Austen: Pleasure, Passion, and Possessiveness in the Jane Austen Community* (2013), and Kylie Mirmohamadi's *The Digital Afterlives of Jane Austen: Janeites at the Keyboard* (2014).[3]

The need for ongoing research is even more pressing in a digital era. Browsing among the countless Jane Austen fan sites, blogs, online communities and forums shows that the image of a bonnets-and-balls Austen travels far and fast. It speaks for the stubbornness of this image that even the cover of the DVD of a brave version of *Persuasion* such as the one by Dear and Michell shows Anne and Wentworth under a rose bower with the estate intact and the caption: 'A fairytale for adults! A splendid motion picture!' Not surprisingly, watching adaptations of her novels has become a yearly communal ritual among the initially iconophobic Janeites. With Austen becoming a favourite of the Hollywood machinery, the number of her devotees within and outside of academia has exploded. It remains the challenge and joy of future criticism to provide readings of her novels, in their literary or filmic versions, that enhance their readers and viewers' own interpretative powers.

Notes

INTRODUCTION

1. Jane Austen to Cassandra Austen, 24 January 1809, in *Jane Austen's Letters*, ed. and coll. by Deirdre Le Faye (Oxford: Oxford University Press, 1997), p. 169.
2. Kathryn Sutherland, 'Chronology of Composition and Publication,' in Janet Todd (ed.), *Jane Austen in Context* (Cambridge: Cambridge University Press, 2005), pp. 12–22.
3. Alexander Pope, *Essay on Man*, ed. Maynard Mack (New Haven: Yale University Press, 1950), Epistle 1, l. 294.
4. Kathryn Sutherland, *Austen's Textual Lives: From Aeschylus to Bollywood* (Oxford: Oxford University Press, 2005), p. 36.
5. Claudia Johnson, *Jane Austen's Cults and Cultures* (Chicago: Chicago University Press, 2012), p. 122.
6. Sue Parrill, *Jane Austen of Film and Television: A Critical Study of the Adaptations* (Jefferson, NC: McFarland, 2002), p. 155.

1 FROM PEN TO PRINT

1. Barbara M. Benedict and Deirdre Le Faye, Introduction to *Northanger Abbey* (Cambridge University Press, 2006), pp. xxiii–lxii, p. xxix.
2. Jane Austen, *Northanger Abbey*, ed. Marilyn Butler (London: Penguin, 2003), p. 13. Hereafter referred to as *NA*. Future references will be given parenthetically within the body of the text.
3. Jan Fergus, *Jane Austen: A Literary Life* (New York: St. Martin's Press, 1991), p. 22.
4. Jane Austen to James Edward Leigh-Austen, 16 December 1816, Le Faye (1997), p. 323.
5. Deirdre Le Faye, *Jane Austen: A Family Record* (1989; Cambridge: Cambridge University Press, 2004), p. 233.
6. Sutherland, 'Chronology of Composition and Publication' (2005), p. 16.
7. Jane Austen to Fanny Knight, 13 March 1817, Le Faye (1997), p. 333.
8. Janet Todd and Antje Blank, Introduction to Persuasion (Cambridge: Cambridge University Press, 2006), pp. xxi–lxxxii, p. xl.
9. Jane Austen to Fanny Knight, 13 March 1817, Le Faye (1997), p. 333.
10. Jane Austen to Fanny Knight, 25 March 1817, Le Faye (1997), p. 335.
11. Peter Garside, 'The English Novel in the Romantic Era: Consolidation and Dispersal', in Peter Garside, James Raven and Rainer Schöwerling (eds), *The English Novel 1770–1829: A Bibliographical Survey of Prose Fiction Published in the British Isles*, 2 vols (Oxford: Oxford University Press, 2000), vol. 2, pp. 15–103, p. 39.
12. The first edition of *Emma*, however, consisted of 2,000 copies, outnumbering the first edition of *Northanger Abbey* and *Persuasion* by 250.
13. Ioan Williams (ed.), *Novel and Romance, 1700–1800: A Documentary Record* (London: Routledge and Kegan Paul, 1970), p. 27.
14. Williams (1970), p. 27.
15. Clara Reeve, *The Progress of Romance*, 2 vols (Colchester: W. Keymer, 1785), vol. 1, p. 111.
16. Reeve (1785), p. 8.

17. Williams (1970), p. 433.
18. William St. Clair, *The Reading Nation in the Romantic Period* (Cambridge: Cambridge University Press, 2004), p. 20. See also James Raven, 'Book production', in Janet Todd (ed.), *Jane Austen in Context* (Cambridge: Cambridge University Press, 2005), pp. 194–203, p. 195.
19. James Raven, 'Historical Introduction: The Novels Come of Age', in Peter Garside, James Raven and Rainer Schöwerling (eds), *The English Novel 1770–1829: A Bibliographical Survey of Prose Fiction Published in the British Isles*, 2 vols (Oxford: Oxford University Press, 2000), vol. 1, pp. 15–121, p. 114.
20. Samuel Johnson, 'Rambler 4', in Donald Greene (ed.), *Samuel Johnson: Major Works* (Oxford: Oxford University Press, 2008), pp. 175–6.
21. *The Critical Review* (August 1791), p. 477.
22. The word featured in the title of the second edition of the novel *The Castle of Otranto: A Gothic Story* (1765). 'Gothic' at the time signified old-fashioned or obsolete.
23. Horace Walpole, *The Castle of Otranto*, ed. Emma Clery (Oxford: Oxford University Press, 1996), p. 9.
24. Robert Miles, 'The 1790s: The Effulgence of Gothic', in Jerrold Hogle (ed.), *The Cambridge Companion to Gothic Fiction* (Cambridge: Cambridge University Press, 2002), pp. 40–62, p. 42.
25. Jane Austen, *Pride and Prejudice*, ed. Vivien Jones (London: Penguin Classics, 1996), p. 114.
26. Claudia L. Johnson, *Jane Austen's Cults and Cultures* (Chicago: University of Chicago Press, 2012), p. 21.
27. Le Faye (1997), p. 217.
28. Le Faye (1997), p. 277.
29. Jan Fergus, 'The Professional Woman Writer,' in Edward Copeland and Juliet McMaster (eds), *The Cambridge Companion to Jane Austen* (Cambridge: Cambridge University Press, 2011) pp. 1–19, p. 16.

2 CONTEMPORARY RECEPTION, 1818–1840s

1. Garside (2000), vol. 2, p. 75. Only in the 1820s did male novelists dominate the genre again. *The Critical Review* (June 1792), p. 132.
2. *The British Critic* 9 (March 1818), pp. 293–301.
3. *British Critic* (1818), p. 294.
4. *British Critic* (1818), p. 297.
5. *British Critic* (1818), p. 297.
6. *British Critic* (1818), p. 297.
7. *Blackwood's Edinburgh Magazine* 2 (May 1818), pp. 453–55, p. 454.
8. *Blackwood's Edinburgh Magazine* (1818), p. 454.
9. *Blackwood's Edinburgh Magazine* (1818), p. 454.
10. *Blackwood's Edinburgh Magazine* (1818), p. 454.
11. *British Critic* (1818), p. 298.
12. *Blackwood's Edinburgh Magazine* (1818), p. 454.
13. *British Critic* (1818), p. 294.
14. *British Critic* (1818), p. 301.
15. *The Gentleman's Magazine* 88 (July 1818), pp. 52–3, p. 53.
16. *Blackwood's Edinburgh Magazine* (1818), p. 454.
17. *The Quarterly Review* 24 (January 1821), pp. 353–76, p. 357.
18. *Quarterly Review* (1821), p. 357.
19. *Quarterly Review* (1821), p. 358.
20. *Blackwood's Edinburgh Magazine* (1818), p. 454. The *British Critic* praises her 'good sense', p. 298.

21. *British Critic* (1818), p. 298; *Quarterly Review* (1821), p. 376.
22. *British Critic* (1818), p. 298.
23. *Blackwood's Edinburgh Magazine* (1818), p. 454.
24. *Blackwood's Edinburgh Magazine* (1818), p. 455.
25. *British Critic* (1818), p. 301.
26. Maria Edgeworth to Mrs. Ruxton, 21 February 1818. Cited from reprint in Brian Southam (ed.), *Jane Austen: The Critical Heritage*, 2 vols (London: Routledge and Kegan Paul, 1968–87), vol. 1, p. 17.
27. *Quarterly Review* (1821), p. 355.
28. *Quarterly Review* (1821), p. 356.
29. *Quarterly Review* (1821), p. 367.
30. *Quarterly Review* (1821), p. 367.
31. *British Critic* (1818), p. 301; *Blackwood's Edinburgh Magazine* (1818), p. 454.
32. *Quarterly Review* (1821), p. 368.
33. *Quarterly Review* (1821), p. 368.
34. *Quarterly Review* (1821), p. 368.
35. *Quarterly Review* (1821), p. 368.
36. *Quarterly Review* (1821), p. 368; *British Critic* (1818), p. 298.
37. *Quarterly Review* (1821), p. 368.
38. *Quarterly Review* (1821), p. 372.
39. *Quarterly Review* (1821), p. 374.
40. *The Retrospective Review* 7 (1823), pp. 131–5. Cited from reprint in *The Critical Heritage*, vol. 1, p. 113.
41. Mary Shelley to Edward Moxon, 4 April 1839. Mary Shelley, *The Letters of Mary Shelley*, ed. F. L. Jones, vol. 2, p. 133. Cited from reprint in *The Critical Heritage*, vol. 1, p. 23.
42. William Macready (8 July 1836). Cited from reprint in *The Critical Heritage*, vol. 1, p. 118.
43. Henry Crabb Robinson (18 September 1842). Cited from reprint in *The Critical Heritage*, vol. 1, p. 86.
44. Southam (1968), vol. 1, p. 18.
45. *The Edinburgh Review* 53 (July 1830), pp. 448–51. Cited from reprint in *The Critical Heritage*, vol. 1, p. 114.
46. *Edinburgh Review* (1830), CH I, p. 114.
47. Robert Southey (8 April 1830). Cited from reprint in *The Critical Heritage*, vol. 1, p. 116; Sara Coleridge, *Memoirs and Letter of Sara Coleridge*, ed. E. Coleridge (London: H. S. King, 1873), vol. 1, p. 75. Cited from reprint in The Critical Heritage, vol. 1, p. 117.
48. Charlotte Brontë to George Henry Lewes, 18 January 1848. Cited from reprint in *The Critical Heritage*, vol. 1, p. 127.
49. George H. Lewes, 'Recent Novels: French and English', *Fraser's Magazine* 36 (December 1847), p. 687. Cited from reprint in *The Critical Heritage*, vol. 1, p. 124.
50. Charlotte Brontë to George Henry Lewes, 18 January 1848 in T. J. Wise and J. A Symington (eds), *The Brontës: Their Lives, Friendships, and Correspondence* 4 vols (Oxford: Blackwell, 1932), vol. 2, pp. 180–1. Cited from reprint in *The Critical Heritage*, vol. 1, p. 127.

3 VICTORIAN READERS, 1850s–1900s

1. Lewes laments William Hazlitt's omission of Austen in his *Lectures on the Comic Writers* (1819), where Ann Radcliffe, Fanny Burney, Amelia Opie and Maria Edgeworth feature prominently. George Lewes, 'The Novels of Jane Austen', *Blackwood's Edinburgh Magazine* 86 (July 1859), pp. 99–113; cited from reprint in *The Critical Heritage*, vol. 1, pp. 148–66, p. 148.

2. Richard Simpson, 'Memoir', *North British Review* 52 (April 1870), pp. 129–52; cited from reprint in *The Critical Heritage*, vol. 1, pp. 241–65, p. 241.
3. Lewes (1859), *CH I*, p. 149.
4. Lewes (1859), *CH I*, p. 154.
5. Lewes (1859), *CH I*, p. 155.
6. Simpson (1870), *CH I*, pp. 243–4.
7. Lewes (1859), *CH I*, p. 155.
8. Lewes (1859), *CH I*, p. 159.
9. Lewes (1859), *CH I*, p. 161.
10. Julia Kavanagh, 'Miss Austen's Six Novels', in *English Women of Letters* (1862), pp. 251–74; cited from reprint in *The Critical Heritage*, vol. 1, pp. 176–98.
11. William F. Pollock, 'British Novelists – Richardson, Miss Austen, Scott', *Fraser's Magazine* 61 (January 1860), pp. 30–5; cited from reprint in *The Critical Heritage*, vol. 1, pp. 167–74, p. 167.
12. Margaret Oliphant, 'Miss Austen and Miss Mitford', *Blackwood's Edinburgh Magazine* 107 (March 1870), pp. 290–305; cited from reprint in *The Critical Heritage*, vol. 1, pp. 215–26, p. 215.
13. Anonymous (1866), *CH II*, p. 202.
14. Richard Holt Hutton, 'The Memoir of Miss Austen', *Spectator* (25 December 1869), pp. 1533–5; cited from reprint in *The Critical Heritage*, vol. 2, pp. 160–4, p. 163.
15. Leslie Stephen, 'Humour', *Cornhill Magazine* 33 (1876), pp. 324–5; cited from reprint in *The Critical Heritage*, vol. 2, pp. 173–5, p. 175.
16. Simpson (1870), *CH I*, p. 250.
17. Simpson (1870), *CH I*, p. 251.
18. George Pellew, *Jane Austen's Novels* (Boston: Cupples, Upham, 1883); cited from reprint in *The Critical Heritage*, vol. 2, pp. 176–9, p. 178.
19. Pellew (1833), *CH II*, p. 178.
20. George Moore, 'Turgeneff', *Fortnightly Review* 43 (February 1888), pp. 237–51; cited from reprint in *The Critical Heritage*, vol. 2, pp. 187–8, p. 188.
21. William B. S. Clymer, 'A Note on Jane Austen', *Scribner's Magazine* (February 1891), pp. 377–84, p. 378.
22. Goldwin Smith, 'Jane Austen', *Great Writers Series* (1890), pp. 185–91; cited from reprint in *The Critical Heritage*, vol. 2, pp. 189–91, p. 191.
23. Anonymous, 'Jane Austen', in *Eminent Women Series* (1889), pp. 209–10; cited from reprint in *The Critical Heritage*, vol. 2, pp. 188–9, p. 189.
24. Eneas Sweetland Dallas, 'Felix Holt, the Radical', *The Times* (26 June 1866), p. 6; cited from reprint in *The Critical Heritage*, vol. 1, p. 199.
25. Pollock (1860); cited from reprint in *The Critical Heritage*, vol. 1, pp. 167–74, p. 167. John Mackinnon Robertson, 'Jane Austen', *Criticism* 1 (1902), pp. 21–7; cited from reprint in *The Critical Heritage*, vol. 2, pp. 191–8.
26. Simpson (1870), *CH I*, p. 247.
27. Mary Augusta Ward, 'Style and Miss Austen', *Macmillan's Magazine* 51 (1885), pp. 84–91; cited from reprint in *The Critical Heritage*, vol. 2, pp. 180–7, p. 185.
28. Lewes (1859), *CH I*, p. 152.
29. Ward (1885), *CH II*, p. 186.
30. Ward (1885), *CH II*, p. 185.
31. Richard Holt Hutton, 'The Charm of Miss Austen', *Spectator* 64 (22 March 1890), pp. 403–4.
32. Dallas (1866), *CH I*, p. 198.
33. Anonymous (1866), *CH I*, p. 200.
34. Anne Thackeray, 'Jane Austen', *Cornhill Magazine* 34 (1871), pp. 158–74; cited from reprint in *The Critical Heritage*, vol. 2, pp. 164–70, p. 166.
35. Anonymous (1866), *CH I*, p. 200.

36. Simpson (1870), *CH I*, p. 253.
37. Simpson (1870), *CH I*, p. 247.
38. Simpson (1870), *CH I*, p. 249.
39. Simpson (1870), *CH I*, p. 248.
40. Kavanagh (1862), *CH I*, p. 178.
41. Anonymous (1866), *CH I*, p. 214.
42. Dallas (1866), *CH I*, p. 199.
43. Oliphant (1870), *CH I*, p. 216.
44. Oliphant (1870), *CH I*, pp. 216–17.
45. Oliphant (1870), *CH I*, pp. 216–17.
46. Alice Meynell, 'The Classic Novelist', *Pall Mall Gazette* (16 February 1894); cited from reprint in Alice Meynell, *The Second Person Singular and Other Essays* (Oxford: Oxford University Press, 1922), pp. 62–7, p. 63.
47. George E. B. Saintsbury, Preface to *Pride and Prejudice* (London: George Allen, 1894); cited from reprint in *The Critical Heritage*, vol. 2, pp. 214–18, pp. 216–17.
48. George Lewes, 'The Lady Novelists', *Westminster Review* 58 (July 1852), pp. 134–5; cited from reprint in *The Critical Heritage*, vol. 1, pp. 140–1, p. 140.
49. Simpson (1870), *CH I*, p. 246.
50. Simpson (1870), *CH I*, p. 247.
51. Stephen (1876), *CH I*, p. 172.
52. Simpson (1870), *CH I*, p. 242.
53. Simpson (1870), *CH I*, p. 244.
54. Anonymous (1866), *CH I*, p. 206.
55. Kavanagh (1862), *CH I*, p. 178.
56. Kavanagh (1862), *CH I*, p. 179.
57. Agnes Repplier, 'Conversation in Novels', in *Essays in Miniature* (Boston and New York: Houghton, Mifflin and Co., 1895), pp. 59–69, p. 62.
58. Anonymous (1866), *CH I*, p. 206.
59. Anonymous (1866), *CH I*, p. 207; Ward (1885), *CH II*, p. 183.
60. Saintsbury (1894), *CH II*, p. 215.
61. Ward (1885), *CH II*, p. 183.
62. Simpson (1870), *CH I*, p. 255.
63. Simpson (1870), *CH I*, pp. 261–2.
64. Lewes (1859), *CH I*, p. 166.
65. Pollock (1860), *CH I*, p. 174.
66. Henry James to George Pellew, 23 June 1883, in *Letters*, ed. Leon Edel, 4 vols. (Cambridge, MA: Harvard University Press, 1978), vol. 2, p. 423.
67. Hutton (1869), *CH II*, p. 162.
68. Clymer (1891), p. 384.
69. Thackeray (1871), *CH II*, p. 167.
70. Kavanagh (1862), *CH I*, p. 195.
71. Simpson (1870), *CH I*, p. 256.
72. Thackeray (1871), *CH II*, p. 167.
73. Clymer (1891), p. 384.
74. Simpson (1870), *CH I*, p. 256.
75. William Shakespeare, *Twelfth Night*, ed. Keir Elam (London: Arden Shakespeare), 2.4.92–6; 2.4.116–18.
76. Simpson (1870), *CH I*, p. 257.
77. Clymer (1891), p. 383.
78. James (1883), p. 422.
79. Ward (1885), *CH II*, pp. 186–7.
80. Anonymous (1866), *CH I*, p. 210.
81. Anonymous (1866), *CH I*, p. 210.

82. Kavanagh (1862), *CH I*, p. 195.
83. Saintsbury (1894), *CH II*, p. 216
84. Oliphant (1870), *CH I*, p. 225.
85. Simpson (1870), *CH I*, p. 261.
86. Simpson (1870), *CH I*, pp. 262–3.
87. Clymer (1891), p. 381.
88. Clymer (1891), p. 382.

4 THE 'CULT OF JANE' AND THE RISE OF THE NOVEL, 1900s–1950s

1. Henry James, 'The Lesson of Balzac', *The House of Fiction: Essays on the Novel by Henry James* (London: Rupert Hart-Davies, 1957), pp. 62–3.
2. *Blackwood's Edinburgh Magazine* (May 1818), p. 455.
3. Saintsbury (1894), *CH II*, p. 215.
4. A. C. Bradley, 'Jane Austen: A Lecture', in *Essays and Studies by Members of the English Association* 2 (1911), pp. 7–36. Cited from reprint in Ian Littlewood (ed.), *Jane Austen: Critical Assessments*, 4 vols (Robertsbridge: Helm International, 1998), vol. 2, pp. 199–217, p. 199.
5. Rudyard Kipling, 'The Janeites' (1926), in Sandra Kemp (ed.), *Debts and Credits* (Harmondsworth and New York: Penguin, 1987), pp. 119–40, p. 132.
6. Christopher Kent, 'Learning History with, and from, Jane Austen', in David Grey (ed.), *Jane Austen's Beginnings: The Juvenilia and Lady Susan* (Ann Arbor: UMI Research Press, 1989), pp. 59–72, p. 59. Qtd. in Claudia L. Johnson, 'The Divine Miss Austen: Jane Austen, Janeites, and the Discipline of the Novel Studies', *Boundary* 2:23 (1996), pp. 143–63, p. 154.
7. H. W. Garrod, 'Jane Austen: A Deprecation', in *Essay by divers hands, being the Transactions of the Royal Society of Literature of the United Kingdom* 8 (1928), pp. 21–40. Cited from reprint in Littlewood (1998), pp. 226–36.
8. Johnson (2012), p. 6.
9. Garrod (1928), p. 236, ft. 1.
10. Garrod (1928), p. 234.
11. Garrod (1928), p. 231, p. 234.
12. R. W. Chapman, 'Jane Austen: A Reply to Mr. Garrod', *Essay by Divers Hands, being the Transactions of the Royal Society of Literature of the United Kingdom* 10 (1931), pp. 17–34. Cited from reprint in Littlewood (1998), pp. 237–46, p. 238, pp. 244–6.
13. Gamaliel Bradford, 'Portrait of a Lady', *The North American Review* 197:691 (1913), pp. 819–31, p. 819. This view is quite common in these years; see, for example, Warwick James Price, 'Great-Grandmother's Favorite Novel', *Sewanee Review* 2:4 (1913), pp. 480–9, p. 483.
14. Price (1913), p. 483.
15. Bradford (1913), p. 827.
16. D. W. Harding, 'Regulated Hatred: An Aspect of the Work of Jane Austen', *Scrutiny* 8 (1940), pp. 346–62.
17. Harding (1940), p. 347.
18. Harding (1940), p. 347.
19. Harding (1940), p. 349.
20. Harding (1940), p. 350; Chapman (1931), p. 246.
21. Harding (1940), p. 362.
22. Harding (1940), p. 362.
23. R. W. Chapman, *Jane Austen: A Critical Bibliography* (1953; Oxford: Clarendon Press, 1955), 52, entry no. 62.
24. John Louis Haney, '*Northanger Abbey*', *Modern Language Notes* 16:7 (1901), pp. 223–4, p. 223.

25. Michael Sadleir, 'The Northanger Novels: A Footnote to Austen', *Edinburgh Review* 246 (1927), pp. 91–106.
26. Warren Barton Blake, 'Brockden Brown and the Novel', *Sewanee Review* 18:4 (1910), pp. 431–43, p. 437.
27. Reginald Farrer, 'Jane Austen', *Quarterly Review* 228 (1917), pp. 1–30. Cited from reprint in Littlewood (1998), pp. 177–98, pp. 189–90.
28. Annette Hopkins, 'Jane Austen the Critic', PMLA 40:2 (1925), pp. 398–425.
29. Hopkins (1925), pp. 414–15.
30. Hopkins (1925), p. 412.
31. Mary Lascelles, *Jane Austen and Her Art* (1939; London: Athlone, 1995), p. 62.
32. Lascelles (1995), p. 64.
33. Northrop Frye, 'The Four Forms of Prose Fiction', *Hudson Review* 2:4 (1950), pp. 582–95, pp. 584–5. Frye organizes prose fiction into the following categories: novel, confession (autobiography), anatomy (satire) and romance.
34. Frye (1950), p. 586.
35. Marvin Mudrick, *Jane Austen: Irony as Defense and Discovery* (Princeton, NJ: Princeton University Press, 1952), p. 40.
36. Mudrick (1952), p. 53.
37. Mudrick (1952), p. 59.
38. Farrer (1917), p. 190.
39. Virginia Woolf, 'Jane Austen', in *The Common Reader* (London: Hogarth Press, 1925), pp. 168–83. Cited from reprint in Littlewood (1998), pp. 218–25, p. 224.
40. Elizabeth Bowen, '*Persuasion*', *London Magazine* 4 (June 1957), pp. 47–51. Cited from reprint in Brian Southam (ed.), *Northanger Abbey and Persuasion: A Casebook* (London: Macmillan, 1976), pp. 165–70, p. 165.
41. Bowen (1957), p. 165.
42. Lascelles (1995), p. 77.
43. Mark Schorer, 'Fiction and the "Matrix of Analogy"', *The Kenyon Review* 11:4 (1949), pp. 539–60, p. 542.
44. Schorer (1949), pp. 542–3.
45. Schorer (1949), p. 540.
46. John K. Mathison, '*Northanger Abbey* and Jane Austen's Conception of the Value of Fiction', *ELH* 24:2 (1957), pp. 138–52, p. 138.
47. Mathison (1957), p. 150.
48. Lionel Trilling, *The Opposing Self: Nine Essays in Criticism* (1955; New York and London: Harcourt Brace Jovanovich, 1978), p. 207.
49. Andrew Wright, *Jane Austen's Novels: A Study in Structure* (London: Chatto and Windus, 1953), p. 13.
50. Wright (1953), p. 102.
51. Wright (1953), p. 172.
52. R. W. Chapman, *Jane Austen: Facts and Problems* (Oxford: Clarendon Press, 1948), p. 209.
53. Ronald S. Crane, 'Jane Austen: *Persuasion*', in *The Idea of the Humanities and Other Essays, Critical and Historical* (Chicago: University of Chicago Press, 1967), pp. 283–302. Cited from reprint in Southam (1976), pp. 171–92.
54. Bowen (1957), p. 170.
55. Crane (1967), p. 177.
56. Crane (1967), p. 185.
57. Crane (1967), p. 185.
58. Crane (1967), p. 188.
59. Trilling (1978), p. iii.
60. Trilling (1978), pp. 200–1.
61. D. H. Lawrence, *Letters of D. H. Lawrence*, ed. by Aldous Huxley (London: Heinemann; NY: Viking, 1932), p. 614.

62. William Dean Howells, *Criticism and Fiction* (New York: Harper; London: Osgood McIlvane & Co., 1891), p. 38.
63. F. R. Leavis, *The Great Tradition: George Eliot, Henry James, Joseph Conrad* (London: Penguin Books, 1962), p. 16.
64. Leavis (1962), p. 15.
65. Leavis (1962), p. 10.
66. Leavis (1962), p. 17.
67. Leavis (1962), p. 16.
68. Matthew Arnold, *Essays in Criticism* (London and Cambridge: Macmillan, 1865).
69. Ian Watt, *The Rise of the Novel: Studies in Defoe, Richardson, and Fielding* (1957; London: Penguin Books, 1963), p. 11.
70. Watt (1963), p. 18.
71. Watt (1963), pp. 30–1.
72. Watt (1963), p. 310.

5 THE TEXT, THE UNCONSCIOUS AND COMMODITY, 1950s–1990s

1. Joseph M. Duffy, Jr., 'Structure and Idea in *Persuasion*', *Nineteenth-Century Fiction* Vol. 8, No. 4 (Mar., 1954), pp. 272–289.
2. Duffy (1954), p. 273.
3. Duffy (1954), p. 276.
4. Duffy (1954), p. 279.
5. Duffy (1954), p. 289.
6. Howard Babb, *Jane Austen's Novels: The Fabric of Dialogue* (Columbus: Ohio State University, 1962), p. 106, p. 227.
7. Babb (1962), p. 214.
8. Babb (1962), p. 111.
9. Babb (1962), p. 28.
10. A. Walton Litz, *Jane Austen: A Study of Her Artistic Achievement* (Oxford: Oxford University Press, 1965), p. 59.
11. Litz (1965), p. 63.
12. Thomas P. Wolfe, 'The Achievement of *Persuasion*', *Studies in English Literature* 11:4 (1971), pp. 687–700, pp. 689–90.
13. Wolfe (1971), p. 692.
14. Cheryl Ann Weissman, 'Doubleness and Refrain in Jane Austen's *Persuasion*', *The Kenyon Review* 10:4 (1988), pp. 87–91, p. 90.
15. Karl Kroeber, *Styles in Fictional Structure: The Art of Jane Austen, Charlotte Brontë, George Eliot* (Princeton, NJ: Princeton University Press, 1971), p. 79.
16. Deidre Shauna Lynch, *The Economy of Character: Novels, Market Culture, and the Business of Inner Meaning* (Chicago: University of Chicago Press, 1998), p. 154.
17. Lynch (1998), p. 233; Weissman (1988), p. 88.
18. Norman Page, *The Language of Jane Austen* (Oxford: Basil Blackwell, 1972), p. 19.
19. Lloyd Brown, *Bits of Ivory: Narrative Techniques in Jane Austen's Fiction* (Baton Rouge: Louisiana State University Press, 1973), p. 18.
20. Page (1972), p. 17.
21. Page (1972), p. 48.
22. Page (1972), p. 127. K. C. Phillipps, too, discusses the use of free indirect speech (or the *erlebte Rede*); see Kenneth C. Phillipps, *Jane Austen's English* (London: Andre Deutsch, 1970), pp. 206–7.
23. Phillipps (1970), pp. 112–13.
24. Brown (1973), p. 80.
25. Brown (1973), p. 101.

26. Brown (1973), pp. 39–40.
27. James Phelan, *Worlds from Words: A Theory of Language in Fiction* (Chicago: University of Chicago Press, 1981), p. 126.
28. Phelan (1981), p. 148.
29. Sheldon Sacks, 'Novelists as Storytellers', *Modern Philology* 73 (1976), pp. 97–109, p. 108.
30. Michael Boardman, *Narrative Innovation and Incoherence: Ideology in Defoe, Goldsmith, Austen, Eliot, and Hemingway* (Durham, NC and London: Duke University Press, 1992), p. 76.
31. Boardman (1992), p. 103.
32. John Dussinger, 'The Language of "Real Feeling": Internal Speech in the Jane Austen Novel', in Robert W. Uphaus (ed.), *The Idea of the Novel in the Eighteenth Century* (East Lansing, MI: Colleagues Press, 1988), pp. 97–115, p. 99.
33. Dussinger (1988), p. 102.
34. Frank J. Kearful, 'Satire and the Form of the Novel: The Problem of Aesthetic Unity in Northanger Abbey', *ELH* 32:4 (1965), pp. 511–27, p. 519.
35. Kearful (1965), p. 522.
36. George Levine, 'Translating the Monstrous: Northanger Abbey', *Nineteenth-Century Fiction* 30:3 (1975), pp. 335–50, p. 338.
37. Levine (1975), p. 350.
38. Tara Ghoshal Wallace, *Jane Austen and Narrative Authority* (London: Palgrave, 1995), p. 17.
39. Wallace (1995), p. 19.
40. Wallace (1995), p. 29.
41. Maud Ellman, 'Introduction', in Maud Ellman (ed.), *Psychoanalytic Literary Criticism* (London and New York: Longman, 1994), pp. 1–35, p. 7.
42. See Stuart Tave, *Some Words of Jane Austen* (Chicago: University of Chicago Press, 1973), p. 63.
43. Paul Morrison, 'Enclosed in Openness: *Northanger Abbey* and the Domestic Carceral', *Texas Studies in Literature and Language* 33:1 (1991), pp. 1–23.
44. Morrison (1991), p. 7.
45. Morrison (1991), p. 11.
46. Morrison (1991), p. 11.
47. Anita Sokolsky, 'The Melancholy Persuasion', in Maud Ellman (ed.), *Psychoanalytic Literary Criticism* (London and New York: Longman, 1994), pp. 128–42, p. 133.
48. Sokolsky (1994), p. 142.
49. Frances L. Restuccia, 'Mortification: Beyond the Persuasion Principle', in *Melancholics in Love: Representing Women's Depression and Domestic Abuse* (Lanham, MD: Rowman & Littlefield Publishers, 2000), pp. 17–34, p. 20.
50. Restuccia (2000), p. 34.
51. Adela Pinch, 'Lost in a Book: Jane Austen's *Persuasion*', *Studies in Romanticism* 32:1 (1993), pp. 97–113, p. 98.
52. Pinch (1993), p. 102.
53. Pinch (1993), p. 111.
54. Daniel Cottom, *The Civilized Imagination: A Study of Ann Radcliffe, Jane Austen and Sir Walter Scott* (Cambridge: Cambridge University Press, 1985), p. 122.
55. Pinch (1993), p. 114.
56. Raymond Williams, *The English Novel from Dickens to Lawrence* (New York: Oxford University Press, 1970), p. 21.
57. Alistair Duckworth, *The Improvement of the Estate: A Study of Jane Austen's Novels* (Baltimore, MD: Johns Hopkins University Press, 1971), pp. 202–3.
58. John Vernon, *Money and Fiction: Literary Realism in the Nineteenth and Early Twentieth Centuries* (Ithaca, NY and London: Cornell University, 1984), p. 20.

160 NOTES

59. Vernon (1984), p. 59.
60. Vernon (1984), p. 59.
61. Vernon (1984), p. 64.
62. Judith Weissman, 'Jane Austen: Loving and Leaving', in *Half Savage and Hardy and Free: Women and Rural Radicalism in the Nineteenth-Century Novel* (Middletown: Wesleyan University Press, 1987), pp. 47–75, p. 74.
63. Weissman (1987), p. 75.
64. James Thompson, *Between Self and World: The Novels of Jane Austen* (University Park and London: Pennsylvania State University, 1988).
65. Georg Lukács, *The Theory of the Novel*, trans. Anna Bostock (1971; Cambridge: MIT Press, 1978), p. 34.
66. Thompson (1988), p. 13, p. 15.
67. Thompson (1988), p.15.
68. Thompson (1988), p. 91.
69. Thompson (1988), p. 91.
70. Thompson (1988), p. 66.

6 POLITICAL AND HISTORICAL AUSTEN, 1950s–1990s

1. Duckworth (1971), p. 4.
2. Duckworth (1971), p. 5.
3. Duckworth (1971), p. 25.
4. Duckworth (1971), p. 180.
5. Duckworth (1971), p. 183.
6. Nina Auerbach, 'O Brave New World: Evolution and Revolution in *Persuasion*', *ELH* 39:1 (1972), pp. 112–28, p. 120.
7. Auerbach (1972), p. 119.
8. David Monoghan, 'The Decline of the Gentry: A Study of Jane Austen's Attitude to Formality in *Persuasion*', *Studies in the Novel* 7:1 (1775), pp. 73–87.
9. David Spring, 'Interpreters of Jane Austen's Social World', in Janet Todd (ed.), *Jane Austen: New Perspectives* (New York and London: Holmes & Meier, 1983), pp. 53–72, p. 65.
10. Monoghan (1975), p. 75.
11. Marilyn Butler, *Jane Austen and the War of Ideas* (Oxford: Clarendon Press, 1975), p. 279.
12. Butler (1975), p. 290.
13. Butler (1975), p. 285.
14. Claudia Johnson, *Jane Austen: Women, Politics, and the Novel* (Chicago: University of Chicago Press, 1988), p. 27.
15. Johnson (1988), p. 145.
16. Johnson (1988), p. 146, p. 153.
17. Johnson (1988), p. 36.
18. Johnson (1988), p. 39.
19. Johnson (1988), p. 47.
20. Johnson (1988), p. 166.
21. Butler (1975), p. 180.
22. Butler (1975), p. 175.
23. Robert Hopkins, 'General Tilney and the Affairs of State: The Political Gothic of *Northanger Abbey*', *Philological Quarterly* 57 (1978), pp. 213–24. Cited from reprint in Ian Littlewood (ed.), *Jane Austen: Critical Assessments*, 4 vols (Robertsbridge: Helm International, 1998), vol. 3, pp. 175–85, p. 176.
24. Hopkins (1978), p. 181.
25. Hopkins (1978), p. 181.
26. Hopkins (1978), p. 182.

27. Margaret Kirkham, *Jane Austen, Feminism and Fiction* (Brighton: The Harvester Press, 1983), p. 89.
28. Kirkham (1983), pp. 89–90.
29. Mary Wollstonecraft, *A Vindication of the Rights of Woman*, ed. by Anne Mellor and Noelle Chao (New York: Longman, 2007), p. 187.
30. Kirkham (1983), p. 149.
31. Kirkham (1983), p. 153.
32. Mary Poovey, *The Proper Lady and the Woman Writer: Ideology as Style in the Works of Mary Wollstonecraft, Mary Shelley, and Jane Austen* (Chicago: Chicago University Press, 1984), p. 233.
33. Poovey (1984), p. 236.
34. Laura Mooneyham White, '(Jane Austen and the Marriage Plot: Questions of Persistence', in Devoney Looser (ed.), *Jane Austen and Discourses of Feminism* (New York: St. Martin's Press, 1995), pp. 71–86, p. 75.
35. Poovey (1984), p. 239.
36. White (1995), p. 79.
37. White (1995), p. 80.
38. Julia Prewitt Brown, 'The Radical Pessimism of *Persuasion*', in Judy Simons (ed.), *Mansfield Park and Persuasion: A Casebook* (New York: St. Martin's Press, 1997), pp. 124–36, p. 133.
39. Brown (1997), p. 136.
40. John Wiltshire, *Jane Austen and the Body: 'The Picture of Health'* (Cambridge: Cambridge University Press, 1992), p. 168.
41. Wiltshire (1992), p. 174.
42. Maria Jencik, 'In Defense of the Gothic: Rereading *Northanger Abbey*', in Devoney Looser (ed.), *Jane Austen and Discourses of Feminism* (New York: St. Martin's Press, 1995), pp. 137–49, p. 142.
43. Jencic (1995), p. 147.
44. Diane Hoeveler, 'Vindicating *Northanger Abbey*: Mary Wollstonecraft, Jane Austen, *Northanger Abbey*', in Devoney Looser (ed.), *Jane Austen and Discourses of Feminism* (New York: St. Martin's Press, 1995), pp. 117–35, p. 119.
45. Hoeveler (1995), p. 121.
46. Hoeveler (1995), p. 122.
47. Jan Fergus, *Jane Austen and the Didactic Novel: Northanger Abbey, Sense and Sensibility and Pride and Prejudice* (London and Basingstoke: Macmillan Press, 1983), p. 37.
48. Fergus (1983), p. 15. This is also Laura Mooneyham's view in *Romance, Language and Education in Jane Austen's Novels* (New York: St. Martin's Press, 1988), p. 23.
49. Miranda J. Burgess, 'Domesticating Gothic: Ann Radcliffe, Jane Austen, National Romance', in Thomas Pfau and Robert F. Gleckner (eds), *Lessons of Romanticism: A Critical Companion* (Durham: Duke University Press, 1998), pp. 392–412, p. 405.
50. Mary Waldron, *Jane Austen and the Fiction of Her Time* (Cambridge: Cambridge University Press, 1999), p. 28.
51. Waldron (1999), p. 34.
52. Ann Radcliffe, *The Mysteries of Udolpho*, ed. by Frederick Garber (Oxford: Oxford University Press, 1980), p. 672.
53. Waldron (1999), p. 35.
54. Mark Loveridge, 'Northanger Abbey; Or, Nature and Probability', *Nineteenth-Century Literature* 46:1 (1991), pp. 1–29, p. 7.
55. Loveridge (1991), p. 12.
56. Loveridge (1991), p. 12.
57. Devoney Looser, '(Re)making History and Philosophy: Austen's *Northanger Abbey*', *European Romantic Review* 4:1 (1993), pp. 34–56, p. 39.
58. Looser (1993), p. 40.

59. Looser (1993), p. 45.
60. Hopkins, 'Moral Luck and Judgment in Jane Austen's *Persuasion*', *Nineteenth-Century Literature* 42:2 (1987), pp. 143–57.
61. Hopkins (1987), p. 150. This is Barbara Hardy's conclusion in *A Reading of Jane Austen* (New York: New York University Press, 1976), p. 191.
62. Hopkins (1987), pp. 153–4.
63. Poovey (1984), p. 224.
64. Hopkins (1987), p. 156.
65. Arthur Walzer, 'Rhetoric and Gender in Jane Austen's *Persuasion*', *College English* 57:6 (1995), pp. 688–707, p. 693.
66. Jane Austen, *Pride and Prejudice*, ed. and notes by Vivien Jones (London: Penguin Classics, 1996), p. 44.
67. Walzer (1995), pp. 700–701.
68. Walzer (1995), p. 705.
69. Waldron (1999), p. 151.
70. Waldron (1999), p. 138.
71. Waldron (1999), p. 141.
72. Waldron (1999), p. 155.
73. Susan Morgan, *In the Meantime: Character and Perception in Jane Austen's Fiction* (Chicago: University of Chicago Press, 1980), p. 51. For other discussions of Austen's status within Romantic literatures, consult 'Romantic Austen', a special issue of *Wordsworth Circle* 7:4 (1974).
74. Robert Kiely, *The Romantic Novel in England* (Cambridge, MA: Harvard University Press, 1972), p. 119.
75. Kiely (1972), p. 122.
76. Kiely (1972), pp. 122–3.
77. Kiely (1972), p. 134.
78. Anne K. Mellor, 'Why Women Didn't Like Romanticism: The Views of Jane Austen and Mary Shelley', in Gene W. Ruoff (ed.) *The Romantics and Us: Essays on Literature and Culture* (New Brunswick, NJ: Rutgers University Press, 1990), pp. 275–87, p. 279.
79. Gary Kelly, *English Fiction of the Romantic Period, 1789–1830* (London and New York: Longman, 1989), p. 114.
80. Clifford Siskin, *The Historicity of Romantic Discourse* (Oxford: Oxford University Press, 1988), p. 143.
81. A. Walton Litz, '*Persuasion*: Forms of Estrangement', in John Halperin (ed.), *Jane Austen: Bicentenary Essays* (Cambridge: Cambridge University Press, 1975), pp. 221–32, p. 224.
82. Litz (1975), pp. 226–7.
83. Litz (1975), p. 228.
84. Litz (1975), p. 231.
85. Peter Knox-Shaw, '*Persuasion*, Byron and the Turkish Tale', *Review of English Studies* 44:173 (1993), pp. 47–69, p. 48.
86. Knox-Shaw (1993), p. 50.
87. Knox-Shaw (1993), p. 69.

7 NEW MILLENNIUM, NEW DIRECTIONS

1. Michael Kramp, *Disciplining Love: Austen and the Modern Man* (Columbus: Ohio University Press, 2007), p. 36.
2. Kramp (2007), p. 36.
3. Kramp (2007), p. 3.
4. Jill Heydt-Stevenson, *Austen's Unbecoming Conjunctions: Subversive Laughter, Embodied History* (Basingstoke: Palgrave, 2005), p. 114.
5. Heydt-Stevenson (2007), p. 119.

6. Heydt-Stevenson (2007), p. 117.
7. Heydt-Stevenson (2007), p. 197.
8. Christopher R. Miller, 'Jane Austen's Aesthetics and Ethics of Surprise', *Narrative* 13:3 (2005), pp. 238–60, p. 238.
9. Miller (2005), p. 254, p. 255.
10. Miller (2005), p. 257.
11. Anne K. Mellor, *Mothers of the Nation: Women's Political Writing in England, 1780–1830* (Bloomington: Indiana University Press, 2000), p. 126.
12. Joseph A. Kestner, 'Jane Austen: Revolutionizing Masculinities', *Persuasions* 16 (1994), pp. 147–60, p. 155.
13. Jocelyn Harris, *A Revolution Almost beyond Expression: Jane Austen's Persuasion* (Newark: University of Delaware Press, 2007), p. 99.
14. Peter Knox-Shaw, *Jane Austen and the Enlightenment* (Cambridge: Cambridge University Press, 2005), p. 110. Knox-Shaw's chapter on *Northanger Abbey* in this monograph is based on his article '*Northanger Abbey* and the Liberal Historians', *Essays in Criticism* 49:4 (1999), pp. 319–43.
15. Knox-Shaw (2005), p. 111.
16. Knox-Shaw (2005), p. 116.
17. Knox-Shaw (2005), pp. 117–18.
18. Knox-Shaw (2005), p. 126.
19. Janine Barchas, *Matters of Fact in Jane Austen: History, Location, and Celebrity* (Baltimore, MD: Johns Hopkins University Press, 2012), p. 78.
20. Barchas (2012), p. 94.
21. Claire Tomalin, *Jane Austen: A Life* (New York: Alfred A. Knopf, 1997), p. 88.
22. Barchas (2012), p. 115. For Johnson's phrase, see James Boswell, *The Life of Samuel Johnson*, 4 vols (London: H. Baldwin & Son, 1799), vol. 2, p. 371.
23. Barchas (2012), p. 116.
24. Linda Bree reads the revision in similar terms, speaking of Anne's move from 'a position of marginality to respected centrality'. Linda Bree, 'Belonging to the Conversation in *Persuasion*', in Stuart Tave and Lynn Weinlos Gregg (eds), *The Talk in Jane Austen* (Edmonton: University of Alberta, 2002), pp. 149–65, p. 150.
25. Harris (2007), p. 52.
26. Harris (2007), p. 61.
27. Harris (2007), p. 71
28. Tandon Bharat, *Jane Austen and the Morality of Conversation* (London: Anthem Press, 2003), p. 233.
29. D. A. Miller, *Jane Austen, or The Secret of Style* (Princeton, NJ: Princeton University Press, 2003), p. 69.
30. Miller (2003), p. 71.
31. Miller (2003), p. 71.
32. Penny Gay, *Jane Austen and the Theatre* (Cambridge: Cambridge University Press, 2002), p. 147.
33. Gay (2002), p. 149.
34. Gay (2002), p. 163.
35. Gay (2002), p. 164.
36. Southam discusses the probability of significant alterations in 1816. Brian Southam (ed.), *Jane Austen: Northanger Abbey and Persuasion: A Casebook* (London: Macmillan, 1976), p. 18.
37. Narelle Shaw, 'Free Indirect Speech and Jane Austen's 1816 Revision of *Northanger Abbey*', *Studies in English Literature, 1500–1900* 30:4 (1990), pp. 591–601.
38. Shaw (1990), p. 596.
39. Caroline Franklin, '"The Interest Is Very Strong Especially for Mr. Darcy": Jane Austen, Byron, and Romantic Love', *The Female Romantics: Nineteenth-Century Women Novelists and Byronism* (New York: Routledge, 2014), pp. 83–102, p. 84.

40. John Wiltshire, *The Hidden Jane Austen* (Cambridge: Cambridge University Press, 2014), p. 153.
41. Clara Tuite, *Romantic Austen: Sexual Politics and the Literary Canon* (Cambridge: Cambridge University Press, 2002), p. 72.
42. Tuite (2002), p. 62.
43. Tuite (2002), p. 62.
44. Tuite (2002), p. 63.
45. Pierre Bourdieu, 'The Field of Cultural Production', in *The Field of Cultural Production: Essays on Art and Literature* (Oxford: Polity Press, 1993), p. 31.
46. Tuite (2002), p. 63.
47. Gay (2002), p. 54.
48. Gay (2002), p. 71.
49. Gay (2002), p. 63.
50. Gay (2002), p. 66.
51. Natasha Duquette, '"Motionless Wonder": Contemplating Gothic Sublimity in *Northanger Abbey*', *Persuasions On-Line* 30:2 (2010).
52. Lord Byron, '*The Giaour*', in Jerome McGann (ed.), *The Major Works of Lord Byron* (Oxford: Oxford University Press, 2008), pp. 207–47, p. 237.
53. Franklin (2014), p. 92.
54. Franklin (2014), p. 93.
55. Anne Frey, 'Nation without Nationalism: The Reorganization of Feeling in Austen's *Persuasion*', *Novel: A Forum on Fiction* 38:2/3 (2005), pp. 214–34, p. 216.
56. In *Jane Austen and Representations of Regency England*, Sales calls *Persuasion* a 'Condition-of-England novel', see Sales (1994), p. 199; Mellor allots to Austen and, in particular to Anne, the role of a 'Mother of the Nation'; see 'The Politics of Fiction', in *Mothers of the Nation* (2000), pp. 103–40.
57. Frey (2005), p. 216.
58. Frey (2005), p. 227, p. 224.
59. Frey (2005), p. 218.
60. Frey (2005), p. 219. Brian Southam, *Jane Austen and the Navy* (New York: Hambledon and London, 2000), pp. 257–98.
61. Frey (2005), p. 230.
62. See Benedict Anderson, *Imagining Communities: Reflections on the Origin and Spread of Nationalism* (London: Verso, 1983); Linda Colley, *Britons: Forging a Nation, 1707–1837* (New Haven, CT: Yale University Press, 1992).
63. Johnson (2012), p. 104. The idea of brotherhood emerges in Humberstall's words: 'Brethren, there's no one to touch Jane when you're in a tight place.'
64. Johnson (2012), p. 106.
65. Barchas (2012), p. 206.
66. Barchas (2012), p. 254.
67. Katherine Kickel, 'General Tilney's Timely Approach to the Improvement of the Estate', *Nineteenth-Century Literature* 63:2 (2008), pp. 145–59, p. 150.
68. Kickel (2008), p. 164.
69. William Deresiewicz, 'Early Phase Versus Major Phase: The Changing Feelings of the Mind', in *Jane Austen and the Romantic Poets* (New York: Columbia University Press, 2004), pp. 18–55.
70. Deresiewicz (2004), p. 150.
71. Deidre Lynch, '"Young ladies are delicate plants": Jane Austen and Greenhouse Romanticism', *ELH* 77:3 (2010), pp. 689–729, p. 690.
72. The term was proposed by Jonathan Bate in *Romantic Ecology: Wordsworth and the Environmental Tradition* (London: Routledge, 1991); it was drawn upon by James C. McKusick, *Green Writing: Romanticism and Ecology* (New York: St. Martin's Press, 2002).

73. Lynch (2010), p. 692. For other interpretations dealing with the phenomenon of the hothouses, see Brian Southam, 'General Tilney's Hot-houses,' *Ariel* 2 (1971), pp. 52–62; and Kickel (2008), pp. 145–59.
74. Lynch (2010), p. 709.
75. Lynch (2010), p. 715.
76. Lynch (2010), p. 714.
77. Lynch (2010), p. 719.
78. Sonia Hofkosh, 'The Illusionist: *Northanger Abbey* and Austen's Uses of Enchantment', in Claudia L. Johnson and Clara Tuite (eds), *A Companion to Jane Austen* (Oxford: Blackwell, 2009), pp. 101–11, p. 104.
79. Hofkosh (2009), p. 101.
80. Anne K. Mellor, *Romanticism and Gender* (Bloomington: Indiana University Press, 1988).
81. Enit Karafili Steiner, *Jane Austen's Civilized Women: Morality, Gender and the Civilizing Process* (London: Pickering and Chatto, 2012), p. 155.
82. Mary Wollstonecraft, *A Vindication of the Rights of Woman and The Wrongs of Woman, or Maria*, edited by Anne K. Mellor and Noelle Chao (New York: Longman, 2007), p. 247. The term 'heroinism' was coined by Ellen Moers in *Literary Women* (New York: Doubleday & Co., 1976). It seeks to validate the experience of the woman writer and that of her female protagonists.
83. Steiner (2012), p. 170.
84. Steiner (2012), p. 174.
85. Melissa Sodeman, 'Domestic Mobility in *Persuasion* and *Sanditon*', *Studies in English Literature* 45:4 (2005), pp. 787–812, p. 788.
86. Sodeman (2005), p. 788.
87. Sodeman (2005), pp. 792–3.
88. Sodeman (2005), p. 797.

8 FROM WORDS TO IMAGE AND SOUND

1. Sara Cardwell, *Adaptation Revisited: Television and the Classic Novel* (Manchester: Manchester University Press, 2002), p. 134.
2. Sutherland, *Austen's Textual Lives: From Aeschylus to Bollywood*, p. 341.
3. Mary A. Favret, 'Being True to Jane Austen', in John Kucich and Diane F. Sadoff (eds), *Victorian Afterlife: Postmodern Culture Rewrites the Nineteenth Century* (Minneapolis and London: University of Minnesota Press, 2000), p. 66, pp. 64–82.
4. Fredric Jameson, *Signatures of the Visible* (New York: Routledge, 1990), p. 192.
5. John Wiltshire, 'From Drama, to Novel, to Film: Inwardness in *Mansfield Park* and *Persuasion*', in *Recreating Jane Austen* (Cambridge: Cambridge University Press, 2001), pp. 77–98.
6. Sue Parrill, *Jane Austen on Film and Television. A Critical Study of the Adaptations* (Jefferson, NC and London: McFarland & Co., 2002), p. 174, p. 182.
7. Parrill (2002), p. 175.
8. Bruce Stovel, 'Northanger Abbey at the Movies', *Persuasions* 29 (1998), pp. 236–47, p. 237.
9. Stovel (1998), p. 242.
10. Stovel (1998), p. 245.
11. Marilyn Roberts, '*Catherine Morland*: Gothic Heroine after All?', *Topic: A Journal of the Liberal Arts* 48 (1997), pp. 22–30, pp. 23–6.
12. Jade Wright, 'Last Night's TV', *Liverpool Echo*, 26 March 2007.
13. Tamara Wagner, '"Would you have us laughed out of Bath?": Shopping Around for Fashion and Fashionable Fiction in Jane Austen Adaptations', in Tiffany Potter (ed.),

Women, Popular Culture, and the Eighteenth Century (Toronto: Toronto University Press, 2012), pp. 257–73, p. 262.
14. Wagner (2012), p. 263.
15. Jonathon Shears, '"Why Should I Hide My Regard?": Erotic Austen', in Beth Johnson, James Aston and Basil Glynn (eds), *Television, Sex and Society: Analyzing Contemporary Representations* (London: Continuum, 2012), pp. 127–42, p. 127.
16. Shears (2012), p. 138.
17. Shears (2012), p. 141.
18. Ginia Bellafante, 'A Most Proper Marriage: Jane Austen and PBS,' *The New York Times*, 19 January 2008.
19. Sutherland, *Austen's Textual Lives: From Aeschylus to Bollywood*, p. 346.
20. Wiltshire (2001), p. 91.
21. Sarah Cardwell, 'Persuaded? The Impact of Changing Production Contexts on Three Adaptations of *Persuasion*', in Jonathan Bignell and Stephen Lacey (eds), *British Television Drama: Past, Present and Future* (Basingstoke and New York: Palgrave, 2014), pp. 84–97, p. 86.
22. Cardwell (2014), p. 90.
23. Wiltshire (2001), p. 95.
24. Wiltshire (2001), p. 95.
25. Roger Sales, 'In Face of All the Servants: Spectators and Spies in Austen', in Deidre Lynch (ed.), *Janeites: Austen's Disciples and Devotees* (Princeton, NJ: Princeton University Press, 2000), pp. 188–205, p. 189.
26. Sales (2000), p. 192.
27. Carol M. Dole, 'Austen, Class and the American Market', in Linda Troost and Sayre Greenfield (eds), *Jane Austen in Hollywood* (Lexington: University of Kentucky Press, 1998), pp. 58–78, p. 59.
28. Tara Goshal Wallace, 'Filming Romance: *Persuasion*', in Gina Macdonald and Andrew F. Macdonald (eds), *Jane Austen on Screen* (Cambridge: Cambridge University Press, 2003), pp. 127–43, pp. 128–9.
29. Rebecca Dickson, 'Misrepresenting Jane Austen's Ladies: Revising Texts (and History) to Sell Films', in Linda Troost and Sayre Greenfield (eds), *Jane Austen in Hollywood* (Lexington: University of Kentucky Press, 1998), pp. 44–57, p. 45.
30. Devoney Looser, 'Feminist Implications of the Silver Screen', in Linda Troost and Sayre Greenfield (eds), *Jane Austen in Hollywood* (Lexington: University of Kentucky Press, 1998), pp. 159–76, p. 168.
31. Dickson (1998), p. 47.
32. Dole (1998), p. 62.
33. Amanda Collins, 'Jane Austen, Film and The Pitfalls of Modern Nostalgia', in Linda Troost and Sayre Greenfield (eds), *Jane Austen in Hollywood* (Lexington: University of Kentucky Press, 1998), pp. 79–89, pp. 83–5.
34. Favret (2000), p. 78.
35. Collins (1998), p. 87.
36. Gay (2002), p. 164.
37. Wallace (2003), p. 132.
38. Cardwell (2014), pp. 92–3.
39. Cardwell (2014), p. 93.
40. Cardwell (2014), p. 94.
41. Cardwell (2014), p. 94.
42. M. Gilbert, 'New *Persuasion* Tries a Little Too Hard', *The Boston Globe* (12 January 2008).
43. Cardwell (2014), p. 96.
44. Cardwell (2014), p. 94.
45. John Wiltshire, 'Afterword: On Fidelity', in David Monaghan, Ariane Hudelet and John Wiltshire (eds), *The Cinematic Jane Austen: Essays on the Filmic Sensibility of the Novels* (Jefferson, NC, and London: McFarland & Co., 2009), pp. 160–70, p. 170.

46. Wiltshire (2009), p. 167.
47. Wiltshire (2009), p. 170.
48. Wiltshire (2009), p. 161.

CONCLUSION

1. For an outline of the research proposed in this conference, see Gillian Dow and Susan Allen Ford, '"New Directions in Austen Studies": A Conference, a Publication and Some Thoughts on Bicentenaries', *Persuasions On-Line* 30:2 (2010).
2. Kathryn Sutherland, 'Jane Austen's Manuscripts', British Library, http://www.bl.uk/romantics-and-victorians/videos/jane-austens-manuscripts, date accessed 31 July 2015.
3. Johnson (2012); Laurence Raw and Robert G. Dryden, *Global Jane Austen: Pleasure, Passion, and Possessiveness in the Jane Austen Community* (Basingstoke and New York: Palgrave, 2013); Kylie Mirmohamadi, *The Digital Afterlives of Jane Austen: Janeites at the Keyboard* (Basingstoke and New York: Palgrave, 2014).

Bibliography

NINETEENTH-CENTURY SOURCES
REVIEWS
Blackwood's Edinburgh Magazine 2 (May 1818), pp. 453–5.
The British Critic 9 (Mar 1818), pp. 293–301.
The Gentleman's Magazine 88 (July 1818), pp. 52–3.
The Quarterly Review 24 (Jan 1821), pp. 353–76.
The Retrospective Review 7 (1823), pp. 131–5.

CRITICISM
Clymer, William B. S., 'A Note on Jane Austen', *Scribner's Magazine* (February 1891), pp. 377–84.
Howells, William Dean, *Criticism and Fiction* (New York: Harper; London: Osgood McIlvane & Co., 1891).
Hutton, Richard Holt, 'The Memoir of Miss Austen', *Spectator* (25 December 1869), pp. 1533–5.
Hutton, Richard Holt, 'The Charm of Miss Austen', *Spectator* 64 (22 March 1890), pp. 403–4.
Kavanagh, Julia, 'Miss Austen's Six Novels', *English Women of Letters* (1862), pp. 251–74; cited from reprint in Brian Southam (ed.), *Jane Austen: The Critical Heritage*, 2 vols (London: Routledge and Kegan Paul, 1968–87), vol. 1, pp. 176–98.
Lewes, George Henry, 'The Novels of Jane Austen', *Blackwood's Edinburgh Magazine* 86 (July 1859), pp. 99–113; cited from reprint in Brian Southam (ed.), *Jane Austen: The Critical Heritage*, 2 vols (London: Routledge and Kegan Paul, 1968–87), vol. 1, pp. 148–66.
Meynell, Alice, 'The Classic Novelist', *Pall Mall Gazette* (16 February 1894), p. 4; cited from reprint in Alice Meynell, *The Second Person Singular and Other Essays* (Oxford: Oxford University Press, 1922), pp. 62–7.
Oliphant, Margaret, 'Miss Austen and Miss Mitford', *Blackwood's Edinburgh Magazine*, 107 (March 1870), pp. 290–305; cited from reprint in Brian Southam (ed.), *Jane Austen: The Critical Heritage*, 2 vols (London: Routledge and Kegan Paul, 1968–87), vol. 1, pp. 215–26.
Pollock, W. F., 'British Novelists – Richardson, Miss Austen, Scott', *Fraser's Magazine* 61 (January 1860), pp. 30–5; cited from reprint in Brian Southam (ed.), *Jane Austen: The Critical Heritage*, 2 vols (London: Routledge and Kegan Paul, 1968–87), vol. 1, pp. 167–74.
Repplier, Agnes, 'Conversation in Novels', in *Essays in Miniature* (Boston and New York: Houghton, Mifflin and Co., 1895), pp. 59–69.
Simpson, Richard, 'Memoir', *North British Review* 52 (April 1870), pp. 129–52; cited from reprint in Brian Southam (ed.), *Jane Austen: The Critical Heritage*, 2 vols (London: Routledge and Kegan Paul, 1968–87), vol. 1, pp. 241–65.

Smith, Goldwin, 'Jane Austen', in *Great Writers Series* (1890), pp. 185–91; cited from reprint in Brian Southam (ed.), *Jane Austen: The Critical Heritage*, 2 vols (London: Routledge and Kegan Paul, 1968–87), vol. 2, pp. 180–7.
Stephen, Leslie, 'Humour', *Cornhill Magazine* 33 (1876), pp. 324–5; cited from reprint in Brian Southam (ed.), *Jane Austen: The Critical Heritage*, 2 vols (London: Routledge and Kegan Paul, 1968–87), vol. 2, pp. 173–5.
Thackeray, Anne, 'Jane Austen', *Cornhill Magazine* 34 (1871), pp. 158–74; cited from reprint in Brian Southam (ed.), *Jane Austen: The Critical Heritage*, 2 vols (London: Routledge and Kegan Paul, 1968–87), vol. 2, pp. 164–70.
Ward, Mary Augusta, 'Style and Miss Austen', *Macmillan's Magazine* 51 (1885), pp. 84–91; cited from reprint in Brian Southam (ed.), *Jane Austen: The Critical Heritage*, 2 vols (London: Routledge and Kegan Paul, 1968–87), vol. 2, pp. 180–7.

1900–1950 SOURCES

Blake, Warren Barton, 'Brockden Brown and the Novel', *Sewanee Review* 18:4 (1910), pp. 431–43.
Bowen, Elizabeth, '*Persuasion*', *The London Magazine* 4 (June 1957), pp. 47–51.
Bradford, Gamaliel, 'Portrait of a Lady', *The North American Review* 197:691 (1913), pp. 819–31
Bradley, A. C., 'Jane Austen: A Lecture', in *Essays and Studies by Members of the English Association* (Oxford: Clarendon, 1911), vol. 2, pp. 7–36.
Chapman, R. W., 'Jane Austen: A Reply to Mr. Garrod', in *Essays by Divers Hands: Being the Transactions of the Royal Society of Literature of the United Kingdom* 10 (1931), pp. 17–34.
Chapman, R. W., *Jane Austen: Facts and Problems. The Clark Lectures* (Oxford: Clarendon Press, 1948).
Crane, Ronald S., 'Jane Austen: *Persuasion*', in *The Idea of the Humanities and Other Essays, Critical and Historical* (Chicago: University of Chicago Press, 1967), pp. 283–302.
Farrer, Reginald, 'Jane Austen', *Quarterly Review* 228 (1917), pp. 1–30.
Frye, Northrop, 'The Four Forms of Prose Fiction', *The Hudson Review* 2:4 (1950), pp. 582–95.
Garrod, H. W., 'Jane Austen: A Deprecation', in *Essays by Divers Hands: Being the Transactions of the Royal Society of Literature of the United Kingdom* 8 (1928), pp. 21–40.
Haney, John Louis, '*Northanger Abbey*', *Modern Language Notes* 16:7 (1901), pp. 223–4.
Harding, D. W., 'Regulated Hatred: An Aspect of the Work of Jane Austen', *Scrutiny* 8 (1940), pp. 346–62.
Hopkins, Annette, 'Jane Austen the Critic', *PMLA* 40:2 (1925), pp. 398–425.
Howells, William Dean, 'Editor's Easy Chair', *Harper's Magazine* (November 1913), p. 958.
Howells, William Dean, *Heroines of Fiction* (New York and London: Harper and Brothers, 1901).
Kipling, Rudyard, 'The Janeites', in Sandra Kemp (ed.), *Debts and Credits* (Harmondsworth and New York: Penguin, 1987), pp. 119–40.
Lascelles, Mary, *Jane Austen and Her Art* (1939; Oxford: Clarendon Press, 1995).
Mathison, John K., '*Northanger Abbey* and Jane Austen's Conception of the Value of Fiction', *ELH* 24: 2 (1957), pp. 138–52.
Mudrick, Marvin, *Jane Austen: Irony as Defense and Discovery* (Princeton, NJ: Princeton University Press, 1952).

Price, Warwick James, 'Great-Grandmother's Favorite Novel', *Sewanee Review* 21:4 (1913), pp. 480–9.
Sadleir, Michael, 'The Northanger Novels: A Footnote to Austen', *Edinburgh Review* 246 (1927), pp. 91–106.
Schorer, Mark, 'Fiction and the "Matrix of Analogy"', *The Kenyon Review* 11:4 (1949), pp. 539–60.
Tompkins, J. M. S., *The Popular Novel in England, 1770–1800* (London: Constable, 1932).
Trilling, Lionel, *The Opposing Self: Nine Essays in Criticism* (1955; New York: Viking, 1978).
Woolf, Virginia, 'Jane Austen', in *The Common Reader* (London: Hogarth Press, 1925), pp. 168–83.
Wright, Andrew, *Jane Austen's Novels: A Study in Structure* (London: Chatto and Windus, 1953).

1950–2000: THE TEXT, THE UNCONSCIOUS AND COMMODITY

Babb, Howard, *Jane Austen's Novels: The Fabric of Dialogue* (Columbus: Ohio State University, 1962).
Boardman, Michael, *Narrative Innovation and Incoherence: Ideology in Defoe, Goldsmith, Austen, Eliot, and Hemingway* (Durham, NC and London: Duke University Press, 1992).
Brown, Lloyd, *Bits of Ivory: Narrative Techniques in Jane Austen's Fiction* (Baton Rouge: Louisiana State University Press, 1973).
Cottom, Daniel, *The Civilized Imagination: A Study of Ann Radcliffe, Jane Austen and Sir Walter Scott* (Cambridge: Cambridge University Press, 1985).
Duckworth, Alistair, *The Improvement of the Estate: A Study of Jane Austen's Novels* (Baltimore: Johns Hopkins University Press, 1971).
Duffy, Joseph M., 'Structure and Idea in *Persuasion*', *Nineteenth-Century Fiction* 8:4 (1954), pp. 272–89.
Dussinger, John, 'The Language of "Real Feeling": Internal Speech in the Jane Austen Novel', in Robert W. Uphaus (ed.), *The Idea of the Novel in the Eighteenth Century* (East Lansing, MI: Colleagues Press, 1988), pp. 97–115.
Ellman, Maud, 'Introduction', in Maud Ellman (ed.), *Psychoanalytic Literary Criticism* (London and New York: Longman, 1994), pp. 1–35.
Kearful, Frank J., 'Satire and the Form of the Novel: The Problem of Aesthetic Unity in *Northanger Abbey*', *ELH* 32:4 (1965), pp. 511–27.
Kroeber, Karl, *Styles in Fictional Structure: The Art of Jane Austen, Charlotte Brontë, George Eliot* (Princeton, NJ: Princeton University Press, 1971).
Leavis, F. R., *The Great Tradition: George Eliot, Henry James, Joseph Conrad* (London: Penguin Books, 1962).
Levine, George, 'Translating the Monstrous: *Northanger Abbey*', *Nineteenth-Century Fiction* 30:3 (1975), pp. 335–50.
Litz, A. Walton, *Jane Austen: A Study of Her Artistic Achievement* (Oxford: Oxford University Press, 1965).
Lukács, Georg, *The Theory of the Novel*, trans. Anna Bostock (1971; Cambridge: MIT Press, 1978).
Lynch, Deidre Shauna, *The Economy of Character: Novels, Market Culture, and the Business of Inner Meaning* (Chicago: University of Chicago Press, 1998).
Morrison, Paul, 'Enclosed in Openness: *Northanger Abbey* and the Domestic Carceral', *Texas Studies in Literature and Language* 33:1 (1991), pp. 1–23.

Page, Norman, *The Language of Jane Austen* (Oxford: Basil Blackwell, 1972).
Phelan, James, *Worlds from Words: A Theory of Language in Fiction* (Chicago: University of Chicago Press, 1981).
Phillipps, Kenneth C., *Jane Austen's English* (London: Andre Deutsch, 1970).
Pinch, Adela, 'Lost in a Book: Jane Austen's *Persuasion*', *Studies in Romanticism* 32:1 (1993), pp. 97–113.
Restuccia, Francesca, 'Mortification: Beyond the Persuasion Principle', in *Melancholics in Love: Representing Women's Depression and Domestic Abuse* (Lanham, MD: Rowman & Littlefield Publishers, 2000), pp. 17–34.
Sacks, Sheldon, 'Novelists as Storytellers', *Modern Philology* 73 (1976), pp. 97–109.
Sokolsky, Anita, 'The Melancholy Persuasion', in Maud Ellman (ed.), *Psychoanalytic Literary Criticism* (London and New York: Longman, 1994), pp. 128–42.
Tave, Stuart, *Some Words of Jane Austen* (Chicago: University of Chicago Press, 1973).
Thompson, James, *Between Self and World: The Novels of Jane Austen* (University Park and London: Pennsylvania State University, 1988).
Vernon, John, *Money and Fiction: Literary Realism in the Nineteenth and Early Twentieth Centuries* (Ithaca, NY and London: Cornell University, 1984).
Wallace, Tara Ghoshal, *Jane Austen and Narrative Authority* (London: Palgrave, 1995).
Weissman, Cheryl Ann, 'Doubleness and Refrain in Jane Austen's *Persuasion*', *The Kenyon Review* 10:4 (1988), pp. 87–91.
Weissman, Judith, 'Jane Austen: Loving and Leaving', in *Half Savage and Hardy and Free: Women and Rural Radicalism in the Nineteenth-Century Novel* (Middletown: Wesleyan University Press, 1987), pp. 47–75.
Williams, Raymond, *The English Novel from Dickens to Lawrence* (New York: Oxford University Press, 1970).
Wolfe, Thomas P., 'The Achievement of *Persuasion*', *Studies in English Literature* 11:4 (1971), pp. 687–700.

1950–2000: POLITICAL AND HISTORICAL AUSTEN

Auerbach, Nina, 'O Brave New World: Evolution and Revolution in *Persuasion*', *ELH* 39: 1 (1972), pp. 112–28.
Brown, Julia Prewitt, 'The Radical Pessimism of *Persuasion*', in Judy Simons (ed.), *Mansfield Park and Persuasion: A Casebook* (New York: St. Martin's Press, 1997), pp. 124–36.
Burgess, Miranda J., 'Domesticating Gothic: Ann Radcliffe, Jane Austen, National Romance', in Thomas Pfau and Robert F. Gleckner (eds), *Lessons of Romanticism: A Critical Companion* (Durham, NC: Duke University Press, 1998), pp. 392–412.
Butler, Marilyn, *Jane Austen and the War of Ideas* (Oxford: Clarendon Press, 1975).
Chapman, R. W., *Jane Austen: A Critical Bibliography* (1953; Oxford: Clarendon Press, 1955).
Fergus, Jan, *Jane Austen and the Didactic Novel: Northanger Abbey, Sense and Sensibility and Pride and Prejudice* (London and Basingstoke: Macmillan Press, 1983).
Fergus, Jan, *Jane Austen: A Literary Life* (New York: St. Martin's Press, 1991).
Hardy, Barbara, *A Reading of Jane Austen* (New York: New York University Press, 1976).
Hoeveler, Diane, 'Vindicating *Northanger Abbey*: Mary Wollstonecraft, Jane Austen, *Northanger Abbey*', in Devoney Looser (ed.), *Jane Austen and Discourses of Feminism* (New York: St. Martin's Press, 1995), pp. 117–35.
Hopkins, Robert, 'General Tilney and the Affairs of State: The Political Gothic of *Northanger Abbey*', *Philological Quarterly* 57 (1978), pp. 213–24.

Hopkins, Robert, 'Moral Luck and Judgment in Jane Austen's *Persuasion*', *Nineteenth-Century Literature* 42:2 (1987), pp. 143–57.
Jencic, Maria, 'In Defense of the Gothic: Rereading *Northanger Abbey*', in Devoney Looser (ed.), *Jane Austen and Discourses of Feminism* (New York: St. Martin's Press, 1995), pp. 137–49.
Johnson, Claudia L., 'The Divine Miss Austen: Jane Austen, Janeites, and the Discipline of Novel Studies', *Boundary* 2:23 (1996), pp. 143–63.
Johnson, Claudia L., *Jane Austen: Women, Politics, and the Novel* (Chicago: University of Chicago Press, 1988).
Kelly, Gary, *English Fiction of the Romantic Period, 1789–1830* (London and New York: Longman, 1989).
Kent, Christopher, 'Learning History with, and from, Jane Austen', in David Grey (ed.), *Jane Austen's Beginnings: The Juvenilia and Lady Susan* (Ann Arbor: UMI Research Press, 1989), pp. 59–72.
Kestner, Joseph A., 'Jane Austen: Revolutionizing Masculinities', *Persuasions* 16 (1994), pp. 147–60.
Kiely, Robert, *The Romantic Novel in England* (Cambridge, MA: Harvard University Press, 1972).
Kirkham, Margaret, *Jane Austen, Feminism and Fiction* (Brighton: The Harvester Press, 1983).
Knox-Shaw, Peter, '*Northanger Abbey*, and the Liberal Historians', *Essays in Criticism* 49:4 (1999), pp. 319–43.
Knox-Shaw, Peter, '*Persuasion*, Byron and the Turkish Tale', *Review of English Studies* (1993), pp. 47–69.
Littlewood, Ian (ed.), *Jane Austen: Critical Assessments*, 4 vols (Robertsbridge: Helm International, 1998).
Litz, A. Walton, '*Persuasion*: Forms of Estrangement', in John Halperin (ed.), *Jane Austen: Bicentenary Essays* (Cambridge: Cambridge University Press, 1975), pp. 221–32.
Looser, Devoney, '(Re)making History and Philosophy: Austen's *Northanger Abbey*', *European Romantic Review* 4:1 (1993), pp. 34–56.
Loveridge, Mark, '*Northanger Abbey*; Or, Nature and Probability', *Nineteenth-Century Literature* 46:1 (1991), pp. 1–29.
Mellor, Anne K., 'Why Women Didn't Like Romanticism: The Views of Jane Austen and Mary Shelley', in Gene W. Ruoff (ed.), *The Romantics and Us: Essays on Literature and Culture* (New Brunswick, NJ: Rutgers University Press, 1990), pp. 275–87.
Mellor, Anne K., *Mothers of the Nation: Women's Political Writing in England, 1780–1830* (Bloomington: Indiana University Press, 2000).
Monoghan, David, 'The Decline of the Gentry: A Study of Jane Austen's Attitude to Formality in *Persuasion*', *Studies in the Novel* 7:1 (1775), pp. 73–87.
Mooneyham, Laura, *Romance, Language and Education in Jane Austen's Novels* (New York: St. Martin's Press, 1988).
Morgan, Susan, *In the Meantime: Character and Perception in Jane Austen's Fiction* (Chicago: University of Chicago Press, 1980).
Poovey, Mary, *The Proper Lady and the Woman Writer: Ideology as Style in the Works of Mary Wollstonecraft, Mary Shelley, and Jane Austen* (Chicago: Chicago University Press, 1984).
Sales, Roger, *Jane Austen and Representations of Regency England* (New York: Routledge, 1994).
Shaw, Narelle, 'Free Indirect Speech and Jane Austen's 1816 Revision of *Northanger Abbey*', *Studies in English Literature, 1500–1900* 30:4 (1990), pp. 591–601.

Siskin, Clifford, *The Historicity of Romantic Discourse* (Oxford: Oxford University Press, 1988).
Southam, Brian (ed.), *Jane Austen: Northanger Abbey and Persuasion: A Casebook* (London: Macmillan, 1976).
Southam, Brian (ed.), *Jane Austen: The Critical Heritage*, 2 vols (London: Routledge and Kegan Paul, 1968–87).
Southam, Brian, 'General Tilney's Hot-houses', *Ariel* 2 (1971), pp. 52–62.
Southam, Brian, *Jane Austen and the Navy* (New York: Hambledon and London, 2000).
Spring, David, 'Interpreters of Jane Austen's Social World', in Janet Todd (ed.), *Jane Austen: New Perspectives* (New York and London: Holmes & Meier, 1983), pp. 53–72.
Tomalin, Claire, *Jane Austen: A Life* (New York: Alfred Knopf, 1997).
Waldron, Mary, *Jane Austen and the Fiction of Her Time* (Cambridge: Cambridge University Press, 1999).
Walzer, Arthur, 'Rhetoric and Gender in Jane Austen's *Persuasion*', *College English* 57:6 (1995), pp. 688–707.
Watt, Ian, *The Rise of the Novel: Studies in Defoe, Richardson, and Fielding* (1957; London: Penguin Books, 1963).
White, Laura Mooneyham, 'Jane Austen and the Marriage Plot: Questions of Persistence', in Devoney Looser (ed.), *Jane Austen and Discourses of Feminism* (New York: St. Martin's Press, 1995), pp. 71–86.
Williams, Ioan (ed.), *Novel and Romance, 1700–1800: A Documentary Record* (London: Routledge and Kegan Paul, 1970).
Wiltshire, John, *Jane Austen and the Body: 'The Picture of Health'* (Cambridge: Cambridge University Press, 1992).

EARLY TWENTY-FIRST CENTURY SOURCES

Barchas, Janine, *Matters of Fact in Jane Austen: History, Location, and Celebrity* (Baltimore: Johns Hopkins University Press, 2012).
Bautz, Annika, *The Reception of Jane Austen and Walter Scott: A Comparative Longitudinal Study* (London: Continuum, 2007).
Benedict, Barbara M. and Deirdre Le Faye, *Introduction to* Northanger Abbey (Cambridge: Cambridge University Press, 2006), pp. xxiii–lxii.
Bharat, Tandon, *Jane Austen and the Morality of Conversation* (London: Anthem Press, 2003).
Bree, Linda, 'Belonging to the Conversation in *Persuasion*', in Stuart Tave and Lynn Weinlos Gregg (eds), *The Talk in Jane Austen* (Edmonton: University of Alberta, 2002), pp. 149–65.
Deresiewicz, William, 'Early Phase Versus Major Phase: The Changing Feelings of the Mind', in *Jane Austen and the Romantic Poets* (New York: Columbia University Press, 2004), pp. 18–55.
Dow, Gillian and Susan Allen Ford, '"New Directions in Austen Studies": A Conference, a Publication and Some Thoughts on Bicentenaries', *Persuasions On-Line* 30.2 (2010), http://www.jasna.org/persuasions/on-line/vol30no2/editors.html, accessed July 31, 2015.
Duquette, Natasha, '"Motionless Wonder": Contemplating Gothic Sublimity in *Northanger Abbey*', *Persuasions On-Line* 30:2 (2010), http://www.jasna.org/persuasions/on-line/vol30no2/duquette.html, accessed July 31, 2015.
Fergus, Jan, 'The Professional Woman Writer', in Edward Copeland and Juliet McMaster (eds), *The Cambridge Companion to Jane Austen* (Cambridge: Cambridge University Press, 2011), pp. 1–19.

Franklin, Caroline, '"The Interest is Very Strong Especially for Mr. Darcy": Jane Austen, Byron, and Romantic Love', in *The Female Romantics: Nineteenth-Century Women Novelists and Byronism* (New York: Routledge, 2014), pp. 83–102.

Frey, Anne, 'Nation without Nationalism: The Reorganization of Feeling in Austen's *Persuasion*', *Novel: A Forum on Fiction* 38:2/3 (2005), pp. 214–34.

Gay, Penny, *Jane Austen and the Theatre* (Cambridge: Cambridge University Press, 2002).

Harris, Jocelyn, *A Revolution Almost beyond Expression: Jane Austen's Persuasion* (Newark: University of Delaware Press, 2007).

Heydt-Stevenson, Jill, *Austen's Unbecoming Conjunctions: Subversive Laughter, Embodied History* (Basingstoke: Palgrave, 2005).

Hofkosh, Sonia 'The Illusionist: *Northanger Abbey* and Austen's Uses of Enchantment', in Claudia L. Johnson and Clara Tuite (eds), *A Companion to Jane Austen* (Oxford: Blackwell, 2009), pp. 101–11.

Johnson, Claudia L., *Jane Austen's Cults and Cultures* (Chicago: University of Chicago Press, 2012).

Kickel, Katherine, 'General Tilney's Timely Approach to the Improvement of the Estate', *Nineteenth-Century Literature* 63:2 (2008), pp. 145–59.

Knox-Shaw, Peter, *Jane Austen and the Enlightenment* (Cambridge: Cambridge University Press, 2005).

Kramp, Michael, *Disciplining Love: Austen and the Modern Man* (Columbus: Ohio University Press, 2007).

Le Faye, Deirdre, *Jane Austen: A Family Record* (Cambridge: Cambridge University Press, 2004).

Lynch, Deirdre, '"Young ladies are delicate plants": Jane Austen and Greenhouse Romanticism', *ELH* 77:3 (2010), pp. 689–729.

Mellor, Anne K., *Romanticism and Gender* (Bloomington: Indiana University Press, 1988).

Miles, Robert, 'The 1790s: The Effulgence of Gothic', in Jerrold Hogle (ed.), *The Cambridge Companion to Gothic Fiction* (Cambridge: Cambridge University Press, 2002), pp. 40–62.

Miller, Christopher R., 'Jane Austen's Aesthetics and Ethics of Surprise', *Narrative* 13:3 (2005), pp. 283–60.

Miller, D. A., *Jane Austen, or The Secret of Style* (Princeton, NJ: Princeton University Press, 2003).

Raven, James, 'Book Production', in Janet Todd (ed.), *Jane Austen in Context* (Cambridge: Cambridge University Press, 2005), pp. 194–203.

Raw, Laurence and Robert G. Dryden, *Global Jane Austen: Pleasure, Passion, and Possessiveness in the Jane Austen Community* (Basingstoke and New York: Palgrave: 2013)

Sodeman, Melissa, 'Domestic Mobility in *Persuasion* and *Sanditon*', *Studies in English Literature* 45:4 (2005), pp. 787–812.

St. Clair, William, *The Reading Nation in the Romantic Period* (Cambridge: Cambridge University Press, 2004).

Steiner, Enit Karafili, *Jane Austen's Civilized Women: Morality, Gender and the Civilizing Process* (London: Pickering and Chatto, 2012).

Sutherland, Kathryn, 'Chronology of Composition and Publication', in Janet Todd (ed.), *Jane Austen in Context* (Cambridge: Cambridge University Press, 2005), pp. 12–22.

Sutherland, Kathryn, *Austen's Textual Lives: From Aeschylus to Bollywood* (Oxford: Oxford University Press, 2005).

Todd, Janet and Antje Blank, *Introduction to* Persuasion (Cambridge: Cambridge University Press, 2006), pp. xxi–lxxxii.

Tuite, Clara, *Romantic Austen: Sexual Politics and the Literary Canon* (Cambridge: Cambridge University Press, 2002).

Wiltshire, John, *The Hidden Jane Austen* (Cambridge: Cambridge University Press, 2014).

CRITICISM ON ADAPTATIONS

Bellafante, Ginia, 'A Most Proper Marriage: Jane Austen and PBS', *The New York Times* (19 January 2008).

Cardwell, Sara, *Adaptation Revisited: Television and the Classic Novel* (Manchester: Manchester University Press, 2002).

Cardwell, Sarah, 'Persuaded? The Impact of Changing Production Contexts on Three Adaptations of *Persuasion*', in Jonathan Bignell and Stephen Lacey (eds), *British Television Drama: Past, Present and Future* (Basingstoke and New York: Palgrave, 2014), pp. 84–97.

Collins, Amanda, 'Jane Austen, Film and The Pitfalls of Modern Nostalgia', in Linda Troost and Sayre Greenfield (eds), *Jane Austen in Hollywood* (Lexington: University of Kentucky Press, 1998), pp. 79–89.

Dickson, Rebecca, 'Misrepresenting Jane Austen's Ladies: Revising Texts (and History) to Sell Films', in Linda Troost and Sayre Greenfield (eds), *Jane Austen in Hollywood* (Lexington: University of Kentucky Press, 1998), pp. 44–57.

Dole, Carol M., 'Austen, Class and the American Market', in Linda Troost and Sayre Greenfield (eds), *Jane Austen in Hollywood* (Lexington: University of Kentucky Press, 1998), pp. 58–78.

Favret, Mary A., 'Being True to Jane Austen', in John Kucich and Diane F. Sadoff (eds), *Victorian Afterlife: Postmodern Culture Rewrites the Nineteenth Century* (Minneapolis and London: University of Minnesota Press, 2000), pp. 64–82.

Gilbert, M., 'New *Persuasion* Tries a Little Too Hard', *The Boston Globe*, 12 January 2008.

Looser, Devoney, 'Feminist Implications of the Silver Screen', in Linda Troost and Sayre Greenfield (eds), *Jane Austen in Hollywood* (Lexington: University of Kentucky Press, 1998), pp. 159–76.

Mirmohamadi, Kylie, *The Digital Afterlives of Jane Austen: Janeites at the Keyboard* (Basingstoke and New York: Palgrave, 2014).

Parrill, Sue, *Jane Austen on Film and Television: A Critical Study of the Adaptations* (Jefferson, NC and London: McFarland & Co., 2002).

Roberts, Marilyn, '*Catherine Morland*: Gothic Heroine after All?', *Topic: A Journal of the Liberal Arts* 48 (1997), pp. 22–30.

Sales, Roger, 'In Face of All Servants: Spectators and Spies in Austen', in Deirdre Lynch (ed.), *Janeites: Austen's Disciples and Devotees* (Princeton: Princeton University Press, 2000), pp. 188–205.

Shears, Jonathon, '"Why Should I Hide My Regard?": Erotic Austen', in Beth Johnson, James Aston and Basil Glynn (eds), *Television, Sex and Society: Analyzing Contemporary Representations* (London: Continuum, 2012), pp. 127–42.

Stovel, Bruce, '*Northanger Abbey* at the Movies', *Persuasions* 29 (1998), pp. 236–47.

Wagner, Tamara, '"Would you have us laughed out of Bath?": Shopping Around for Fashion and Fashionable Fiction in Jane Austen Adaptations', in Tiffany Potter (ed.), *Women, Popular Culture, and Eighteenth Century* (Toronto: Toronto University Press, 2012), pp. 257–73.

Wallace, Tara Goshal, 'Filming Romance: *Persuasion*', in Gina Macdonald and Andrew F. Macdonald (eds), *Jane Austen on Screen* (Cambridge: Cambridge University Press, 2003), pp. 127–43.
Wiltshire, John, 'Afterword: On Fidelity', in David Monaghan, Ariane Hudelet and John Wiltshire (eds), *The Cinematic Jane Austen: Essays on the Filmic Sensibility of the Novels* (Jefferson, NC, and London: McFarland & Co., 2009), pp. 160–70.
Wiltshire, John, 'From Drama, to Novel, to Film', in *Recreating Jane Austen* (Cambridge: Cambridge University Press, 2001), pp. 77–98.
Wright, Jade, 'Last Night's TV', *Liverpool Echo* (26 March 2007).

FILMOGRAPHY
Northanger Abbey
1987 *Northanger Abbey*
Arts & Entertainment Network, BBC 90 min
Directed by Giles Foster
Produced by Louis Marks
Screenplay by Maggie Wadey
Music by Ilona Sekacz
Principal Actors:
Katherine Schlesinger – Catherine Morland
Peter Firth – Henry Tilney
Cassie Stuart– Isabella Thorpe

2007 *Northanger Abbey*
ITV, 84 min
Directed by Jon Jones
Produced by Rebecca Eaton and Charles Elton
Screenplay by Andrew Davies
Music by Charlie Mole
Principal Actors:
Geraldine James – Jane Austen
Felicity Jones – Catherine Morland
JJ Feild – Henry Tilney
Carey Mulligan – Isabella Thorpe

Persuasion
1961 *Persuasion*
BBC, mini-series, black and white
Directed and produced by Campbell Logan
Screenplay by Barbara Burnham and Michael Voysey
Principal Actors:
Daphne Slater – Anne Elliot
Paul Daneman– Captain Wentworth
Fabia Drake– Lady Russell

1971 *Persuasion*
BBC, mini-series, 225 min
Directed and produced by Howard Baker

Screenplay by Julian Mitchell
Principal Actors:
Ann Firbank – Anne Elliot
Bryan Marshall – Captain Wentworth
Marian Spencer – Lady Russell

1995 *Persuasion*
BBC, 107 min
Directed by Roger Michell
Produced by Rebecca Eaton and George Faber
Screenplay by Nick Dear
Music by Nicholas Bucknall et al.
Principal Actors:
Amanda Root – Anne Elliot
Ciarán Hinds – Captain Wentworth
Susan Fleetwood – Lady Russell

2007 *Persuasion*
ITV, 120 min
Directed by Adrian Shergold
Produced by Rebecca Eaton and Murray Ferguson
Screenplay by Simon Burke
Music by Martin Phipps
Principal Actors:
Sally Hawkins – Anne Elliot
Rupert Penry-Jones – Captain Wentworth
Alice Krige – Lady Russell

Index

'Advertisement' (*NA*), 7–9
'The Elliots' (*P*), 10
adaptations
　casting, (*NA*) 131, 133; (*P*) 138, 139
　eroticism, 134, 138, 147
　fidelity and inventiveness, 135–6
　novel reader as movie critic, 142
Addison, Joseph (1672–1719), 44
Althusser, Louis Pierre (1918–1990), 123
Aristotle (384–322 BC), 24
Austen, Cassandra (1773–1845), 9–11, 15, 27
Austen, Henry (1771–1850), 7–9, 15–17, 35, 47
　biographical notice, 7, 15–17
Austen, Jane (1775–1817)
　defence of the novel, 11–12, 58, 70, 100
　fame, 20, 28, 47, 130 (*see also* Janeites)
　financial profit, 10, 16–17
　intuition, 17, 50
　juvenilia, 8, 55, 108, 111
　manuscripts, 2, 8–10, 27, 113–15, 149
　notoriety, 16
　online, 150
Austen-Leigh, James Edward (1798–1874), 14, 29, 38, 41, 47

Balzac, Honoré de (1799–1850), 30, 43
Bath, 9, 56, 78, 97–8, 104, 109, 112–13, 119–20
bawdy language, 108
Behn, Aphra (1640–1689), 31
Bildungsroman, 59
biography, 14–17, 22, 29, 47–8
Brontë, Charlotte (1816–1855), 28, 30, 41, 103, 138
Burke, Edmund (1729–1797), 89, 98, 120–1, 143

Burney, Fanny (1752–1840), 17, 54, 63, 74, 102, 118
Byron, George Gordon (1788–1824), 10, 82, 103, 105–6, 115, 117, 121, 125
　constancy, 105–6

caricature, 34, 40, 52
characters, 22, 24, 43
　rounded, 71
　secondary, 40, 43–4
Cinderella trope, 52, 68
class
　Navy, 71, 83–4
　politics, 87–93
　romance, 55
Coleridge, Samuel Taylor (1772–1834), 28, 125–7
comedy, 17, 50, 56–8, 76–7, 95, 99
commerce and property, 57–8, 148
commodity, 83–6
Congreve, William (1670–1729), 10–11
Conrad, Joseph (1857–1924), 63, 64
constancy, 42, 69, 75, 105, 114, 128
consumers, 85, 108, 133, 148
consumption, 85, 108, 133, 148
conversation, 22, 39, 45, 69, 142, 149
　foreshadowing, 72
copyright, 9, 27
courtship plot, 32, 54, 86, 94 (*see also* marriage)
cynicism, 28, 36–7, 49–50

death, 52, 68, 81–2, 116, 131
desire, 108–9, 119, 134
　body, 96, 131
　gender, 41, 148
　self-discipline, 34–6
Dickens, Charles (1812–1870), 30, 48, 62, 83, 95
domesticity, 20, 129 (*see also* English realism)

dramatic, 19, 24, 28–9, 99, 115, 136
  dialogue, 69, 73
  dramatization of consciousness, 70, 73
  ventriloquism, 30, 32
dualism, 65, 85

economy of style, 30, 32
Edgeworth, Maria (1768–1849), 17, 20, 22, 23
Eliot, George (1819–1880), 32, 61, 64, 96
Emma (1815), 7, 10, 17, 29, 43, 84
erotic desire, 41, 109, 134, 139, 147
estrangement, 62, 85, 95, 105, 146
  films, 134, 138, 147 (*see also* adaptations)
  novels, 41, 109

family names, 83, 112, 124
Fielding, Henry (1707–1754), 20, 24, 50, 64–6, 76, 114
Forster, E. M. (1879–1970), 95, 97
Foucault, Michel (1926–1984), 88, 108
free indirect discourse, 73, 76, 105, 116–17, 131, 136–7
French Revolution, 89–90, 92–3, 98
Freud, Sigmund (1856–1939), 65, 79–82, 133

genre criticism, 76–9
Gothic
  domesticity, 79–80
  gendered readers, 80, 93–7 (*see also* reading)
  market share, 13
  political, 92
  realism, 13
  sublime, 118–21
  The Castle of Otranto (1764), 13

Hegel, Friedrich (1770–1831), 63
heroism/heroinism, 35, 128, 165
Hollywood
  fairy tale, 150
  marriage plot, 95 (*see also* marriage; courtship plot)
home(lessness), 27, 80, 87–8, 124, 147
Hume, David (1711–1776), 111

imagination, 19, 35–6, 46
  judgement, 70
  nation, 122–3

individualism, 63, 65, 88, 90, 128
industrialism, 84, 125, 147
interpellation, 123
intertextuality, 53–4, 141–2
invention, 20, 111–13
irony, 15, 27, 64, 131, 144
  morality, 59–60, 61–3 (*see also* morality)
  NA, 55–6, 59, 70, 117, 134
  P, 57–8, 60, 76, 102, 115, 117
  restraint, 35–9
  Romantic, 117–19

James, Henry (1843–1916), 34, 40, 43, 47–9, 64, 95
Janeites (*see also* Austen and fame)
Johnson, Samuel (1709–1784), 12, 73–4, 113

Lacan, Jacques (1901–1981), 133
Lamb, Charles (1775–1834), 36, 126
language as clothing, 85–6
Lennox, Charlotte (1730–1804), 98

marriage, 58, 66–9, 88, 96, 128 (*see also* courtship)
masculinity, 36, 97, 101–2
materiality, 58, 65, 84
melancholia, 9, 57, 70, 81, 146
  dead mother, 82
melodrama, 97, 115–16, 136, 139
metaphoric indirection, 68–9
mimesis, 18–20, 108, 91, 123
mobility, 78, 89, 128
morality, 20–3
  imagination, 70
  irony, 59–60, 61–3 (*see also* irony)
  luck, 100–1
  modernity, 62–3 (*see also* personality)
  serious comedy, 60
  unlimited rejection, 56
More, Hannah (1745–1833), 103, 128

Napoleonic Wars (1796–1815), 6, 13, 110, 146
narrator, 30, 44–5, 70, 127, 143
Northrop, Frye (1912–1991), 54–5
nostalgia, 5–6, 138–9, 149

novel
  estrangement, 85
  gender, 18, 93–7
  tradition of the novel, 26, 41, 63–6, 73, 76, 88

originality, 8, 30, 41, 63, 65, 120

parody, 38–9, 53–8, 78, 81, 118–19
  class, 78
  serious drama, 53, 55
  symbolism, 101–2
personality, 19, 33, 56, 62–3, 85 (*see also* modernity)
persuadability, 75, 101–2
philosophy and historians, 111, 113
portraiture, 33, 48, 52, 117
Pride and Prejudice (1813), 15, 29, 40, 44, 84, 101, 139
privacy, 85, 111–14
probability, 13, 19, 23–4, 99
professional class, 68, 83, 89, 110, 147
professional sublime, 121–4
psyche, 28, 33, 65, 79–83
publication history, 10–12
punctuation, 5, 115, 149

quotations, 82–3, 105

Radcliffe, Ann, 11, 38–9, 55, 96–9, 111, 113, 118–21
reading (*see also* gendered readers)
  as critique, 59
  as experience 59, 77–8, 82–3
realism
  English realism, 20, 31 (*see also* domesticity; Gothic)
  selective realism, 26, 29–32
Reeve, Clara (1729–1807), 11
revisions, 85, 113–18
Richardson, Samuel (1689–1761), 11, 20, 64–6, 76, 114
Robinson, Henry Crabb (1775–1867), 28
romance-novel debate, 10–11
Romanticism, 103–7, 117, 125–7
  greenhouse Romanticism, 126–7

satire
  anti-Jacobin, 91–2
  Cervantean, 54

harsh, 37–9, 44, 51
incongruity, 77
innocent, 22
sentimentality, 77
Schimmelpenninck, Mary Anne (1778–1856), 120
Scott, Walter (1771–1832), 10, 16–17, 20, 125
sensationalism, 53, 132
Sense and Sensibility (1811), 16, 40–2, 106, 125, 139
sensibility
  autonomy, 71
  conduct books, 100, 102
  gender, 41
  nature, 57
  property, 58
Shakespeare, William (1564–1616), 24–8, 30, 38, 62, 138
  The Merry Wives of Windsor (1602), 24
  Twelfth Night (1602), 24, 42–3
Shelley, Mary (1797–1851), 27, 94
Shelley, Percy Bysshe (1792–1822), 42, 62, 95, 103
Smith, Adam (1723–1790), 32, 100
Smith, Charlotte (1749–1806), 54
Southey, Robert (1774–1843), 28
stereotypes, 33, 40, 102, 113, 120
style and conversation, 72
sublime
  landscape, 98, 104, 108
  love, 117
subversion, 50–3, 93
Swift, Jonathan (1667–1745), 35, 77
symbolism, 68, 74–5

tense, 73–4
title page, 7, 10, 12

uncanny, 79–80, 132, 143

vocabulary, 5, 33, 58, 72
Voltaire (1694–1778), 111

Wollstonecraft, Mary (1759–1797), 90, 93–5, 97–8, 104, 121, 127–8, 146
Wordsworth, William (1770–1850), 28, 85, 103–5, 125–6
writing process, 1, 115